GAṄGEŚA'S
THEORY OF TRUTH

GAṄGEŚA'S

Theory of Truth

Containing the Text of
Gaṅgeśa's Prāmāṇya (jñapti) vāda

With an English Translation, Explanatory Notes and an Introductory Essay

JITENDRA NATH MOHANTY

MOTILAL BANARSIDASS PUBLISHERS
PRIVATE LIMITED • DELHI

Reprint: Delhi, 2006
Second Revised Edition: Delhi, 1989
First Edition: Santiniketan, 1966

ISBN: 81-208-0618-2

MOTILAL BANARSIDASS
41 U.A. Bungalow Road, Jawahar Nagar, Delhi 110 007
8 Mahalaxmi Chamber, 22 Bhulabhai Desai Road, Mumbai 400 026
203 Royapettah High Road, Mylapore, Chennai 600 004
236, 9th Main III Block, Jayanagar, Bangalore 560 011
Sanas Plaza, 1302 Baji Rao Road, Pune 411 002
8 Camac Street, Kolkata 700 017
Ashok Rajpath, Patna 800 004
Chowk, Varanasi 221 001

Printed in India
BY JAINENDRA PRAKASH JAIN AT SHRI JAINENDRA PRESS,
A-45 NARAINA, PHASE-I, NEW DELHI 110 028
AND PUBLISHED BY NARENDRA PRAKASH JAIN FOR
MOTILAL BANARSIDASS PUBLISHERS PRIVATE LIMITED,
BUNGALOW ROAD, DELHI 110 007

PREFACE TO THE SECOND EDITION

The main text remains the same in this edition. I have corrected several typographical errors and a couple of serious substantive mistakes—to most of which my attention was drawn by Lawrence Davis.

Karl Potter organized a discussion on *Gaṅgeśa's Theory of Truth*—to which he contributed the leading paper—at the annual meetings of the American Association of Asian Studies in 1983 in San Francisco. My response to Potter's paper is being reprinted in this edition as an appendix.

I wish to thank Shri N.P. Jain of Motilal Banarsidass, Publishers, for taking the initiative in bringing out this new edition, and their Editors for having taken pains in improving the work.

Temple University
Philadelphia

J.N. Mohanty

PREFACE TO THE FIRST EDITION

It is well known that *Prāmāṇyavāda* is the second chapter of the first part i.e. the *Pratyakṣakhaṇḍa* of Gaṅgeśa's *Tattvacintāmaṇi.* A discussion of the four *pramāṇas* or sources of true knowledge is preceded by this chapter on Truth in general. There is a certain logical propriety in this order, for the concept of true knowledge logically involves that of truth. *Prāmāṇyavāda* has three subdivisions: the first deals with the knowiedge (*jñapti*) of truth, the second with the origin (*utpatti*) of truth, and the third with the definition (*lakṣaṇa*) of truth. Here again there is an obvious reason behind this arrangement. Unless the sceptic's objection that truth cannot at all be ascertained is satisfactorily set aside and the method of ascertaining truth laid down, it would be idle to discuss the nature and the origin of it. The text included here is concerned with the knowledge of truth: it constitutes the first subdivision of *Prāmāṇyavāda*. The reason why I have chosen this rather than any or both of the other two is that in my opinion it deals with philosophically the more important question. In the Introductory Essay I have argued that the question of the origin of truth is much less important. However, I do consider the problem of defining truth a highly exciting task, and I have in my Introduction taken note of Gaṅgeśa's contributions to this problem.

I came to deal with this text of Gaṅgeśa's not so much in connection with my studies in the Nyāya as in course of my systematic investigations into the problems of meaning and truth. My approach to Gaṅgeśa's text has not been that of an expositor but that of a critical philosopher, and I am sure that is the best way of dealing with so outstanding a critical philosopher as Gaṅgeśa. I do think that the Nyāya theories of knowledge and truth contain valuable philosophical insights which any systematic philosopher can ill-afford to lose sight of. At the same time, one must know where to draw the line between what is living and what is dead, a task which has yet to be done with regard to much of Indian philosophy.

I have made use of the following three editions of *Prāmāṇya-vāda*:

(*i*) the Kanchi edition containing also the *Dīdhiti* and *Gādādharī*;

(*ii*) the Asiatic Society edition containing Mathurānātha's *Rahasya*;

(*iii*) the Darbhanga edition containing Pakṣadhara's *Āloka*.

Where there are different readings I have chosen the reading which I have used only on philosophical grounds. In preparing the explanatory notes I have depended on all the commentaries which were at my disposal but chiefly on Raghunātha and Mathurānātha.

A few words about the method adopted in preparing the text: I have divided Gaṅgeśa's text into paragraphs each having a number. The explanatory notes are then numbered in accordance with the number of the paragraph in the text. (Thus, for example, the notes on para 2 are numbered 2.1, 2.2, 2.3, and so on.) This system, I hope, will facilitate cross-reference and also connecting the notes with the appropriate places in the text.

My English rendering of Gaṅgeśa's text has been free in the sense that I have tried not to distort the English language, as far as possible, by forcibly adapting it to the complicated pattern of Navya Nyāya Sanskrit. I have taken care however to see that the original meanings remain precisely the same. How far I have succeeded is for the readers to judge.

In translating the Nyāya technical terms I have largely followed Ingalls*, though I have also occasionally departed from him. In some cases I have preferred to retain the Sanskrit terms as such, not being happy with any of the suggested renderings. Amongst the Sanskrit terms I have retained as such are: '*anuvyavasāya*' (I am not happy with 'introspection' and have reserved 'secondary knowledge' for a more generic purpose so as to in-

*D.H.H. Ingalls, *Materials for the Study of Navya Nyāya Logic*, Harvard, 1951, reprinted by Motilal Banarsidass, 1988.

clude all kinds of knowledge of knowledge, e.g. the inference-from-knownness of the Bhāṭṭas), '*sādhya*' and '*pakṣa*' (I have distaste for the Latin equivalents often used). I have rendered '*dharmī*' into 'substantive', but '*viśeṣya*' into 'qualificandum' (following Ingalls); '*dharma*' into 'property' or 'attribute', but '*prakāra*' into 'qualifier' again a la Ingalls. My aim is to keep the ontological categories distinct from the logical and the epistemological.

A word about the use of quotation marks: double quotation marks " " have been used to quote from an author. Single quotation marks ' ' have been used for a variety of purposes, either when a word is being mentioned but not used, or when it is being used in the formal, logical or epistemological signification. Thus, for example, when a property is treated ontologically, its name is used without quotation marks, but when the same property is regarded as a concept or as a qualifier of a knowledge, its name is used within single quotation marks.

My greatest obligation is to Pandit Ananta Kumar Tarkatīrtha who unfortunately did not live to see this work completed. He taught me whatever little I know of the Nyāya, but what is more, he taught me to raise fundamental questions in philosophy and made Indian philosophy living for me. He made me search for the real philosophical truths behind the maze of technicalities in which the Navya Nyāya works abound. I send this for publication with the tantalising thought, if he would have been satisfied, were he alive now, with this work as it is, and if he would not have solved to my satisfaction many of the problems which I have raised. However, of one thing I feel sure: he would have fully approved of the critical spirit in which this work has been undertaken.

I wish also to express my gratitude to Principal Gaurinath Sastri of the Sanskrit College, Calcutta (for providing me with all facilities to work in his college both during and after my tenure of service there), Pandits Viswabandhu Nyāyācāryya and Narayana Chandra Goswami (with both of whom I have studied Nyāya texts on various occasions) and my colleague Sri Sivajeeban Bhattacharyya with whom I always had very stimulating discussions. I owe also a special debt of gratitude to Sri Sudhi Ranjan Das, formerly Vice-Chancellor of the Visva-Bharati University, and Professor Kalidas Bhattacharyya, Vice-Chancellor of the Visva-Bharati University and Director of the Centre of Advanced Study in Philosophy there for sponsoring the publication of this book.

J.N.M.

CONTENTS

INTRODUCTION

THE PURPOSE of this introductory study is to clarify the concept of truth in Indian philosophy, especially in the Mīmāṃsā and the Nyāya systems, and also to attempt a critical appraisal of the *prāmāṇya* theories. In both these respects the task before us is bewildering. Not much attention has been paid by scholars to a precise explication of the concept of truth in Indian philosophy. If we could throw some light on this and clarify the concepts, we could also to some extent clarify the amazingly complicated tangle of discussions that have grown up throughout the ages around the apparently simple question: Is *prāmāṇya svataḥ* or *parataḥ*? This is one of those questions to which every school worth the name came forward with an official answer. Arguments and counter-arguments were produced in never-ending stream. What we propose to do with regard to this vast mass of material at our disposal is in the first place to clarify the nature of the issue round which the theorics centre, and then to examine the nature of the arguments that have been advanced by the different schools in support of their contentions. Since the primary purpose of this study is clarification of concepts, no attempt will be made here to take sides. But it is quite possible that certain conclusions are likely to emerge which would reflect our attitude towards this entire problem. It is needless to say that Gaṅgeśa's great contribution to the problem would be brought to the foreground wherever possible. To anticipate a general conclusion that is likely to emerge, it is very much plausible that the views of the rival schools are not really mutually incompatible as they at the first sight certainly appear to be. They may even be regarded in the long run as supplementing each other. The apparent incompatibility between these views then may partly be due to the fact that though it would seem they were giving different answers to the same questions, they were not always unanimous in their formulation of the problems, so that sometimes they were really answering very different questions.

I. Preliminary Distinctions

Certain fairly well known distinctions may be mentioned at the very beginning.

1. *Two senses of 'prāmāṇya'*: The word '*prāmāṇya*' may mean either the property of being instrumental in bringing about true knowledge (*pramākaraṇatva*), or simply the truth of a knowledge (*pramātva*). In the former sense, *prāmāṇya* belongs to the various instrumental causes of true knowledge. In the latter sense, it characterizes a knowledge itself, if that knowledge is true. Of these two senses the second one is logically prior inasmuch as the very idea of being an instrumental cause of true knowledge cannot be understood without understanding what is meant by true knowledge and in effect without understanding what is meant by truth. The theories of *prāmāṇya*—the well known *svataḥ* and *parataḥ* theories—are concerned with *prāmāṇya* in the second sense, i.e. with the truth of a knowledge.[1]

2. *Two kinds of pramātva*: The Vedāntins who form a major group of participants in the controversy prefer to distinguish between two kinds of truth[2]: metaphysical truth (*tāttvika prāmāṇya*) and empirical truth (*vyāvahārika prāmāṇya*). A knowledge is metaphysically true if it can never be falsified at any time, past, present or future. *Metaphysical* truth then consists in *traikālika abādhitatva*. The truth which the Advaitins take to be *svataḥ* (in the sense or senses to be explained below) is not this metaphysical truth, but *empirical* truth[3], whose nature has yet to be made precise. It is this empirical truth which besides is, according to the Mīmāṃsaka, the cause of unwavering activity (*niṣkampa pravṛtti*). This shows that although the Advaita metaphysics has the conception of an eternal truth, this does not lead the Advaitin to the utter scepticism of regarding all other knowledge falling short of the knowledge of Brahman as false. The *svataḥ* and the *parataḥ* theories are concerned with the *empirical truth* of—it is needless to add—the knowledge of finite human

1. The idea of 'instrumental cause of a true knowledge' has been subjected to a quite different controversy between the Nyāya and the Bauddha schools.

2. Madhusūdana Sarasvatī, *Advaitasiddhi* (Nirnayasagar edn.), p. 499.

3. Madhusūdana Sarasvatī, *Advaitaratnarakṣaṇam* (Nirnayasagar edn.), p. 32.

beings, and are not concerned with any other more perfect kind of knowledge, be it knowledge belonging to a God or be it the knowledge of Brahman.

3. *The theory of prāmāṇya and the theory of prakāśa*: The theory of *prāmāṇya* should be distinguished from a connected but quite different theory, namely, the theory of *prakāśa*. The latter is concerned with the apprehension not of truth but of the knowledge itself whose truth or falsity may at any time be under consideration. The *prāmāṇya* theory asks, how does a knowledge become true, and how is its truth ascertained? The theory of *prakāśa*, on the other hand, asks the question, how is the knowledge itself known? How do I know that I know? One way of bringing home the fact that they are two distinct theories is to look into the various ways in which the different views about *prāmāṇya* have been combined with the different views about *prakāśa*. Bearing in mind that in each case we have a *svataḥ* theory and a *parataḥ* theory we may expect that there should be four different combinations. This expectation in fact stands confirmed. The four combinations are:

i. the theory of *svataḥprakāśa* combined with the theory of *svataḥprāmāṇya* (upheld by Advaita and Prābhābara Mīmāṃsā);
ii. the theory of *parataḥprakāśa* combined with the theory of *svataḥprāmāṇya* (upheld by the Miśra and the Bhāṭṭa schools of Mīmāṃsā);
iii. the theory of *svataḥprakāśa* combined with the theory of *parataḥprāmāṇya* (upheld by the Bauddhas); and
iv. the theory of *parataḥprakāśa* combined with the theory of *parataḥprāmāṇya* (upheld by the Nyāya school).

The theory of *prakāśa* is in fact logically prior to the theory of *prāmāṇya*. The question about the apprehension of a knowledge is logically prior to, and independent of, the question about the origin and the apprehension of the truth of that knowledge. For unless the knowledge itself is known, no question can even be raised about its truth. The theory of *prakāśa* is also wider in scope inasmuch as it pertains to all states of consciousness and not merely to knowledge.

4. '*Svataḥ*' *and* '*parataḥ*': The Vedānta and the Mīmāṃsā theory is known as the theory that truth is *svataḥ* whereas falsity is *parataḥ*. As opposed to this we have the Nyāya theory that both truth and falsity are *parataḥ*. The key terms in this controversy are '*svataḥ*' and '*parataḥ*', literally meaning 'from within' and 'from without' respectively. We would sometimes use the English words '*intrinsic*' and '*extrinsic*' more for reasons of convenience than for their accuracy in rendering the two Sanskrit terms.

When the Mīmāṃsā-Vedānta theory holds that truth is intrinsic to knowledge it means either or both of two things. It may mean on the one hand that the originating conditions of the truth of knowledge are precisely the same as the originating conditions of the knowledge itself. On the other hand, the theory also holds that the knowledge and its truth are apprehended together. Thus, 'intrinsic' means both 'intrinsic with regard to origin' and 'intrinsic with regard to apprehension', both *utpattitaḥ* and *jñaptitaḥ*.

Similarly, when the Nyāya holds that truth is extrinsic to knowledge, it means both of two things. On the one hand it holds that the generating conditions of the truth of a knowledge are more than the generating conditions of the knowledge itself. It also holds that the apprehension of a knowledge *does not always* amount to the apprehension of its truth. Thus 'extrinsic' means both 'extrinsic with regard to origin' and 'extrinsic with regard to apprehension', *utpattitaḥ* and *jñaptitaḥ*.

With regard to origin, it should be borne in mind that the Nyāya does *not* hold that the truth of a knowledge is produced *after* the knowledge itself has come into being. The Nyāya rather holds (or, at least the majority of the Naiyāyikas do) that though a knowledge and its truth are produced together, their generating conditions are yet not quite the same, nor are they apprehended as a rule together.

Pārthasārathi Miśra in his *Nyāyaratnamālā*[4] mentions two meanings of the word '*svataḥ*' which may mean either 'what is related to oneself' or simply 'from oneself'. Raghunātha Śiromaṇi

4. Pārthasārathi Miśra, *Nyāyaratnamālā* (ed. by Mm. Pt. Gangadhar Sastri, Chowkhamba Sanskrit Series, Banaras), p. 30-1.

in his *Dīdhiti* on Gaṅgeśa's *Prāmāṇyavāda* also distinguishes between two meanings of '*svataḥ*': 'from oneself' (*svasmāt*) and 'from what is one's own' (*svakīyāt*).[5] It seems to me that the distinction does not introduce anything new and so may be overlooked for our purpose.

It goes to Gaṅgeśa's credit to have shown that the words '*sva*' and '*para*' are relative terms, so that what is *sva* in one context may be regarded as *para* in another. Gaṅgeśa therefore (see para 35 of Gaṅgeśa's text) formulates his thesis independent of these terms though that means a more circuitous mode of speech.

II. Different Forms of the *Svataḥprāmāṇya* Theory

Although they all agree that truth of a knowledge originates precisely from those causal conditions which also give rise to the knowledge, the different advocates of the *svataḥprāmāṇya* theory nevertheless differ amongst themselves as to the nature of the apprehension of truth. Even with regard to this latter question they all no doubt agree that a knowledge is as a rule apprehended together with its truth.[6] They differ, however, in the first place, with regard to the nature of knowledge and, secondly, as to the nature of our apprehension of a knowledge. Accordingly, we might distinguish between four different forms of the theory: the Prābhākara, the Vedānta, the Bhāṭṭa and the Miśra.

(*a*) *The Prābhākara theory*: The Prābhākara stands alone in thinking that there is no positive error. Strictly speaking, the problem of truth *and* error is simply meaningless on his theory, for there is no cognitive error. Is then the ordinary usage about truth *and* error without any significance? The Prābhākara would say that the only point about this distinction lies in the practical side of knowledge. When we say a knowledge is false we really mean—the Prābhākara seems to be saying—that it leads to unsuccessful behaviour?[7] On the cognitive side all knowledge is

5. *Prāmāṇyavāda* (Kanchi ed.), p. 15.

6. Gaṅgeśa: "*svatastve prāmāṇyavata eva jñānasya grahāt*" (*Prāmāṇyavāda*).

7. Rāmānujācāryya: "*yatra vyavahāravisaṃvādaḥ tatra pūrvajñānasya bhrāntatvam*". (*Tantrarahasya*, Gaekwad's O.S., p. 3)

true. Even the so called false knowledge is, for every knowledge has its object which it manifests.[8] Bearing this in mind, we might say that the Prābhākara Mīmāṃsā distinguishes between three levels of truth and error:

In the broadest sense of the term 'truth', all awareness, and therefore all knowledge, is true. In a narrower sense of the term, all awareness other than memory is true. In a still narrower sense of the term, only those knowledges are true that lead to successful practice whereas those that lead to unsuccessful practice are false. Rāmānujācāryya uses three different terms for these three different kinds of truth: *yāthārthya*, *prāmāṇya* and *samyaktva*. *Yāthārthya* belongs to all awareness[9] (including memory and what ordinarily passes for erroneous apprehension), *prāmāṇya* to all awareness[10] excepting memory (but including even the so-called erroneous apprehension) and *samyaktva* only to such knowledge other than memory which leads to successful practice.[11] *Yāthārthya*, or truth in the widest sense, is coextensive with the property of being an awareness of..., or of being true to its object (*sarvasya jñānasyārthāvyabhicāritva*). The criterion of *prāmāṇya* is independence in manifesting the object; memory is not *pramā* since it does not independently manifest its object.[12] The test of *samyaktva* is the absence of contradicted practice.

Now, how does all this bear on the Prābhākara version of the *Svataḥprāmāṇya* theory? Ganganath Jha has raised a pertinent issue against the Bhāṭṭa theory of *prāmāṇya*[13] without himself realising that the objection is equally valid against the Prābhākara notion. For, if the test of *prāmāṇya* is independence in manifesting its object or, in other words, if *prāmāṇya* is the property of apprehending something not apprehended before (*anadhigatatva*), then *prāmāṇya* is not *svatogrāhya*. The appre-

8. Rāmānujācāryya: "*yasyāṃ saṃviti yaḥ artha avabhāsate sa tasya viṣayaḥ, nānyaḥ asya tatrānavabhāsāt.*" (*loc. cit.*, p. 2)

9. "*tasya sarvasaṃvitsādhāraṇatvāt.*" (*loc. cit.*, p. 2)

10. "*anubhūtiḥ pramāṇam*". (*loc. cit.*, p. 2)

11. "*yatra tu na (vyavahāravisaṃvādaḥ) tatra samyaktvam.*" (*loc. cit.*, p. 3).

12. "*na svātantryeṇārtham paricchinattīti na pramāṇam*". (Śālikanātha, *Prakaraṇa Pañcikā*, p. 42)

13. Jha, *Prābhākara Mīmāṃsā.*

hension of the *prāmāṇya* of a knowledge would in that case await the ascertainment of this further condition. Or, to put it differently, if *prāmāṇya* is the property of being other than memory, it could not be said to be apprehended along with the apprehension of the knowledge (whose *prāmāṇya* it is). It is clear therefore that neither *prāmāṇya* nor *samyaktva* are apprehended *ab initio*. If therefore the Prābhākara Mīmāṃsā advocates the theory of *svataḥprāmāṇya* that could only be with regard to *yāthārthya*;[14] for it is only in this broadest sense of 'truth' that every awareness is awareness of its own object and to apprehend a knowledge is *eo ipso* to apprehend it as knowledge of its own object.

(*b*) *The Bhāṭṭa theory*: The Bhāṭṭa school, agreeing though in the fundamental point of *svataḥprāmāṇya*, differs from the Prābhākaras in the following points.

The Bhāṭṭas regard knowledge as an imperceptible activity and not as something self-luminous. We come to know about our knowledge therefore—on the Bhāṭṭa theory—only through an inferential process which immediately follows upon the knowledge. The inferential process has the following character. The activity of knowing, itself imperceptible, is directed towards and terminates in the object which thereby comes to acquire a new property of 'being known'. This property called by the Bhāṭṭas

14. I am indebted, in bringing out this threefold sense of 'truth', to P. Sastri's *Introduction to the Pūrvamīmāṃsā* (Calcutta, 1923). It would be seen that I agree with that learned scholar in thinking that it is truth only in the broadest sense of the term that, on the Mīmāṃsā theory, could be *svataḥ*. I however have differed from him in the precise formulation of these three senses. The difference between his analysis and mine may be represented thus:—

On Sastri's analysis:

1. Truth as common to all cognitions (*pramā*, *apramā* and memory)
2. Truth as common to memory and *anubhūti* (=*bādhakābhāvatva*)
3. Truth as belonging only to *anubhūti* (*bādhakābhāvatva*+*anadhigatatva*)

On my analysis:

1. *Yāthārthya* (common to all awareness quâ awareness of some object)
2. *Prāmāṇya*, as common to all knowledge, right or wrong, but excepting memory (=*anadhigatatva*).
3. *Samyaktva*, as characterizing only right *anubhūti* (*anadhigatatva* + *bādhakābhāvatva*).

'*jñātatā*' or '*knownness*' serves as the mark for our inference of the act of knowing which is its imperceptible cause. Unlike most other inferences, this inference of the knowledge from the *jñātatā* in the object does not wait upon my desire to infer: it automatically—unless hindered by more powerful factors—follows upon knowledge and in that sense no knowledge goes unknown, though again none is directly perceived.

Now, truth—according to the Bhāṭṭas—is apprehended *svataḥ* in the sense that the same inference from *jñātatā* which makes us aware of a knowledge also makes us aware of the truth of that knowledge. Truth of course has its origin in the very same factors which also give rise to the knowledge whose truth it is but like the knowledge its truth also remains unknown at the beginning. The knowledge manifests its object without itself or its truth being apprehended till of course the above-mentioned inference brings both to light.[15,15a]

But what does the Bhāṭṭa mean by '*prāmāṇya*'? Kumārila has not given anywhere a precise definition of it. We could only fall back on the line: "*tasmād bodhātmakatvena svataḥ prāptā pramāṇatā*"[16] which suggests the conjecture[17] that also for Kumārila, as for the Prābhākara, *prāmāṇya* is the same as awareness-of-the-object (= *bodhātmakatva*). In this sense of course every knowledge is intrinsically true. Other members of the school however are not as reticent as Kumārila, nor are they all unanimous on this point.

Umbeka, commenting on the *Ślokavārtika*, rejects the identification of *prāmāṇya* with *bodhakatva* on the plea that though the latter is intrinsic to all knowledge yet it does not serve to distinguish right from wrong knowledge,[18] for even the erroneous knowledge of a rope-snake has the property of *bodhakatva* inas-

15. *Ślokavārtika*, 2.83.

15a. It should be remembered however that though the said inference reveals truth, truth is not inferred. Thus Gāgā Bhaṭṭa writes: "*Pramātvasyānanumeyatvāt jñānānumāne samānasaṃvitsaṃvedyatayā jñānatvavatpramātvasya svatastvasaṃbhavāt*" (*Bhāṭṭacintāmaṇi*, p. 13).

16. *Ślokavārtika*, 2.53.

17. Sastri, loc. *loc. cit.*, 68-9.

18. It must be remembered that the Bhāṭṭa unlike the Prābhākara does distinguish between right knowledge and error so that his account of *prāmāṇya* should be expected to distinguish the one from the other.

much as it also manifests its own object. Umbeka concludes by defining '*prāmāṇya*' as *arthāvisaṃvāditvam*, that is to say, as the 'property of being uncontradicted in its object'.[19] Mere manifestation of an object is not enough. A true knowledge must be uncontradicted in its object. Umbeka adds that it is this truth which is *svataḥ* in the sense of being produced by the cause of the knowledge itself.

Gāgā Bhaṭṭa goes further to define a true knowledge as a knowledge whose object was previously unknown and which is uncontradicted by another knowledge;[20] in this sense, *prāmāṇya* is the same as *samyaktva* of the Prābhākaras. But can truth in this sense as also in the sense of Umbeka be *svataḥ*?

Pārthasārathi suggests a new distinction between two senses of 'truth': truth as pertaining to the knowledge, and truth as pertaining to the object. Apparently, his purpose is to circumvent the following difficulty. My knowledge of truth would take the form 'This knowledge is true'. Now on the Bhāṭṭa theory both the original knowledge and its truth are apprehended together. The original knowledge however being previously unknown, the judgment 'This knowledge is true' is not possible. Awareness of truth would therefore presuppose a prior apprehension of the knowledge—which would of course contradict the central thesis of the *svataḥprāmāṇya* theory. This difficulty is evaded by suggesting that the *prāmāṇya* is nothing other than *viṣayatathātva* or the "suchness of the object", in which case the ascription of *prāmāṇya* to the knowledge cannot but be secondary[21,22].

Now it seems to me that Pārthasārathi's distinction is hardly to the point. For, truth is an epistemological notion, and it is

19. *Ślokavārtika* with the commentary of Umbeka (Madras Univ. Sanskrit Series, no. 13, 1940), p. 54.

20. "*Ajñātaviṣayakaṃ bādhakajñānarahitajñānaṃ pramā*". (*Bhāṭṭacintāmaṇi*, p. 13)

21. "*Na jñānasaṃbandhitvena prāmāṇyaṃ gṛhyate iti brūmaḥ, kiṃtu viṣayatathātvaṃ tadvijñānasya prāmāṇyaṃ tannibandhanatvājjñāne prāmāṇya-buddhiśabdayoḥ, tat ca ajñātādeva jñānāt svata eva gṛhītamityanarthakaṃ pramāṇāntaramiti*". (*Nyāraratnākara* on *Ślokavārtika*, edtd. by Ram Sastri, Benares, 1898, p. 71)

22. *Nyāyaratnākara*, p. 61. Again *Nyāyaratnamālā*, p. 33 (Banaras edition, 1900): "*arthatathātvamidameva hi jñānasya prāmāṇyam.*"

only as an epistemological notion that truth concerns us here. Truth in this sense, i.e. as the 'suchness of the object' or as the pure nature of the object hardly concerns the issue under consideration. The fact is that '*viṣaya*' itself is an epistemological concept, so that '*viṣayatathātva*' could only mean faithfulness or adequacy of the knowledge to its object.

We may then say that the Bhāṭṭas have suggested two notions of *prāmāṇya*, (*i*) of *prāmāṇya* as equal to *anadhigatatva*+*abādhitatva* and (*ii*) of *prāmāṇya* as nothing other than *viṣayatathātva*. Of these two notions, it is (*i*) whose claim to be apprehended *ab initio* must be rejected, for the two constituent notions are sufficiently complex so as to require subsequent deliberation.[23] It is therefore (*ii*) which might put forward a reasonable claim for being *svataḥ*. But in that case the meaning of *viṣayatathātva* has to be made more precise. One thing seems to be clear: it is not the same as the *yāthārthya* of the Prābhākaras. For *yāthārthya*, as we have seen, belongs to all awareness as such, to right knowledge and error alike, while Pārthasārathi's notion is meant to distinguish right knowledge from error. If *viṣayatathātva* in this sense is to be *svataḥ*, then we have to take it that every knowledge quâ knowledge claims to be true to its object.

It must be added that though *viṣayatathātva* is meant to distinguish right knowledge from error, nevertheless—Pārthasārathi reminds us—when the Mīmāṃsaka seeks to establish the intrinsic truth of all knowledge, he has in view all knowledge and not merely the right ones.[24] This is in fact, as we shall have occasions to emphasize later on, one of the puzzling situations with which the *svataḥprāmāṇya* theory is faced.

(*c*) *The Miśra theory*: The third form of the theory is ascribed to the school of Mīmāṃsā associated with the name of Murāri

23. Pārthasārathi recognizes this in *Nyāyaratnamālā*. To the question whether truth also belongs to memory, he replies that strictly speaking it does not, but in the context of the present discussion (*asmin tu prakaraṇe*) truth is taken as what is common to right knowledge and memory. For, he goes on to tell us "*ananusandhīyamānatvaṃ tadayogānupalabdhigamyatvena na jñānasvarūpād gamyate*" (p. 35): The knowledge of a jar, for example, does not tell us that it is knowledge of what has not been previously apprehended.

24. "*Sarvavijñānaviṣayamidam*" (*Nyāyaratnamālā*, p. 35). Also: "*jñānamātraṃ tu adhikṛtya svataḥ prāmāṇye parataścāprāmāṇye sādhyamāne*" (*ibid*, p. 35).

Miśra none of whose writings is handed down to us but who is mentioned in Nyāya and Mīmāṃsā treatises.[25] This school is represented as combining the Nyāya doctrine of *anuvyavasāya* with the Mīmāṃsā theory of intrinsic truth. Again there is no difference as to the origin of truth, about which all the three Mīmāṃsā schools agree. The difference centres round the question of apprehension. The primary knowledge whose truth is under consideration is apprehended in its *anuvyavasāya* or introspective awareness; this secondary knowledge also apprehends the truth of the primary knowledge.[26]

Hardly any arguments of the school survive. Gaṅgeśa however gives one argument in favour of the view. This is to the effect that since a knowledge is specified only by its object (*viṣayanirūpya*), the *anuvyavasāya* apprehending a primary knowledge should also apprehend that primary knowledge as being knowledge of such and such object, which in fact amounts to apprehending it as a true knowledge.[27] The underlying conception of truth seems to be, on the face of it, not very far from the Naiyāyika's. Truth is defined as *tadvadviśeṣyakatve sati tatprakārakatvam*, and both these component properties—to be explained later on—are said to be knowable in introspection. Gaṅgeśa therefore takes great pains to show that truth is *more than the mere co-existence* of (1) the property of having a qualifier and (2) the property of having a qualificandum which possesses that qualifier. For this see pp. 43. *infra*.

(*d*) *The* Vedāntic *theory*: The *Vedāntic* form of the *svataḥprāmāṇya* theory owes some of its peculiarities to the background of the Vedāntic metaphysics. For our present purpose, it would suffice to draw attention to two of its main features before raising the really critical issues that are at stake. In the first place, the Vedāntin's conception of knowledge is very different from the Mīmāṃsaka's. The word 'knowledge' means, in the

25. Compare Gaṅgeśa in *Prāmāṇyavāda*, Gāgā Bhaṭṭa's *Bhāṭṭacintāmaṇi*, Viśvanātha's *Siddhāntamuktāvalī* etc.

26. Thus Gāgā Bhaṭṭa: "*Murārimiśrāstu ghaṭādijñānottaraṃ ghaṭaṃ jānāmityādyanuvyavasāyo jāyate tena ghaṭatvavadviśeṣyakaghaṭatvaprakārakarūpaprāmāṇyagraha ityāhuḥ*". (*loc. cit.*, p. 19)

27. "*Viṣayanirūpyaṃ hi jñānaṁ ato jñānavittivedyo viṣaya iti vyavasāye bhāsamāne dharmadharmivat tadvaiśiṣṭyamapi viṣayaḥ*". (*Prāmāṇyavāda*)

Advaita works, either of four things: (*i*) a modification of the inner sense (*antaḥkaraṇavṛtti*) or (*ii*) consciousness as limited by a modification of the inner sense (*antaḥkaraṇavṛttyavacchinna-caitanya*) or (*iii*) the witness self (*sākṣī*) or, finally (*iv*) the pure undifferentiated consciousness free from all limiting adjuncts and determinations. Of these four, the question of truth or falsity does not concern either (*iii*) or (*iv*); not (*iv*), for it has no object and truth or falsity pertains to the relation of knowledge to its object[28]; not (*iii*), for the witness self to which, on the Vedāntic theory, everything is given either as known or as unknown is by itself neither true nor false.[29] It is really (*i*) and (*ii*) of which we could meaningfully predicate truth or falsity. Curiously enough, (*i*) is not self-revealing, for being a modification of the inner sense it is, on the Vedāntic principles, *jaḍa* or non-conscious. But there is the saving consideration that (*i*) never remains unknown, being in direct touch with the self-luminous witness self. Knowledge in the sense of (*i*) is therefore self-revealing only in a derivative sense. It is not revealed by itself, but it is revealed directly, i.e. without the mediation of another *vṛtti*, by the *sākṣī*. It is (*ii*) which is knowledge in the strictest sense and which is self-luminous in a sense that is more direct than the sense in which (*i*) is so.

Secondly, *svataḥprāmāṇya* on the Vedāntic theory means that the truth of a knowledge is apprehended through the same *sākṣī*-awareness through which the knowledge itself is apprehended.

The really pertinent question however is, what does the Vedāntin mean by '*prāmāṇya*' in this context? In other words, in what precise sense of '*prāmāṇya*' does the Vedāntin take it to be intrinsic to a knowledge?

The usual definitions of '*prāmāṇya*' are in terms of the uncontradicted character (*abādhitatvam*) and the originality (*anadhigatatvam*) of a knowledge.[30] We have however said before that the *anadhigatatvam* is a character whose ascertainment depends upon subsequent reflection and cannot be apprehended *ab initio*.

28. Cp. *Advaitasiddhi*, p. 311.

29. Thus *Advaitasiddhi*: "*Sākṣijñānasya bhramapramāsādhāraṇatvena*" etc. (p. 351).

30. Thus, for example, Vācaspati Miśra: "*Abādhitānadhigatāsandigdha-bodhajanakatvaṃ hi pramāṇatvaṃ pramāṇānām*" (*Bhāmatī*, 1·4).

It remains to be shown that the same could as well be said of *abādhitatvam*. This is practically admitted by Madhusūdana Sarasvatī. Uncontradictedness refers not merely to the absence of contradiction at the time of knowing[31] but also to the absence of contradiction in future. Now, Madhusūdana recognizes that though present uncontradictedness may be apprehended along with the knowledge, yet it is absurd to suppose that a knowledge is apprehended *ab initio* as incapable of contradiction in future.[32,33]

Vivaraṇa regards *prāmāṇya* in the sense of the capacity of manifesting (its) object as being intrinsic to a knowledge.[34] But is not this capacity for manifesting (its object) common to both right knowledge and error, as Umbeka has rightly pointed out? For erroneous apprehension, like all apprehension, is of an object, and it also manifests its object. This sense of truth therefore does not serve to distinguish true from false knowledge. If it be said, that is just the reason why all knowledge is intrinsically true in this sense, we could only reply that truth in this sense could never possibly be absent in an apprehension so that the Vedāntin would not be entitled to hold the further position, which in fact he holds, that a knowledge may be rendered false through extrinsic circumstances. For, no matter what extrinsic circumstances might present themselves, no matter if a knowledge is proved to be erroneous, the apprehension still remains apprehension of

31. "*Vyavahārakālābādhyatva*" (*Advaitasiddhi*, p. 351).

32. "*Bhāvikālabādhatadabhāvau ca na mānaṃ vinā sākṣiṇā grahītuṃ śakyate tasya vidyamānamātragrāhitvāditi*" (*ibid*., p. 35). *Gauḍabrahmānandī* admits that validity also in the sense of *viśeṣyāvṛttyaprakārakatva* (i. e. the property of not having a form e.g. 'snakehood' which does not reside in the substantival object, e.g. in a rope) is not apprehended *svataḥ*, the reason apparently being that such a property consisting of a double negation cannot but be the object of subsequent deliberation (*Advaitasiddhi*, p. 312).

33. This future uncontradictedness is not to be confused with that absolute uncontradictedness (*trikālābādhyatva*) which belongs only to Brahman and which cannot be apprehended by any means (*Advaitasiddhi*, p. 499). The latter is called *tāttvikaprāmāṇya* or metaphysical truth and is distinguished from empirical truth. We are here concerned only with empirical truth. But in what precise sense of truth is empirical truth *svatogrāhya*?

34. "*Nāpi prāmāṇyamarthaparicchedasāmarthyaṃ kāraṇaguṇajñānātparatovagamyate*" (Viz. ed., p. 102). "*Prāmāṇyaṃ nāma jñānasyārthaparicchedasāmarthyam*" (*Vivaraṇaprameyasaṃgraha*, Vasumati edition, Bk, II, p. 223).

something. When therefore the Mīmāṃsaka and the Vedāntin maintain that truth is intrinsic to a knowledge whereas falsity is extrinsic, they ought to understand the two notions of truth and falsity in such a manner that the one remains the contradictory of the other.

Should we then say that truth, for the Vedāntin, is nothing other than the *tadvati tatprakārakatva* of the Naiyāyika? According to this meaning of 'truth', a knowledge 'S is p' is true when p really belongs to S, that is to say, when S (p) is known as p. When p does not really belong to S, the knowledge 'S is p' is false. In Gaṅgeśa's opinion it is only in this sense that truth may be regarded as being apprehended *ab initio*.[35] But the consensus of opinion of the Advaita writers seems to be that *tadvati tatprakārakatva* is common to both right knowledge and error and therefore does not constitute the sense of 'truth' in which all knowledge is intrinsically true (but not intrinsically false). Madhusūdana at least of all writers is emphatically clear on this point.[36] It is curious that though Gaṅgeśa considers *tadvati tatprakārakatva* as the feature which distinguishes right knowledge from error, Madhusūdana and many Advaita writers regard it as belonging to all apprehensions, not excluding error. There is reason therefore to suspect that the Naiyāyika and the Vedāntin do *not* mean quite the same by '*tadvati tatprakārakatva*'.[37] But for the present we shall leave the matter there with the hope that this question would receive further clarification in part III of this Introduction.

A way out is suggested by adding a qualification to *tadvati tatprakārakatva*. Not bare *tadvati tatprakārakatva* but that as qualified by the property of leading to successful activity is what serves

35. "*Tathāpi tadvati tatprakārakajñānatvaṃ tadvati tadvaiśiṣṭyajñānatvaṃ vā prāmāṇyaṃ tacca jñānagrāhakasāmagrīgrāhyam*". (*loc. cit.*, p. 110)

36. Madhusūdana Sarasvatī, *Advaitaratnarakṣaṇam* (*Advaitasiddhi* edn., pp. 29-30). Compare also a modern writer Anantakrishna Sastri: "*yadyapi vedāntinām mate tadvati tatprakārakatvarūpam prāmāṇyaṃ bhramasādhāraṇameva, tathāpi saṃvādipravṛttijanakatvaviśiṣṭaṃ tat na tatsādhāraṇamiti* (*Paribhāṣāprakāśikā* on *Vedāntaparibhāṣā*, Calcutta 1927, p. 263).

37. One reason for this may be that the Advaitin admits a false object which is the object of false apprehension, so that e.g. the false silver does possess the generic character of silverhood.

to distinguish right knowledge from error.[38] This may indeed be so,[39] but can we take such a complex property as capable of being apprehended *ab initio*? On the other hand, it seems reasonable to suggest that at least the property of being the cause of successful activity *cannot* in any case be a feature which one apprehends *ab initio*, for like *abādhitatva*, *saṃvādipravṛttijanakatva* also refers to a future possibility which could at best only be anticipated now.

The exact sense of '*prāmāṇya*' in which the Advaitin could speak both of '*svataḥprāmāṇya*' and of '*parataḥaprāmāṇya*' has to be specified in some other manner. There are two other suggestions that we are to consider; the one gives a psychological account and saves the theory, the other suggests a definition and renders the theory valid *but analytically trivial*.

Gauḍabrahmānandī, after showing that *prāmāṇya* in the sense of *abādhitatva* cannot be regarded as *svataḥ*, suggests that '*prāmāṇya*' for that purpose should be regarded as being the same as 'the property of being a knowledge of anything which has not been known to be false'.[40] In this sense, a knowledge is true insofar as—and in the sense that—it is not known to be false. This is a psychological sense of 'truth', for truth here consists in one's ignorance that a knowledge is false. Now, this has the merit that it accounts for the fact that truth is apprehended *ab initio without obliterating* the distinction between right knowledge and error. For, certainly we cannot call a knowledge 'knowledge' unless it is unaccompained by an awareness of its own falsity; in this respect, every knowledge, even an erroneous apprehension prior to the detection of its erroneous character, is accompanied by an awareness of its own truth. In connection

38. This is the suggestion of Anantakrisna Sastri in the passage quoted in footnote 37.

39. *Gauḍabrahmānandī* recognizes that the simple property of causing an activity—and the activity, we may add, may also be *niṣkampa*—is common to right knowledge and error: "*pravṛttiprayojakatvarūpaṃ... pramātvaṃ bhramasyāpi vidyate*". Hence the qualification should be: " the property of causing successful activity". (*Advaitasiddhi*, p. 319)

40. "*Prāmāṇyam vyavahārakālāvacchinnasya mithyātvaniścayāviṣayatvasya ya āśrayaḥ tadviṣayakadhisvarūpam*". Again: "*Mithyātvena ajñātaṃ yat tadviṣayakajñānatvarūpapramātvasya jñānasāmānyagrāhakasākṣigrāhyatvarūpasvatogrāhyatvasambhavāt*". (*Advaitasiddhi*, pp. 351-352)

with the definition of 'truth' as *arthaparicchedasāmarthya* it was pointed out that this feature is intrinsic to all awareness quâ awareness and not quâ true knowledge, so that it characterizes an erroneous apprehension even if the latter is recognized as erroneous. Now the present psychological definition of 'truth' has the advantage that in this sense truth belongs to an erroneous apprehension only so long as its erroneous character is not detected. Truth in this sense does not characterize all awareness but certainly belongs to all knowledge, and continues to characterize a knowledge so long as extrinsic circumstances do not divest that knowledge of its character of being a knowledge by exposing its pretensions and in effect by reducing it to a mere awareness. It is thus a good account of the meaning of 'truth' within the limits of the *svataḥprāmāṇya*-and-*parataḥaprāmāṇya* theory.

Its defects however—if they are at all to be regarded as defects—are twofold. First, the sense given to 'truth' is chiefly psychological, and secondly, the definition is a negative one. Were the definition merely negative, we could pass it over; what is worse is that it smacks even of circularity. For, 'truth' is defined in terms of 'falsity', as if the idea of falsity is logically more fundamental or epistemically clearer. If however a knowledge is to be called 'false' when it is not true (or if an object is to be called false if it is not the object of a true knowledge), then the definition is plainly circular. Nevertheless as a psychological account of every knowledge-situation, it is based on a sound phenomenological basis.

The other definition is suggested by Madhusūdana in his *Advaitaratnarakṣaṇam*. After rejecting some definitions of 'truth' as unsatisfactory on the ground that they apply to error as well, Madhusūdana proceeds to define 'truth' as 'the property of being a certain apprehension of an object which was previously unknown'.[41] Truth in this sense, Madhusūdana claims, satisfies three needs: it serves to distinguish right knowledge from error, it is capable of being apprehended *svataḥ* as the theory demands, and further it can account for unwavering activity (*niṣkampa pravṛtti*) as the phenomena demand. It does not belong to error, for

41. "*Ajñātārthaniścayātmakatvameva prāmāṇyamasmatpakṣe*". (*loc. cit.*, p. 32)

the content of erroneous apprehension, e.g. the snake in rope-snake illusion, exists only when it is being perceived and therefore has no unknown existence (*ajñātasattā*). Of the object of erroneous apprehension we cannot then say that it was unknown before: hence truth in the above sense does not belong to erroneous apprehension. It is capable of being apprehended *ab initio*, for—according to the Advaita epistemology—the prior unknown existence of what now comes to be known is an object of *sākṣī*-awareness. (What is now known through any of the means of true knowledge is at the same time known as having been unknown before.) Hence, the property of being a certain apprehension of what was previously unknown is something that is apprehended together with any knowledge and by the same *sākṣī*-consciousness.

One very curious feature of the Mīmāṃsā-Vedānta theory is that truth, on this theory, is apprehended *ab initio*, in all knowledge including erroneous apprehension prior to the detection of its erroneous character. But as soon as what so long passed as knowledge is now known to be erroneous, it is divested of its pretensions to be knowledge. Thus truth should on the one hand be common to all apprehensions including error, and yet it should also serve to distinguish right knowledge from error. The theory seeks to satisfy these two apparently conflicting demands. With regard to Madhusūdana's definition of 'truth', we may say that prior to the detection of its erroneous character, even an error passes for true knowledge insofar as even the erroneous object is felt to have had a prior unknown existence; but as soon as the error is recognised as an error, its object is at once seen to possess only a *prātibhāsika* being, i.e. to say being only while it was being experienced. Being without unknown existence, it cannot be an object of a true knowledge.

Understood in this way, Madhusūdana's theory also gives us a psychological account of truth. For, a knowledge, on this theory, is true so long as it is taken to be opposed to *ajñāna* (i.e. to say *ajñānavirodhi*); negatively speaking, a knowledge is true so long as we are *not* aware of it as *ajñāna-avirodhi*, which is the same as saying that a true knowledge is the apprehension of something which has not been known to be false (*mithyātvena ajñātaṃ yat tadviṣayakajñāna*).[42] The latter is the definition of *Gauḍabrahmānandī* and has been discussed above.

Madhusūdana, however, proceeds in a direction quite different from the above psychological interpretation of his theory. He goes on *to define* '*jñānatva*' in terms of '*pramātva*', so that invalid apprehension is regarded as lacking even the generic character of *jñānatva*.[43] Error is really pseudo-knowledge, not knowledge proper.[44] To the well-known argument of the Naiyāyika that if truth originated from the same conditions as give rise to the knowledge, false apprehension should also become true, for the generating conditions of knowledge are also the generating conditions of false apprehension, the latter being, like true apprehension, a species of knowledge, Madhusūdana confidently replies that this need not be so, for false apprehension is not a species of knowledge.[45] Error is not knowledge. It follows *analytically* that truth is intrinsic to knowledge.[46]

We may now sum up the conclusions towards which the above discussions have been leading us.

There are two ways of defining '*prāmāṇya*', so as to render the *svataḥprāmāṇya*-and-*parataḥaprāmāṇya* theory a plausible one.

On the one formulation, *prāmāṇya* is explained in the psychological language with reference to the knower's *unawareness* as to the falsity of the knowledge under consideration. On the other formulation, *prāmāṇya* is identified with the very generic character of *jñānatva*, so that a false apprehension is, by *definition*, not knowledge at all.[47] On both formulations, to know is to know truly, and to know a knowledge is to know it as true.

42. See footnote 40 above.

43. "*Apramāyā ajñānavirodhitvarūpajñānatvābhāvena...*" (*loc. cit.*, 33).

44. "*Na hi hetvābhāso heturbhavati, tadvanna jñānābhāsasya jñānatvam*" (*loc. cit.*, p. 33). For the Naiyāyika, this is not so. Hence the Naiyāyika would regard *pramātva* as belonging only to one species of knowledge and not as coextensive with *jñānatva*.

45. "*Na ca jñānasāmagrīmātrajanyatve apramāpi pramā syāditi vācyaṃ; tasya jñānasāmagrījanyatvābhāvāt. Na ca—evaṃ sati sa jñānamapi na syāditi vācyaṃ, iṣṭāpatteḥ*". (*loc. cit.*, p. 34)

46. "*Jñānamātre jñānatvavat pramātvasyāpyanugamāt sāmānyasāmagrīmātraprayojyatā...*". (*loc. cit.*, p. 34)

47. The late K.C. Bhattacharyya has proposed a similar theory in his paper "Knowledge and Truth", included in the Second Volume of his *Studies in*

In the former sense, *prāmāṇya* belongs in common to all knowledge, right or erroneous, but in the long run, as the erroneous character of the error is detected, it deserts the erroneous apprehension. It would not be correct to ascribe to this theory the view that a knowledge is true if it is not false: that would be trivial. The theory rather says that knowledge is true (*not taken as true*) if it is *not known* to be false. Thus, on this account, truth is a derivative concept and fits in with the Advaita metaphysics that nothing empirical is real. Empirical truth, therefore, is a concept which is logically definable only in terms of falsity. It must be said that to avoid the above mentioned charge of circularity, the Advaitin must give a positive account of falsity (which indeed he claims to have given!).

The second formulation, at the first glance, makes the *svataḥprāmāṇya* theory an analytic consequence of the suggested *definition* of 'knowledge' in terms of '*pramātva*'. But the definition is more than an arbitrary linguistic recommendation: there is an important sense in which it is also phenomenologically descriptive. For, there is a certain absurdity in saying both 'I know that S is p' and 'S is p is false'. One cannot know and yet be in error with regard to what he knows. If something is known, it follows necessarily that it is true. Thus, according to Ayer,[48] in order that I may be able to say 'I know that S is p', three and only three conditions need to be fulfilled. These are: (*i*) that 'S is p' is true, (*ii*) that I am sure of (*i*); and (*iii*) that I who know have the right[48a] to be sure. Knowledge, according to Ayer, is intrinsically true in the sense that if something is known, it follows necessarily that it is true.[49] This follows, we are

---

Philosophy (Calcutta, 1958). Thus he writes: "Two propositions may be stated about knowledge—that knowing is known only as implied in the explicit awareness of truth and that truth is asserted only of a content that is known. Knowledge and truth have to be defined in terms of each other". (p. 154) Again, "There is...no such thing as false knowledge" (p. 157), so that "if it now appears to be not true, it is never said to have been known but taken at best to have been believed" (p. 158).

48. A.J. Ayer, *The Problem of Knowledge* (London, 1956), Ch. I.

48a. In the Indian *svataḥprāmāṇya* theories this 'right to be so sure' need not be apprehended *ab initio*.

49. *Ibid*, p. 22.

told, from the 'linguistic *fact*' that what is not true cannot properly be *said to be* known.[50] What happens if subsequently I detect that. I was really in error? It would follow that I really did not *know*, that I had mistaken a pseudo-knowledge (*jñānābhāsa*) for a knowledge. Hence, it is not a knowledge which becomes falsified, but it is really a pseudo-knowledge whose pretensions to be knowledge are now exposed. Hence the curiously paradoxical situation that although the *svataḥprāmāṇya* theory defined 'knowledge' in terms of 'truth' thereby condemning error as pseudo-knowledge, yet in its attempt to establish its position it includes under its '*pakṣa*' all that *claims* to be knowledge including knowledge in the true sense and pseudo-knowledge.

It should be added that if the *svataḥprāmāṇya* theory is stated in this way, then truth can be taken to be *svataḥ* only with regard to its apprehension (*jñaptitaḥ*) and not with regard to its origination (*utpattitaḥ*). It is only the Prābhākara who is constrained to accept that truth is *svataḥ* even with regard to its origin, for if he did not subscribe to this he would be contradicting his own cardinal doctrine that all knowledge is true, that there is strictly speaking no error at all. Others like the Bhāṭṭas and the Vedāntins may or may not[51] subscribe to this part of the *svataḥ* theory; they may remain content with a moderate form by regarding truth to be *svataḥ* only with regard to apprehension.

All others (except the Prābhākaras) believe that there is erroneous apprehension. While believing in this, they may choose to subscribe to either of the following two explanations: (*a*) they may hold that all apprehensions are initially true but some of them become subsequently, owing to extraneous circumstances, erroneous; or (*b*) they might hold that all knowledge is initially *apprehended* as true, though some of these are, right from the beginning, erroneous and therefore not knowledge at all but are

50. Thus the late K.C. Bhattacharyya bases his suggested definition of 'knowledge' in terms of 'truth' upon the phenomenological evidence that knowing is known never as an "indifferent psychical fact", but always as "the implicate of the awareness of truth" from which it follows that truth "cannot be taken simply as additional confirmation of what already is known indifferently". (*loc. cit.*, p. 157).

51. Thus, for example Pārthasārathi in *Nyāyaratnamālā* accepts the intrinsic character of truth only with regard to its apprehension.

pseudo-knowledge whose falsity comes to be recognised later on owing to extraneous circumstances.

The alternative (*a*) is most consistently held by those for whom an objective definition of 'truth' is not possible and who would consequently define 'truth' in psychological terms as indicated above. But since in this sense truth is not an objective property so that calling a knowledge true is nothing other than not knowing it as false, it is apparent that to claim truth to be *svataḥ* with regard to its origination is rather trivial. This is so for the reason that on this theory *being true* and being *apprehended* as true are the same.

The alternative (*b*) is most consistently held by those who also believe in two other propositions: (*i*) that truth originates *svataḥ* in all knowledge, but not in erroneous apprehensions; and (*ii*) that nevertheless both knowledge and pseudo-knowledge are *ab initio* apprehended as true.

Both the Prābhākaras and those amongst the others who subscribe to (*b*) believe truth to be intrinsic to all knowledge. But this apparent agreement is reached by radically different approaches—in the case of the Prābhākaras by rejecting error and consequently by regarding all certain apprehension as amounting to knowledge, and in the case of the upholders of (*b*) by admitting error but at the same time by excluding error from the purview of the term 'knowledge'.

The Prābhākaras *extend* the scope of 'knowledge' to include all apprehension; the others subscribing to (*b*) *contract* its scope so as to include only right apprehension. It goes without saying that (*b*) is on a safer ground. For, the Prābhākaras by including under the scope of 'knowledge' all apprehensions—not excluding the *so-called* erroneous ones—can save their theory only at the cost of introducing an equally extended sense of 'truth' according to which all knowledge is true since all knowledge is an "*awareness* of...." It hardly needs be emphasised that in this last mentioned sense of 'truth', the *svataḥ* theory, though irrefutable, becomes trivial.

The Naiyāyikas also do not accept the distinction between knowledge and pseudo-knowledge in the manner of (*b*), nor do they accept either the psychological definition of 'truth' advocated in (*a*) or the trivial account of the Prābhākaras. For the Naiyāyika, true and false knowledge form two *species* of knowledge, agreeing in the generic character of being knowledge but differing in the specific characters of truth and falsity. It follows that for him, truth *cannot* be intrinsic to knowledge as such, though it is left to be seen why he also does not regard truth as *svataḥ* even with regard to apprehension. This shall require a precise delimitation of the Nyāya concepts of knowledge and truth, to which the next part of this introduction is to be devoted. It is only after we are able to fix the precise sense of 'truth' in which the Nyāya regards truth to be extrinsic that any attempt to assess the traditional arguments and counter-arguments on both sides could bear fruitful results.

I should conclude this examination of the *svataḥprāmāṇya* theory by noting down a caution against a misinterpretation of this theory which has been most common but which strangely enough has not been challenged. It has been usual to regard this theory as but an Indian version of what passes in Western philosophy as the self-evidence theory of truth. Self-evidence, on the Western theory, is still *a criterion* of truth, a criterion which serves to distinguish truth from error. A *criterion of truth* is always double-edged; it is also a criterion of error. It is precisely the contention of the *svataḥprāmāṇya* theory however that *there is no criterion of truth, though there are criteria of error.* Knowledge as such is true or is apprehended as true; the criteria, when applied, cannot any more *prove* its truth. They may however establish the erroneous character of what so long had passed for knowledge. Error is proved to be error, but knowledge cannot be proved to be true. For the self-evidence theory, on the other hand, truth is proved to be true (or falsehood proved to be false) by the criterion of clearness and distinctness (or, by its opposite). This is far too simple to be a faithful account of the complex phenomena of the progress of human knowledge.

III. The Nyāya Theory of *Parataḥ-prāmāṇya*

In the preceding part of this essay, we have analysed the various notions of *prāmāṇya* upheld by the different advocates of the theory of *svataḥprāmāṇya*. Now we may take up the theory of *paratahprāmāṇya*, especially as upheld by its principal advocates, the Nyāya school of philosophy. It is only after the fundamental concepts and presuppositions—ontological, logical and epistemic—are thus laid bare that we could fruitfully attempt a critical appraisal of the entire *svataḥ-parataḥ* controversy.

The following exposition of the Nyāya theory of *parataḥ-prāmāṇya* has four parts. We start with an account of the Nyāya conception of *jñāna*, for when dealing with *prāmāṇya*, we are in fact concerned with something which is a property of *jñāna*. Next, we shall pass over to the conception of *prāmāṇya* in the Nyāya system. With the notions of *jñāna* and *prāmāṇya* clarified, we would be in a position to offer an account of the Nyāya theory of *paratahprāmāṇya*. In the last two parts, we shall enquire into the basic presuppositions of this theory.

(*a*) *The Nyāya Conception of Knowledge* (*Jñāna*)

(*i*) With regard to the Nyāya conception of *jñāna*, it is necessary for us to bear in mind firstly that *jñāna*, in the Nyāya ontology, has the status of a *guṇa* (which can be rendered into 'quality' only at the risk of grave misunderstanding). Every *guṇa*, in accordance with the definition of '*guṇa*' in the Nyāya ontology, rests in a substance and the substance, in the present case, is none other than the self. Since we are not, in the present context, concerned with the notion of self which therefore need not detain us, we may turn for a moment back to the notion of *guṇa* which, as has already been remarked in parenthesis, does not mean 'quality'. One only needs to remember that the Nyāya includes in its list of *guṇas* such things as *saṃyoga* (or conjunction) which is ordinarily regarded as a relation. Uddyotakara regards "desire, etc." (*icchādayaḥ*) as *guṇas* on the ground that they cannot be subsumed under the rest of the categories (*pāriśeṣyāt*).[52] *Jñāna* is not an activity, but a product;[53] to call it an activity would, firstly, amount to an unusual extension of the ordinary notion of act, involving the notion of movement (*spandana*); but, secondly, it is not admitted by the

52. *Nyāyadarśana* (Calcutta Sanskrit Series), p. 193.

53. Thus Jayanta: "*Na hi kriyāsvabhāvaṃ jñānamapi tu phalasvabhāvameva*" (*Nyāyamañjarī*, Chowkh. ed., p. 16).

definitions underlying the Nyāya ontology.[54] Further, *jñāna* is not a modification of any substance, and therefore it would not be correct to call it a state of a substance, if by 'state' be meant such a modification. For, *jñāna* is a *guṇa* of the self which is not capable of modification in the same sense in which a lump of clay is modified into a pot or in any other literal sense. And, of course, *jñāna* is far from being a mental state, for the mind is only one of the factors in its production but certainly is not that in which what is thereby produced inheres. It must be noted that though the Nyāya gains an advantage by not regarding *jñāna* as a mental state, the incurable privacy of *jñāna* nevertheless persists, for each person's self and therefore his *jñāna* is directly perceivable only by himself and by none else. Thus, a *jñāna* is a product arising out of a collocation of causal conditions. And like all products, it is an occurrent, i.e. to say, arises in time and is replaced by others; the fact that it is not a modification and the fact that it is without any component parts (*niravayava*) are two aspects of the same situation, and being without parts it is also without any ontological form of its own (*nirākāra*).[55] In this respect the Nyāya view stands in sharp opposition to the conception of *jñāna* in Sāṃkhya or Vedānta, according to which it is a modification of a substance called *buddhi* or *antaḥkaraṇa* and *buddhi* or *antaḥkaraṇa* being a composite substance assumes the shape and the form of the object. Not so in the Nyāya: the *jñāna* being a *guṇa* and therefore without parts does not assume any form or shape (*ākāra*). Similarly not being a *kriyā*, it does not bring about any change in the object that is known, as the Bhāṭṭas wrongly regard it as doing.

(*ii*) While thus ontologically, *jñāna* is a *guṇa* of the self, a product of various causal conditions, and yet itself without component parts and so without shape and form, epistemologically it refers beyond itself to its object. This last feature is what serves to distinguish *jñāna* from the other *guṇas* of the self, i.e.

54. This second point needs emphasis. The Nyāya ontology is not a defence of ordinary usage, but a system constructed with its own categories and their definitions. For the idea of such an ontology, see N. Goodman, *The Structure of Appearance* (Cambridge, Mass., 1951).

55. Udayana: "*Arthenaiva viśeṣo hi nirākāratayā dhiyām*" (*Kusumāñjali*, 4.4).

from desire, aversion, effort, pleasure, pain, etc. *Jñāna* alone, of all the other *guṇas* of the self, has this self-transcending reference to an object, and this reference—or intentionality, as Brentano would call it—is intrinsic to *jñāna* quâ *jñāna*.[56] Others, a desire, an aversion for example, may refer to an object but only indirectly, i.e. through the *via media* of a *jñāna*.[57]

But, is not such self-transcending reference or intentionality intrinsic to consciousness as such? And, if so, are not pleasure and pain, desire and aversion states of consciousness, and therefore also intentional? The Nyāya answer is very definite on this point: 'consciousness' and '*jñāna*' are, for the Nyāya, synonymous expressions.[58] To be conscious is to be conscious of something which again is the same as having a *jñāna* of that something. Pleasure and pain, desire and aversion then are not as such states of consciousness, though we are—or, more accurately, become—conscious of them.[59]

What has been said above indicates the very wide sense in which the Nyāya, along with most other systems of Indian thought, uses the word '*jñāna*', so that to render this Sanskrit word '*jñāna*' into the English 'knowledge' would be—and, in fact, has proved—definitely misleading. In fact, it is really the other word '*pramā*'—which denotes ordinarily only a species of *jñāna*—that permits itself to be translated 'knowledge.' It is redundant therefore to say—as has, more often than not, been held—that '*pramā*' means true knowledge. '*Pramā*' certainly means true *jñāna* but since '*jñāna*' is not synonymous with 'knowledge' and since, in accordance with the English usage, to

56. Thus Vācaspati: "*tasmādarthapravaṇebhyo jñānebhyastadapravaṇatayā bhinna-jātīyāḥ sukhādayo...*". (*Tātparyaṭīkā*, p. 108)

Also Vallabhācārya: "*jñānatve cecchādivyāvṛttasvabhāvasya viṣayapravaṇatvamapekṣitamiti*". (*Nyāyalīlāvatī*, Chowkh. ed., p. 814)

57. Śaṅkara Miśra: "*icchādau tu jñānaupādhikaṃ tat*". (*Kaṇṭhābharaṇa* on *Nyāyalīlāvatī*, p. 812)

58. Thus, "*Buddhirupalabdhijñānamityanarthāntaram*" (*Nyāya Sūtra* 1. 1.15). Also, Vācaspati: "*buddheḥ svābhāvikaṃ caitanyamāstheyam*" (*Tātparyaṭīkā* on 1.1.15). Vallabha: "*prakāśo buddhiḥ*". (*loc. cit.*, p. 408)

59. See on this point Kalidas Bhattacharyya, "The Indian Theories of Self and Knowledge" (*Our Heritage*, Vol. 2, Part II, especially pp. 221-223). Also B.K. Matilal, *Perception An Essay on Classical Indian Theories of Knowledge*, Oxford, Clarendon Press, 1986, esp. ch. 9.

know that S is p entails that S is p, '*pramā*' could safely be treated as being equivalent to 'knowledge'. That '*jñāna*' and 'knowledge' are not synonymous expressions is further indicated by the fact that the Nyāya would treat doubt as a species of *jñāna* while to doubt is not to know, according to the English usage of 'know', though doubting certainly involves some knowledge which is not itself doubting. It cannot be said that doubt is a complex form of knowledge involving two mutually contradictory predications and as such resolves itself into elements of which each taken by itself is a knowledge; and that if this be so, then the equivalence between '*jñāna*' and 'knowledge' may be restored. Now this indeed is a possible alternative and has been adopted by Mīmāṃsakas in their zeal to establish *svataḥprāmāṇya*. It is also possible that some Naiyāyikas attempted such an explanation of doubt,[60] though the general tradition of the Nyāya regards doubt as an irreducible form of *jñāna*. Moreover, as would be emphasised later on, this latter explanation of doubt fits in better with the Nyāya conception of truth. Thus we may safely conclude that if I am conscious of anything in whatsoever mode it may be, in the Nyāya terminology I may be said to have a *jñāna* of it, although in accordance with the ordinary use of 'know' in the English language I may not be said to know it.

After having warned in the just preceding paragraph that '*jñāna*' and 'knowledge' are not equivalent expressions, I would add that in the following discussion I *propose* to use the English word 'know' (and its substantive form) in exactly the same sense in which '*jñāna*' is used in the Nyāya, so that when I have a doubt, I would *say* I have a knowledge. Consistently with this *proposal*, '*pramā*' would naturally be rendered 'true knowledge' although—as has been pointed out earlier—such a rendering would be redundant if we keep to the ordinary use of 'know'. Now that the exact sense of '*jñāna*' has been sufficiently emphasised, our proposal to use 'know' and 'knowledge' in its place could not possibly mislead us in our philosophical conclusions.

60. This view is generally attributed to the author of *Ratnakoṣa*, an extinct work.

(*iii*) So far we have explained the ontological and the epistemic nature of knowledge, as upheld by the Nyāya school. Now we shall consider it from the logical point of view. We are of course concerned only with the so-called *savikalpa* knowledge, for that alone, being propositional, admits of logical analysis. But before we go deeper into this matter, an initial difficulty must be mentioned. How at all is it possible to attempt a logical analysis of something that is a transitory occurrent, as a knowledge is according to the Nyāya ontology? Being a *guṇa*, a knowledge cannot be shared in common by two selves;[61] it is incurably particular and in a sense private too. Is a logical analysis of anything of such a nature possible ? I am not quite sure what the Nyāya answer to this difficulty would be, but I am sure that whatever would be the answer would also illuminate one of the basic features of the Nyāya attitude towards knowledge. But I presume, the difficulty might be resolved by the Nyāya by denying that the ontological and the logical attitudes are opposed to each other. It is well-known that the Nyāya logic is ontological and, where necessary, psychological too. Logical structure is not something raised above the existent world or belonging to an ideal world of forms—but is itself a product of existent factors and is exhibited in existents and occurrents. If this be so, the Nyāya might contend, the objection is pointless, for a knowledge, though a transitory occurrent, may yet exhibit logical structures: such perhaps is the very nature of knowledge quâ knowledge.

This leads us to the real crux of the situation. We have said above that *savikalpa* knowledge is propositional. In what sense is this so? Let me introduce the following distinctions, well known in Western logic, in order to find out exactly the Nyāya position in this respect:—

(*a*) An indicative sentence, if significant, is said to express a proposition. Two different sentences may express the same proposition. Thus a sentence may be distinguished from the proposition it expresses. A sentence is a physical occurrent; the

61. Thus Uddyotakara: "*Yadi guṇaḥ sa na sādhāraṇaḥ*" (*Vārttika* on 1.1.23).

proposition expressed is the meaning of the sentence; it is a logical structure.

(β) A proposition may be distinguished from a judgment by saying that in a judgment there is a mental act directed towards a proposition; the proposition is either asserted or denied, believed or disbelieved. A sentence is uttered or written, but a proposition is asserted, denied, etc. Now, the distinction between a mental act and the proposition towards which the act is directed owes its plausibility to the following situation: it is possible to retain an identically fixed proposition and to vary the mental acts directed towards it, so that the very same proposition I was at first doubting, I now assert but later on come to deny. A mental act is a particular occurrent, and private too; but a proposition is not an occurrent but, to use that highly provoking expression, a subsistent entity. Not only can I entertain different mental attitudes towards the same proposition, but two different persons may believe in the same proposition as well! Thus a proposition is objective, at least in the minimum sense of being inter-subjective.

Let us now ask: to which of these categories does knowledge, as conceived in the Nyāya, really belong? It is certainly not the sentence, for the sentence, whether spoken or written, uttered aloud or nascent, is not a *guṇa* of the self. Is it then the proposition expressed by the sentence? Again, we have to say, 'no'. For, the Nyāya does not distinguish between the meaning and the reference of an expression, and what an expression means is taken to be the same as that which it refers to, so that the meaning of a sentence is the state of affairs it refers to and not an intermediate, subsistent entity called a proposition. Further, those who believe in propositions distinguish them not only from sentences but also, as we have seen in (β) above, from the mental acts like asserting, denying, doubting, etc. It seems to me that the Nyāya would not also entertain this latter distinction, for it is not entitled to postulate mental acts—not certainly acts of the self—to serve as the designata of such introspective judgments as 'I know', 'I believe', 'I doubt', etc. Again, the Nyāya would not agree with the contention that it is the same content which I at first doubted and which I now assert or which I may later deny. The content of doubt for example is not

'S is p' which I come to assert later on, but involves the two mutually contradictory predicates 'p' and 'not-p'. It seems then that neither the distinction (α) nor those under (β) are acceptable to the Nyāya.

Positively, we may say that, according to the Nyāya, a *savikalpa* knowledge is propositional though not a proposition,[62] and further that the two expressions 'I know that S is p' and 'my knowledge that S is p' refer to the same state of affairs. The two points require some elucidation. By saying that a *savikalpa* knowledge is propositional though not a proposition, I wish to do justice to both the fact that a knowledge is not a sentence but is expressed by it and the fact that it is nevertheless not a self-subsistent objective entity of the sort conveyed by the word 'proposition'. I call it 'propositional' for it is a logical complex analysable into constituent elements and relations. By the second of the above two statements, I wish to draw attention to the fact that it is the same fact, an event or a situation—a *jñāna*—which is the referent of the episodic verb 'I know' as well as of the substantive 'my knowledge', so that the distinction between a mental act of knowing and a content towards which the act is directed would prove to be an illusion fostered by language. Likewise, the expression 'I doubt' and the expression 'my doubt' refer to the same thing and not that the former refers to the act of doubting while the latter to the content. In fact, what is produced (in the self) is an act and a content in one, a *guṇa* having the specific property of intentionality. More accurately speaking, what is produced is a content having an intentional character and it is this intentional character whose linguistic formulation

62. Ingalls seems to hold that the Nyāya analyses, not propositions but, cognitions (*loc. cit.*, pp. 33-4). In the light of what I have said above, I should like to hold that the Nyāya does not distinguish between proposition and sentence on the one hand and knowledge and proposition on the other. It does distinguish between knowledge and sentence. What it analyses then is as much a knowledge as a proposition, but then not the self-subsistent proposition. More accurately, therefore, it analyses cognitions that are propositional in character if they are of the *savikalpa* sort. Whether a *savikalpa* knowledge is, according to the Nyāya, *necessarily* linguistic or not is a difficult problem. This much seems certain that, in the first place, it *can be* expressed in a sentence and, secondly, that it admits of a logical analysis (and so may be said to be propositional).

generates the illusion of its being an activity, which it really is not.

(*iv*) After having ascertained the ontological, the epistemic and the logical status of knowledge, we have now to turn to *the analysis of knowledge* in this system. It has been said before that knowledge, according to the Nyâya, is without any parts and is in this sense without any form (for, form, in this sense of the term, is constituted by the peculiar arrangement of the parts). Though knowledge is in this sense formless, yet it is—as has also been pointed out—capable of being analysed insofar as it has constituent logical elements and relations. There is no contradiction in holding these two views together, for the sense in which form is denied to knowledge is not the same as the sense in which form is again ascribed to it. Knowledge then is capable of analysis.

Analysing a knowledge requires a reflective attitude towards it. To know is to know an object, but not to know one's knowledge of the object at the same time. Knowledge, in other words, is directed towards the object and not towards itself. All this is familiar enough. Only it is important to bear in mind that the Nyāya like most schools of Indian thought advocates a direct realism; this is not however equivalent to saying that for the Nyāya there is no content of knowledge.[63] There is content of knowledge, though this content is brought to awareness in the reflective awareness. In the primary awareness, the contents are *not* the media through which the object is presented or, better, represented; they are rather transparent so that we perceive the object itself through them. In the reflective awareness, it is these contents that are directly perceived while the object is presented as ancillary (*pucchalagna*) to them! Analysing a knowledge involves this reflective awareness plus[64] an analysis of the content of knowledge into its constituent elements and relations. These

63. Contrast Kalidas Bhattacharyya, *loc. cit.*, *Our Heritage*, Vol. 2, Part II.

64. The merely reflective awareness or *anuvyavasāya* does not explicitly yield the analysis (but gives us the datum for analysis). Analysis therefore requires a different attitude. For an independent development of such a notion of content, see my "Remarks on the Content Theory" in the *Visvabharati Journal of Philosophy*, Vol. 2, No. 2 (Reprinted in *Phenomenology and Ontology*, The Hague: M. Nijhoff, 1970).

contents may all be brought under one category, technically called *viṣayatā*. Though the Nyāya speaks, e.g., of "*viṣayatā* that is attached to the pot" (*ghaṭaniṣṭhaviṣayatā*), yet considering the fact that for the Nyāya knowledge does not generate any feature in the object we may presume that the words 'attached to' have to be taken as a sort of transferred epithet, so that strictly speaking the *viṣayatā* attaches to the knowledge, or rather constitutes it. To say that a knowledge is *of* a pot is the same as saying that a knowledge-content intentionally refers to a pot which is again the same as saying that the content as so referring is the *viṣayatā* "that attaches to the pot".

Understanding '*viṣayatā*' in this wide sense as the regional title for all the various types of knowledge-contents, we have to add that '*viṣayatā*' again is subdivided into three sub-categories, technically called '*viśeṣyatā*', '*prakāratā*' and '*saṃsargatā*'. '*Viśeṣyatā*' is the general title for contents referring to the qualificandum, '*prakāratā*' for contents that refer to adjectives, while '*saṃsargatā*' for those that refer to relations (in each case, the contents are to be taken as so referring). The ideas of qualificandum and qualifier have to be here dissociated from the naive ontological ideas of substances that are incurably substantive and attributes that are incurably qualifying. We are on the other hand to recognise the possibility of a so-called substance, say a pot, characterising another substantive, say, the floor, so that in 'the floor with a pot', the pot also functions as an adjective. Much speculation has been done regarding the ontological status of these entities called '*viṣayatā*'. Some have regarded them as independent *padārthas*, others as "tertiary qualities".[65] No doubt they are called *jñānīya*, and no doubt again that they can be regarded both as "knowledgewise" and as "object-wise". But strictly speaking they are not properties of knowledge, but the knowledge-contents themselves: they constitute the knowledge, and are not its properties, for knowledge is not anything over and above these properties.

Against this last contention it might be objected that a *nirvikalpa* knowledge is knowledge though it is without any such *viṣayatā*, for certainly the *nirvikalpa*, according to the Nyāya,

65. Kalidas Bhattacharyya, *Our Heritage*, Vol. 2, Part II, p. 228.

does not contain any qualifier. In reply, we may point out that the real situation is this: the *nirvikalpa* is not any more direct grasp of the object than *savikalpa* is. Both grasp their objects directly as well as bodily, and in both there are contents that are not apprehended in primary awareness. Though however the contents of *savikalpa* become objects of reflective awareness, the contents of *nirvikalpa* do not,—a fact, for the explanation of which the metaphysician could only postulate some obscure *pratibandhya-pratibandhaka* relation.[66] The *nirvikalpa* has also its *viṣayatā*—only it is by definition devoid of any qualifier and if there is no qualifier there is also no sense in saying that there is a qualificandum. Hence though without any *viśeṣyatā* and any *prakāratā*, yet the *nirvikalpa* has its *viṣayatā* for otherwise it would not be a knowledge of...[67]

Now it is one of the cardinal tenets of the Nyāya epistemology that no knowledge that finds linguistic expression can go without a qualifier (*prakāra*). The qualifier may either be explicitly mentioned or remain implicit. Take the example: 'the floor (that is) with the pot' (*ghaṭavad bhūtalam*). Here of course, one of the qualifiers is the 'pot' (*ghaṭa*) which is mentioned; but there is another that is not mentioned, i.e. 'potness' ('*ghaṭatva*')*. This is only an example of a general truth that every knowledge that finds mention has an unmentioned qualifier though the unmentioned qualifier—which is either a universal or a not further analysable property—is apprehended, insofar as it remains unmentioned, in itself. Mention it, and it, on its part, refers back to an unmentioned qualifier. The point under consideration may

66. For the Nyāya, *viṣayatāsambandhena jñānaṃ prati tādātmya-sambandhena nirvikalpakaṃ pratibandhakam.*

67. Lest it might be objected that '*viṣayatā*' is only a generic name for *viśeṣyatā*, *prakāratā*, etc. and hence in the absence of any of the latter, there is no point in claiming that there still is a *viṣayatā*, some Naiyāyikas uphold the view that there is an additional *viṣayatā* over and above *viśeṣyatā*, *prakāratā*, etc. (*atiriktaviṣayatāpakṣa*). Cf. Gaṅgeśa, *Prāmāṇyavāda* (Kanchi edn.), p. 228, and note 41.1 in the text below.

*A terminological Note: in consistency with remarks made in the preceding paragraphs, it hardly needs to be said that when we speak of the 'pot' being a qualifier (in the knowledge 'the floor with the pot'), what is meant is that the knowledge-content referring to the pot belongs to the specific type called *prakāratā*.

serve as a useful reminder that for the Nyāya analysis of knowledge goes beyond the mere analysis of the linguistic expression and that we have to instal ourselves in the attitude of reflective introspection and recall the exact *anubhava* i.e. the phenomenological datum.[68]

Consider again the knowledge expressed in 'the floor with a pot' (*ghaṭavad bhūtalam*). We have said above that there the 'pot' is a qualifier (*prakāra*) and the 'floor' is a qualificandum (*viśeṣya*). In other words, there is a *prakāratā* referring to the pot and a *viśeṣyatā* referring to the floor. The former is technically called 'the *prakāratā* attached to the pot' and the latter 'the *viśeṣyatā* attached to the floor'. Further analysis reveals however that the matter is not as simple as that. The 'pot', though in one respect, i.e. in relation to the 'floor', is a qualifier, yet in another respect, i.e. in relation to 'pot-ness', is a qualificandum of which 'pot-ness' is the unmentioned qualifier. Similarly, the other element, the 'floor', reveals further complexity though with the difference that in both its aspects, it functions as a qualificandum: firstly, in relation to the unmentioned qualifier 'floor-ness' (*bhūtalatva*) and secondly, in relation to the mentioned qualifier 'pot'. Being without any qualifier aspect, the element of 'floor' functions in the knowledge under consideration as the primary qualificandum (*mukhya-viśeṣya*). Analysis of this knowledge reveals thus six components (leaving aside the relational ones):

i. a *prakāratā* attached to the potness,
ii. a *viśeṣyatā* attached to the pot,
iii. a *prakāratā* attached to the pot,
iv. a *viśeṣyatā* attached to the floor,

68. Another such example of the way the Nyāya analysis goes beyond the linguistic is provided by its attitude towards the relational component of a knowledge (*saṃsargatā*). The relational component in knowledge always remains unmentioned. Conversely, if a relation finds mention, it ceases to be a relational component in the knowledge. In 'The hill is fiery' ('*parvato vahnimān*') the unmentioned relational component is '*saṃyoga*.' But in the knowledge 'The hill has *saṃyoga* with fire', '*saṃyoga*' no more functions as a relational component but has got metamorphosed into a qualificandum and/or a qualifier. The relational component now refers to the unmentioned relation of *samavāya*.

v. another *viśeṣyatā* attached to the floor,
vi. a *prakāratā* attached to the floorness.

These six components constitute a unity by virtue of two sorts of epistemic relations. One of these is called the *'nirūpakanirūpita'* relation and the other the *'avacchedaka-avacchinna'* relation, into the precise nature of which we need not enter in the present context. It is important to bear in mind that even for the Nyāya with all its analytical attitude the unity of a knowledge is not entirely analysable into discrete components.[69]

There seems to be disagreement amongst the Naiyāyikas on one vital issue, namely whether variation in the form of expression necessarily points to a variation in knowledge. Some say it does; others say it does not. But we may take a safer position and contend that perception, of all knowledges, being entirely object-determined, every difference in expression does not mean a variation in knowledge so far as perception is concerned. The same perceptual knowledge, for example, may be formulated either as *'ghaṭaviśiṣṭabhūtala'* or as *'bhūtalavṛttitvaviśiṣṭaghaṭa'*. In case of all other kinds of knowledge there is far closer relation between the linguistic form and the knowledge-form, the inseparability being maximum in the case of *śābda* knowledge. In any case the ultimate test in these issues is one's subjective report and not the objective linguistic event.

(b) *The Nyāya Conception of Prāmāṇya*

Since we are concerned with *prāmāṇya* in the sense of *pramātva* and not in the sense of *pramākaraṇatva*, we may as before safely avoid discussion of the concept of *pramāṇa* in the Nyāya system. We must however begin with the concept of *pramā* or true knowledge. Knowledge is generally divided into *pramā* and

69. This is why some Naiyāyikas speak of a total unanalysable *viṣayatā* which is more than its components and which intentionally refers, as it were in one act of intention, to the total object i.e., in the above example, to the floor-as-possessing-the-pot. This unanalysable unity has been called *'vilakṣaṇa viṣayatā'*. It is absent in the case of error, for in error there is no total related object. There is nothing like the-this-as-qualified-by-silverhood in the case of the erroneous cognition 'This is silver'.

apramā.[70] *Apramā* or false cognition (including both error and doubt) is also knowledge. No attempt is made in the system to reduce error and doubt to true knowledge, nor is there any attempt to exclude them from the purview of 'knowledge'. What then is common to true cognition and false cognition? Uddyotakara answers: "the ability to manifest the general" (*sāmānya-paricchedakatvam*).[71] Vācaspati explains it thus: even the erroneous cognition 'This is silver' manifests the yonder object with its general features like whiteness, shining character etc. While this much is common to both, *pramā* has certain characters that distinguish it from *apramā*, and these characters constitute *prāmāṇya*. *Prāmāṇya* therefore is taken by the Nyāya in the sense of that which distinguishes true knowledge from false, and not in the weak sense of being instrumental to practical behaviour (*pravṛttyaupāyikam*), for—as Vācaspati points out—practical behaviour depends upon the mere presentation of the object and does not wait for a true apprehension of it.[72] Practical behaviour may indeed follow even upon doubt.

Further, *prāmāṇya* is a property of knowledge, and not of the object of knowledge. For if it were a property of the object, an erroneous apprehension apprehending its object would also be true and besides any knowledge while apprehending its object would apprehend its truth as well, which however is not the case.[73] Moreover no such property is experienced in the object.[74] *Prāmāṇya* then is a property of knowledge, though not a generic universal or *jāti* for reasons which we shall examine later on.[75]

There seems to be an unbroken line of speculation in the Nyāya school regarding the nature of *pramā*, though with slight variations in emphasis. Vātsyāyana defines it as "whatever is

70. In the Vaiśeṣika literature we find the classification into '*vidyā*' and '*avidyā*'.

71. *Nyāyadarśana* (Calcutta Sanskrit Series), p. 8.

72. "*Arthapratītyadhīnā tu pravṛttiḥ na arthāvadhāraṇādhīnā*" (*ibid.*, p. 9).

73. Thus Vallabha: "*Na ca viṣayadharmabhedaḥ, sarvasādhāraṇyāt*" (*Nyāyalīlāvatī*, Chowkhambā edn., p. 766). "*Sarvasādhāraṇyāt*" is explained by *Kaṇṭhābharaṇa* as meaning "*bhramasādhāraṇyāt*". But he also interprets it in another way. If truth were a property of object, then one person Caitra could apprehend the truth of Maitra's knowledge.

74. "*Viṣaye tādṛśadharmānanubhavādityarthaḥ*" (*Kaṇṭhābharaṇa* on *Nyāyalīlāvatī*, p. 766).

75. *Satyatvaṃ na jñānajātiḥ* (*Nyāyalīlāvatī*, p. 766). Also see Udayana's *Pariśuddhi*, pp. 158-9. For critical remarks on this see pp. 48-50 following.

knowledge of the object" (*yadarthavijñānaṃ sā pramitiḥ*[76]), but removes the ambiguity later on by speaking of it as "the knowledge of that as that" (*tasmiṃstaditi pratyayaḥ*[77]). Uddyotakara defines *pramāṇa* as "the cause of knowledge" (*upalabdhihetu*[78]). Vācaspati tries to make the definition more precise by adding that here what is meant by the word '*pramā*' is the knowledge that does not deviate from its object and that is other than memory.[79] Udayana in his *Pariśuddhi* also emphasises the character of *avyabhicaritatva*,[80] though in his *Nyāyakusumāñjali* he gives a simpler definition of '*pramā*' as 'right apprehension' and as 'independent'.[81] Jayanta takes it to be such knowledge of the object that both does not deviate from the object and is free from doubt.[82] Śrīdhara defines it as a definitive awareness that is uncontradicted.[83] Vallabha defines it as "the true knowledge" and further defines it as "the knowledge of something as not being what is other than it" (*parānātmatayānubhavaḥ*[84]).

Most of these definitions are negative in character, and the negations are intended to exclude error, doubt and memory. The Mīmāṃsaka's device of defining '*pramā*' as a true knowledge whose object was not known before and thereby to exclude memory from being called '*pramā*' is not acceptable to the Naiyāyikas who prefer the less cumbrous way of defining with the help of the notion of independence. Memory has not the ability to manifest its object independently, but always does so through the via media of a prior experience. Vācaspati accepts the validity of the well known objection that if *anadhigatatva* be admitted as a character of *pramā* then in case of a series of knowledges of the same object, the second, third, and all succeeding members of the series become *apramā*. Udayana raises fresh objections against

76. *Nyāyadarśana*, p. 24.
77. Vātsyāyana's *Bhāṣya* on *Nyāya Sūtra* 2.1.36.
78. *Nyāyadarśana*, p. 15.
79. *Ibid.*, p. 16.
80. *Pariśuddhi*, p. 46.
81. *Nyāyakusumāñjali Kārikā* 4/1, 4/5.
82. *Nyāyamañjarī* (Chowkh. edn.), p. 12.
83. *Nyāyakandalī* (Viz. edn.), p. 172.
84. *Nyāyalīlāvatī*, pp. 737-738.

taking memory as *pramā* in his *Pariśuddhi*. But it must be noted that the eagerness to exclude memory is rooted more in the traditional refusal to accept it as a *pramāṇa* than in any intrinsic defect of memory. Vācaspati almost admits this conventional basis when he says "*pramāṇaśabdena tasyāpāstatvāt...na smṛtiḥ pramā, lokādhīnāvadhāraṇo hi śabdārthasambandhaḥ*". Udayana, commenting on this passage, seeks to show that memory is not true, i.e. that it is *ayathārthu*, on the ground that the remembered past is not now. But in the long run he is forced to confess that even if it is *yathārtha* it is not independent.[85]

To exclude doubt, Jayanta explicitly includes in his definition the phrase "free from doubt", while Śrīdhara has to speak of "definitive knowledge". Error is sought to be excluded by such adjectives as "undeviating" or by the more roundabout device of Vallabha.

What is called for is a positive definition which is yet capable of excluding error and doubt. It goes to Gaṅgeśa's credit to have taken up the simple account of Vātsyāyana and made it far more precise. '*Prāmāṇya*' is now defined as *tadvati tatprakārakatva*, a concept which we shall presently analyse. But before we do that we may review in brief the reasons why Gaṅgeśa rejects some other definitions, new and old. Some of the older definitions which were positive in nature made use of the notion of *yāthārthya*. Gaṅgeśa rejects it on the very important ground that there could possibly be no resemblance (which is what is meant by the word 'yathā') between knowledge and its object: *jñāne ghaṭatvādinā yathāśabdārthasādṛśyābhāvāt*. This is a clear rejection of any kind of 'picture' or 'copy' theory of truth. Knowledge could not be a picture or copy of its object. The two are entirely heterogeneous in nature. In his *Prakāśa* on *Pariśuddhi*, Vardhamāna

85. *Nyāyadarśana*, p. 16 and *Pariśuddhi*, pp. 161-166. Two things are here meant by 'lack of independence of memory'. It is meant, in the first place, that memory reveals what is already known in the past and has no independent capacity for manifesting its object. But dependence in this sense does not go against ascribing to it truth in the ordinary sense. The truth that is denied to memory thereby must be truth in some special sense. Udayana also seems to mean that the '*yāthārthya*' of memory is dependent on that of the past experience which is being remembered. If the past experience is *yathārtha*, then memory is also so; if the past experience is not *yathārtha*, then memory also is not, even if memory may be faithful to it. I think it is being unfair to memory.

considers various possible meanings of '*yāthārthya*' and rejects them all.

In his chapter on the definition of truth (*pramālakṣaṇa*), Gaṅgeśa considers a series of definitions. Truth cannot be defined in terms of novelty (as the Mīmāṃsakas tried to do), for this is not what we ordinarily mean by 'truth', and also because this definition would not apply to the case of a series of true knowledges of the same object. Truth cannot be defined as the property of being uncontradicted experience, for the contradicting knowledge (*bādha*) is itself a true, though contradictory, knowledge. Gaṅgeśa is pointing to the fact that merely from the fact that p is contradicted by q it does not follow that p is false or that q is true. He also rejects the definition of truth in terms of coherence (*saṃvāda*), for coherence means nothing other than "being mentioned similarly in another knowledge" (*jñānāntareṇa tathā ullikhyamānatvam*), and this may be found also in cases of error. What he means is that there can very well be a coherent system of false cognitions. It cannot also be defined in terms of successful practice, for such a definition would not apply to cases of true knowledges where due to some reason or other no practice follows, i.e. to cases of *upekṣāpramā* where the knowledge simply is passed over and does not provoke any practical reaction. Further, successful practice may at best constitute a test but not a definition of truth. Truth cannot also be defined as the property of being experience of the real (*tattvānubhavatvam*), for an unreal is never apprehended, not even in error. Truth cannot also be defined as the property of being an experience whose qualifier is a property which is not the counterpositive of an absence residing in the qualificandum (*viśeṣyaniṣṭhātyantābhāvāpratiyogidharmaprakārakānubhavatvam*), for it does not apply to a true knowledge of conjunction, for the conjunction, being on the general Nyāya view *avyāpyavṛtti* or of incomplete occurrence,[86] may be absent in the qualificandum (and thereby may be the counterpositive of an absence residing in the qualificandum). Nor can it be defined as the property of being an experience whose qualifier is not a pro-

86. For this notion of *avyāpyavṛttitva* and its opposite, see Ingalls, *loc. cit.*, pp. 73-74.

perty which limits the counterpositiveness of a mutual absence residing in the qualificandum (*viśeṣyavṛttyanyonyābhāvapratiyogitāvacchedakadharmāprakārakānubhavatvam*), and that for precisely the same reasons as above. For if a tree is one having conjunction with a monkey, it is also one having no conjunction with the monkey (in another part of the tree); so that even a right knowledge 'This tree is one having conjunction with monkey' has a qualifier namely 'conjunction with monkey' whose absence is in the qualificandum. It follows then that there is in the tree also a mutual absence (or, difference) whose counterpositive is 'one having conjunction with monkey', and the limitor of the counterpositiveness is the property of being the said conjunction which is also the qualifier of the true knowledge that the tree has the conjunction. Truth cannot also be defined as the property of being an experience which does not have a qualifier non-resident in the qualificandum (*viśeṣyāvṛttyaprakārakānubhavatvam*). The definition would not apply to the true knowledge 'These are a pot and a cloth', for here the qualifier 'potness' is absent in the cloth, and the qualifier 'clothness' is absent in the pot. It is also not the property of being an experience having a qualifier which is in the same locus as *viṣayatā*, for this property also belongs to the error 'This is a snake' where the qualifier 'thisness' is in the same locus as *viṣayatā*.

We have only given a few of the definitions which Gaṅgeśa rejects. The resulting definition is stated in two stages. First comes a simpler form: If x is in y, then the experience of x in y is true knowledge (*Yatra yadasti tatra tasyānubhavaḥ pramā*). One has to add, as the commentators do, that if x is in y in the relation R, then the experience of x as being in y in the relation R is true knowledge. A more formal definition follows: true knowledge is an experience whose qualifier is such that it belongs to the object (*tadvati tatprakārakatvam*).

Let us suppose, the knowledge is 'S is p'. This knowledge has amongst others two qualifiers, 'S-ness' and 'p-ness'. Now, if the knowledge is to be true then the qualifiers must really belong to S which is the qualificandum. The definition includes one variable i.e. the word '*tat*' which occurs twice, so that what we have is a dummy schemata with empty places which would give rise to a determinate entity only when the empty places have been filled in i.e. when the variable has been given a value.[87] There is a further rather curious feature of the definition. One part of it refers to an ontological situation, the other to an epistemological. The expression '*tatprakārakatva*' refers to an epistemological situation, namely to the fact that the knowledge under consideration has *that* (*tat*) as its qualifier. The expression '*tadvati*' refers to a correlative ontological situation, namely to the fact that that which is the qualifier of the knowledge under consideration (also) *really* belongs to the object of that knowledge. One thing should be obvious even from this preliminary explanation: the entity designated by '*tadvati tatprakārakatva*' is a curious "hybrid" entity, to use A. N. Whitehead's expression. Truth is neither a property of the object nor a mere property of the knowledge. It is rather relational in nature and as such has to be defined with reference to both the relata, the object and the knowledge, and this is what Gaṅgeśa does.

Let us now see how this definition applies to cases of true knowledge and does not apply to cases of false knowledge. Take the case of a true knowledge. I know a piece of silver as silver. The knowledge is expressed in the form 'This is silver'. This knowledge has three qualifiers: 'thisness', 'silver' and 'silverness'. Now let us take the qualifier 'silverness' as the value of the variable '*tat*'. The knowledge in that case is one which has 'silverness' as its qualifier, it is *rajatatvaprakāraka*. Now since, ex hypothesis, the 'this' designates a real silver we can say that the *this* possesses silverness (or, is *rajatatvavat*). The knowledge therefore possesses the property of *rajatatvavati rajatatvaprakārakatva*, which is the same as the truth of this knowledge 'This is silver'.

Consider on the other hand a case of error. I mistake a piece of shell for silver. I express my knowledge in the judgment 'This is silver'. This knowledge has also 'silverness' for its qualifier. As regards the qualifiers there is nothing to distinguish

87. Definitions in the Nyāya are not merely nominal definitions but real definitions in the sense that they are designations of real properties that serve to distinguish the definiendum from all that is other than it. Hence a definiens may be said to designate an entity. In the present case it may be said to designate an entity only when the variable has been given a value.

right knowledge from error. The distinction then has to be sought for elsewhere, i.e. in the fact that in error the 'silverness' which functions as qualifier does not belong to the qualificandum *this*. In other words, the *this* is not *rajatatvavat*. The definition then does not apply to a case of error.

Let us take a case of doubt. A doubt by definition is a knowledge with two mutually contradictory qualifiers. 'Is this a man or not?' is an example of doubt which has amongst others two mutually contradictory qualifiers 'manhood' and 'absence of manhood'. Both of these cannot belong to the thing designated by 'this'. It is then easy to show that the doubt is not *tadvati tatprakāraka*.

It should also be obvious by now that no knowledge is wholly false. Every error, even doubt, contains an element of truth. With the help of Gaṅgeśa's definition we are in a position to give sense to this fact. In the ordinary sense of the words 'whole' and 'part', a knowledge is not a whole with parts. But now we can say that with regard to some one of its qualifiers at least a knowledge must be true. In other words, it is possible in case of every knowledge to give a value to the variable '*tat*' such that the knowledge under consideration may be shown to possess *tadvati tatprakārakatva*. This is possible, for example, in the above illustrations by choosing 'thisness' which certainly belongs to the *this*.[88] In the case of doubt one could show even more than that; if one of the two mutually contradictory qualifiers does not belong to the qualificandum the other one does. Though a false knowledge is thus not false in all respects, a true cognition must be true in all respects, i.e. must have no qualifiers which do not belong to the qualificandum.

In order to bring out the full implications of Gaṅgeśa's concept of truth it is necessary to emphasise, even at the cost of repetition, that truth on this theory is a "hybrid" entity, having both epistemic and ontological components. With this we have to

88. This is the logical significance of the Nyāya dictum that all knowledge is unerring with regard to the substantive (*dharmiṇi abhrāntam*). The Nyāya doctrine referred to above that every false cognition is in some respect at least true must be sharply distinguished from the theory of degrees of truth and falsity as stated by such thinkers as F.H. Bradley.

exclude any possibility of so interpreting '*tadvati tatprakārakatva*' as to reduce it to a purely epistemological property. It is possible, for example, to construe '*tadvati*' as meaning '*tadvadviśeṣyakatve sati*' meaning 'having a *viśeṣya* which possesses *tat*'. '*Viśeṣyatā*' being an epistemological notion, the entire notion becomes an epistemological one, and the force of Gaṅgeśa's definition is gone. It has been attempted, for example, by Madhusūdana Sarasvatī in his *Advaitaratnarakṣaṇam*, to show that in this sense *tadvati tatprakārakatva* is common to both truth and error. This is not surprising, for Gaṅgeśa's notion has been diluted thereby.

Two comments may be made in this connection. In the first place, even on this interpretation the ontological claim is not completely eliminated. '*Viśeṣyatā*' is an epistemological notion no doubt, but the idea of '*tadvattva*' seems incurably ontological.[89] Secondly, the analysis of the definiens into '*tadvadviśeṣyakatve sati tatprakārakatva*' is not correct for still another reason. It does not fully express the unitary nature of the concept of truth. The definiens should then be more accurately analysed, or better, explicated. The explication may proceed through the following stages:

1. *Tadvadviṣayakatve sati tatprakārakatva* (= the property of having 'that' as its qualifier and an object which possesses the *that*)—This is virtually useless, for even error has an object possessing the *that*. It depends upon what is to be called the object of a knowledge. No doubt, 'object' is an epistemological notion. The Prābhākaras then have some justification in claiming that the object of the alleged false cognition 'This is silver' is the silver.

2. *Tadvadviśeṣyakatve sati tatprakārakatva* (= the property of having 'that' as its qualifier while the qualificandum possesses the *that*)—This seems to be the conception of truth of Murāri Miśra and is claimed by him to be something which can be apprehended by introspection, for *viśeṣyatā* like *prakāratā* is an epistemological entity. If *tatprakārakatva* can be apprehended by *anuvyavasāya*—as the Naiyāyikas also admit—then *tadvad-*

89. This, it seems to me, is the main difference of Gaṅgeśa's conception of truth not only from all epistemological and ontological notions but also from the semantic concept of truth of A. Tarski.

viśeṣyakatva may also be so apprehended. Further, consider this case of a false cognition 'These two (a cloth and a jar) are a jar and a cloth', wherein the cloth is taken to be a jar and vice versa. (It is more natural to make such a mistake in the case of a piece of shining shell and a piece of silver. Certainly more suitable cases may be thought out.) Here the qualificandum 'jar' possesses the qualifier 'jarness', and the qualificandum 'cloth' possesses 'clothness'. Nevertheless the cognition is an error, for the cloth has been known as jar and the jar as a cloth. The definition as explicated under 2, illegitimately extends to such cases of error.

3. *Tadvadviśeṣyakatvāvacchinnatatprakārakatva* (= the property of having 'that' as its qualifier which is limited by the property of having a qualificandum which possesses the *that*)—This definition avoids the difficulty last mentioned under 2. In that example, 'clothness' as a qualifier is not limited by the fact of the cloth being the qualificandum, and so also in the case of the other qualifier. The qualifier must qualify with regard to the right qualificandum namely the qualificandum which possesses that property,[90] Further this explication succeeds in bringing out the unitary nature of the notion of truth by making the two components '*tadvattva*' and '*tatprakārakatva*' limit or determine each other.

4. Further, the explication should also take into consideration the relation in which the property serving as the qualifier belongs to the qualificandum. The qualifier also must qualify in the same relation, or better, the qualifierness of that qualifier must be limited by that relation. This helps to exclude a knowledge 'The jar is in its parts in the relation of conjunction' from the purview of 'true knowledge', for according to the Nyāya ontology the jar is actually in its parts in the relation of inherence and not in the relation of conjunction. The resulting explication becomes '*tatsambandhāvacchinnatadvanniṣṭhaviśeṣyatānirūpitatatsambandhāvacchinnatanniṣṭhaprakāratāśālījñānatva*'.

It is important not to lose sight, in the midst of this mystifying jargon and complexity, of the central fact that truth accord-

90. Thus Mathurānātha explains '*avacchinnatva*' in this connection as "*idametad viśeṣyakatvāṃśe etatprakārakamiti pratītisākṣikaḥ svarūpasambandhaviśeṣaḥ*" (*Māthurī*, p. 403).

ing to this definition is a unitary notion having heterogeneous components, not merely epistemological. The relevance, in fact the central place, of this fact for the Nyāya theory of *parataḥ-prāmāṇya* will be brought out in the next part of this introductory essay.

(c) *The Nyāya Theory of Parataḥprāmāṇya*

With the underlying notions of knowledge and truth thus explicated we may now attempt a formulation of the Nyāya theory of *parataḥprāmāṇya*. As in the case of the *svataḥ* theories, this theory has also two aspects, one concerns the origin of truth and the other its apprehension. In its first aspect the theory holds that the truth of a knowledge is not produced by the same conditions that give rise to the knowledge itself. It is rather produced by some extrinsic circumstances, some additional factors, known as *guṇas* or excellences. In its second aspect the theory holds that the truth of a knowledge is apprehended neither by that very knowledge, nor by the *first* apprehension of that knowledge—be that apprehension an introspection as with the Miśras or an inference as with the Bhāṭṭas—but only[91] by a subsequent inference which ensues either upon the confirmatory knowledge or upon the successful termination of the practical behaviour to which the knowledge under consideration leads us, or by the mark of '*tajjātīyatva*' to be explained below.

Amongst the host of arguments which the Nyāya advances in support of its contentions, two are most important. The first is in support of the extrinsic origination of *prāmāṇya*. First explicitly formulated by Udayana, it states that if *prāmāṇya* originated from the same conditions that give rise to the knowledge quâ knowledge, then even an invalid cognition would come to possess *prāmāṇya* since it too has the same originating conditions, and that is plainly absurd. The second argument is in support of the *parataḥ* apprehension of *prāmāṇya*. Also first formulated by Udayana, though made far more precise by Gaṅgeśa, it argues that if with

91. I leave out for the present the position held by some Naiyāyikas, seemingly admitted by Pakṣadhara Miśra and referred to sympathetically by *Dinakarī* that the truth of a primary knowledge may also be apprehended by second *anuvyavasāya*. See p. 66f *infra*.

the first apprehension of a knowledge we also know it as true, then it would be impossible to have any doubt regarding the truth of that knowledge soon afterwards. It is not our purpose to take sides and to decide if these arguments are tenable or not. It is rather our intention to bring out the exact nature of the controversy. We shall examine the nature of the arguments in the next sections. For the present, we are interested in making the Nyāya contention more precise, and for this purpose it is necessary to bear the two arguments, especially the second one, in mind.

The Nyāya is not contending that when a knowledge comes into being, it is at the beginning neither true nor false. Such a contention would have been plainly absurd. It rather contends that every knowledge is either true or false, right at the beginning. Only its truth or falsity—whichever may be the case—is due to a set of conditions that are different from those other conditions that give rise to the knowledge: in the case of truth, these conditions are called '*guṇas*', in the case of falsity they are called '*doṣas*'. The legitimacy of this distinction would be questioned in a later context. For the present, let us confine ourselves to the second aspect of the theory and seek to make it as much precise as possible.

Since according to the second of the above mentioned arguments the truth of a knowledge is not apprehended *ab initio*, for if it were there would have been no room for subsequent doubt, it seems to follow that in those cases where no such doubt takes place truth is apprehended *ab initio*. These cases in fact put the Naiyāyika to great embarrassment. There are at least three such cases; inference, confirmatory knowledge or *phalajñāna* and knowledge with which one has acquired sufficient familiarity (*abhyāsadaśāpanna jñāna*).

As regards inference, Vācaspati clearly admits that it is known right from the beginning as valid, for amongst the originating conditions of inference there is a certainty about the universal major premise. There is no room left therefore for having any subsequent doubt in the validity of the inference.[92] Udayana is

92. Vācaspati—"*Anumānasya tu....nirastasamastavyabhicāraśaṅkasya svata eva prāmāṇyamanumeyāvyabhicāriliṅgasamutthatvāt*" (*Nyāyadarśana*, p. 9).

not so confident and takes up a more halting attitude. He is willing to grant that inference arises by manifesting the suchness of the object.[93] Most reluctantly he concedes that truth is here apprehended *ab initio*. Yet he makes a desperate attempt to reconcile this with the *parataḥ* theory by suggesting that in such cases both may be true.[94] The Navya Naiyāyikas take up a more uncompromising position and deny that the truth of an inference is ever apprehended *ab initio*. For them there is always the possibility of doubt. Under such circumstances one has to review the entire Nyāya theory of inference in order to decide which of these attitudes is more consistent therewith. For the present however one or two features of the theory would help us in assessing the situation.

It is well known that the Nyāya does not draw any distinction between the psychological process of inferring and the logical process. The two in fact are taken to coincide. An inference quâ inference is a logically valid inference. There is strictly speaking no fallacious inference. The so-called *hetvābhāsas* are rather hindrances (*pratibandhakas*) to inference than errors of inference.[95] An inference then as a rule is a valid inference and does not permit any doubt about its validity. But at the same time one may very well be in error about the universal major, and though one makes an inference based upon a certain belief in such a major premise it is likely that on a subsequent occasion one comes to doubt the truth of the major premise and therefore also of the conclusion it had led to. Thus we find on the one hand that in the process of inference one cannot err and yet on the other hand one might possibly have started from a false universal major. That one cannot err in the process of inference is a curious doctrine held by the Naiyāyika and is due to his further belief that the psychological process never deviates from

93. "*Anumitijñānaṃ hyarthasya tathātvaṃ vyavacchindadevotpadyate*" (*Pariśuddhi*, Asiatic Soc. ed., p. 113).

94. Udayana's "*Atyantāyogavyavaccheda*" (*Pariśuddhi*, p. 120) is thus explained by Vardhamāna in his *Prakāśa* on it: "*kutrāpi svatogṛhyate ityarthaḥ*". For Gaṅgeśa's opinions on this, see para 55 of the text.

95. Thus the *hetvābhāsas* are defined in *Siddhāntamuktāvalī* as those which by being known oppose inference (*Yadviṣayakatvena jñānasyānumitivirodhitvam*).

the logical. But it may quite well be that this belief is largely based on a linguistic decision not to call those processes of thought 'inference' which also do not conform to the logical standard. It seems therefore that if by 'inference' be meant the conclusion arrived at it is liable to be doubted as soon as one, for any reason, is led to doubt the truth of the universal major. If however by 'inference' be meant the process of inferring it is intrinsically valid on this theory. Vācaspati's contention contains this much of truth that unlike perception and *śabda* inference arises out of a sense of certainty, so that the least doubt in the truth of the universal major would be frustrating and would not let the inference take place. An inference therefore arises with an apparently unshakable certainty.[96] If by *prāmāṇya* be meant this sense of certainty then certainly it is intrinsic to inference. But the real issue is, whether *prāmāṇya* in the sense of *tadvati tatprakārakatva* is so or not. At least Vācaspati has no sure ground for saying that it is so. I would think that for Nyāya it is not so and this supposition is likely to fit in better with the Nyāya theory of truth.

The eagerness on the part of some Naiyāyikas like Vācaspati to accord to inference an intrinsic truth is due to an embarrassment to which they are otherwise likely to be subjected from another source. The Naiyāyikas believe, as we have said before, that the truth of a knowledge is apprehended by a subsequent inference. Now it is asked by the Mīmāṃsaka, how is the validity of that inference to be established? If by still another inference, how is this second inference to be validated? In order to avoid such an unpleasant infinite regress some would like to treat inference as intrinsically valid and as in no need of validation. But, as we have seen, the Naiyāyika need not go to that extent of holding that its *tadvati tatprakārakatva* is apprehended[97] right from the beginning. He might adopt a more halting attitude and say that inference is accompanied by a sense of certainty

96. Or, as Vācaspati says, "*gṛhītāvybhicāraliṅgasamutthaṃ niṣkampam utpadyate jñānam*" (*loc. cit.*, p. 9).

97. So far as the origin of the validity of an inference is concerned, the Nyāya of course advocates extrinsic origin, the special excellence needed being "*sādhyavati sādhyavyāpyavaiśiṣṭyajñānam*" (*Muktāvalī* on *Kārikā* no. 133).

that comes to be questioned only if the universal major is for some reason or other doubted.

Let us now consider the confirmations or the *phalajñāna*. Here again an embarrassment similar to the above awaits the Naiyāyika. For if the inference through which the truth of the first knowledge comes to be apprehended depends upon the confirmation or the *phalajñāna* (e.g. quenching of the thirst in the case of a perception of water), it may quite well be asked, how are these confirmations themselves to be validated? In reply, Vācaspati points out that the *phalajñāna* is never questioned by the discerning persons.[98] But why? The answer given is that its familiarity leads us to infer its undeviating character through the mark of *tajjātīyatva* (the property of belonging to that class).[99] Thus instead to taking them as intrinsically true and as self-validating[100], Vācaspati includes them in a much wider class of 'familiar' cases whose sheer familiarity rules out any need for further validating them. The entire idea of familiar cases, cases that have become *abhyāsadaśāpanna* and whose truth is immediately inferred—without waiting upon confirmation—through the mark of *tajjātīyatva* is shrouded in obscurity and Udayana's attempts to throw light on this difficult notion hardly succeed in giving a completely satisfactory account.[101] It is obvious that *tajjātīyatva* can serve as a mark of truth only when the knowledge under consideration has become a familiar case. Further this knowledge is a fresh occurrent. To say that it is a familiar case could then only mean that it is a knowledge the like of which has been experienced before and has been known to be true. What apparently distinguishes these cases from new knowledges is that in such cases one takes them for granted and enter-

98. "*Na ca phalajñānaṃ parīkṣyate prekṣāvadbhiḥ*" (*loc. cit.* 9).

99. "*Vayantu brūmaḥ phalajñānamapi abhyāsadaśāpannatayā tajjātīyatvena liṅgena avadhāritāvyabhicārameva*" (*loc. cit.*, p. 9).

100. Thus writes Moritz Schlick about the nature of confirmations: "They are an absolute end. In them the task of cognition at this point is fulfilled. . . it gives us joy to reach them, even if we cannot stand upon them." "The Foundation of Knowledge", included in Ayer (ed.), *Logical Positivism*. The Free Press, Glencoe, Illinois, 1959). Schlick also writes in the essay that in the case of confirmations "I grasp their meaning at the same time as I grasp their truth".

101. *Pariśuddhi*, pp. 102ff.

tains no doubt about their truth whereas a new knowledge demands to be confirmed. But there are two different notions involved, the notion of 'familiarity' and that of 'belonging to the same class', notions that evade logical precision. What is the test of familiarity? How many times must one have similar experiences in order that they may become *abhyāsadaśāpanna*? It is not possible to lay down any general rule. One is unavoidably led to the conclusion that that knowledge is called '*abhyāsadaśāpanna*' in whose case no doubt arises soon afterwards, so that to say that the *abhyāsadaśāpanna* knowledge does not demand validation appears tautological. A further inference based on the mark of *tajjātīyatva* is not called for. One does not infer anything, only one does not in such cases as these doubt. Besides, what does the word '*tat*' in '*tajjātīyatva*' mean? Not certainly the class of true knowledges, for, as Udayana points out, that exactly is what is to be proved by the supposed inference. It does not mean the class of knowledges that give rise to successful practice, for the mark is supposed to operate, if the supposed inference is not to be pointless, prior to confirmation through successful practice. Nor is *tajjātīyatva* any further unanalysable property in such knowledge which we perceptually discern, for no such property is so discerned. Udayana's solution after rejecting these alternatives is as follows: Every knowledge is of some object and the determinations of the object also serve to mark out the knowledge. Thus a body is characterised by hands and feet, etc. Now if I have a knowledge of something having hands and feet, etc. and say 'It is a body', my knowledge is thereby included under a familiar class of knowledge: in this sense *tajjātīyatva* = *tattadupādhiviśiṣṭatattadanubhavatva*.[102] This is a good reflective account of why we take certain knowledges for granted, but it is not corroborated in our unreflective acceptance of a familiar case. Further, if this is the meaning of the mark in the supposed inference then this supposed inference hardly differs from the inferences used to establish the truth even of the unfamiliar cases. Gaṅgeśa also makes use of the mark of *tajjātīyatva* in the series of examples of the latter sort of inference and gives the following example—"This knowledge of the body is true, for it is a knowl-

102. *Pariśuddhi*, p. 105.

edge of the body in what possesses hands and feet, etc."[103] This shows that either there is no inference at all in the case of a familiar knowledge or if there is any in the supposed manner the supposed sort of inference also takes place in the case of knowledges that have not yet become quite familiar!

Thus we find that in none of these knowledges truth is apprehended, on the Nyāya theory, right from the beginning. In every case therefore there is scope for and the necessity of further validation or correction. It has of course to be admitted that the need for validation is the most pressing in the case of 'non-inferential knowledges that are not confirmations and that are of the unfamiliar sort'.

There are yet two other cases where the Naiyāyika is often led to recognise intrinsic truth. These are the knowledge of the substantive (*dharmijñāna*) and the *anuvyavasāya* of the primary knowledge. In both cases, again as before, one of the motives for recognising some sort of intrinsic truth is to avoid infinite regress. In the former case, there is besides a logical basis which has been examined before. Strictly speaking, this need not lead us to a revision of the *parataḥ* theory that in all knowledge truth is extrinsic, for the so-called *dharmijñāna* is not a complete unit of knowledge by itself but is always a constituent of a complete knowledge. If however it be regarded as a possible complete knowledge expressible in the form 'this' or 'This is this', then its infallibility is merely an analytic consequence of its trivial character.

With regard to *anuvyavasāya* the matter is different and it is not at once clear why it should be regarded as infallible. Both Vācaspati and Udayana emphasise that it is never found to err and that hence there is no room for doubt. "No one who does not have a knowledge introspects 'I am knowing'; no one has the introspection 'I am knowing a silver' when in fact he has knowledge of a shell."[104] Vardhamāna adds, "No one has an introspection of a knowledge when in fact he has a state of feeling". All that this empirical argument proves is that we do not generally err in our introspection and that therefore we do not gener-

103. *Prāmāṇyavāda*, para 50.
104. *Pariśuddhi*, p. 117.

ally doubt its truth. There is besides little practical reason that could stimulate such a doubt. Vardhamāna rightly remarks, and is here closer to the spirit of the Nyāya, that by calling all such knowledge *svataḥpramā* what is meant is that there is in such cases no initial apprehension of falsity,[105] and hence no initial doubt to start with.[106]

IV. Critical Examination of the Arguments

(*a*) The *Utpatti* or origination of truth:—

One of the two questions that have been asked is, what is the cause of the truth of a true knowledge? Do the same causes which give rise to a knowledge also produce its truth, or are additional factors needed for the latter purpose? The *svataḥ* theory holds that the truth of a knowledge is produced by the very same conditions which cause that knowledge itself. The *parataḥ* theory holds the opposite view, namely that additional factors, called by the theory '*guṇas*' or 'excellences', are needed to make a knowledge true.

Now, the issue about the apprehension (*jñapti*) of truth is, it must be confessed, more intelligible to us than that about the origin (*utpatti*) of truth. In Western theories of truth two questions are discussed: one of them concerns the nature and the definition of truth (*pramālakṣaṇa*) and the other concerns the test of truth. The latter question is no doubt included in the problem of *jñapti*. But the peculiarly Indian question about the origin of truth, viz. about the originating causes of truth, is somewhat difficult to grasp unless one instals oneself in the peculiarly ontological-causal attitude which prevails in most Indian schools, especially the Nyāya-Vaiśeṣika. Even the epistemology is not free from causal considerations. Knowledge is an occurrent, and like all occurrents it arises out of certain collo-

105. *Aprāmāṇyaśaṅkā nāstīti eva svataḥprāmāṇyagrahārthaḥ* (*Pariśuddhiprakāśa*, p. 118).

106. Jayanta goes to the other extreme and holds the absurd view that every knowledge, prior to confirmation, has the status of a doubt, but in order to show this he has to stretch the meaning of 'doubt' and has to find an explanation of why it is *not* apprehended as a doubt. *Cf. Nyāyamañjarī*, pp. 156-7.

cation of appropriate causal conditions. The same would hold good of true knowledge, which is a species of knowledge. It is sensible therefore to ask, out of what causal conditions does true knowledge arise? It should be borne in mind that the Nyāya conception of *pramāṇa* is both (*i*) the conception of the various kinds of true knowledge, and also (*ii*) the conception of the *causes* of such kinds of true knowledge.

It may be asked, can one speak of the causes of truth itself? True knowledge may have an origin and so may have causal antecedents. But truth being that which is common to all true knowledges and which at the same time marks them off from all false cognitions could not be said to have a causal origin. An individual human being is born; a particular instance of red is caused. But manhood and redness do not have causes, they are not simply things of which a causal enquiry can meaningfully be made. They are eternal universals. Does not the same hold good of truth? Of course, *guṇas* of finite substances are causes, but truth is not a *guṇa*, for knowledge, itself a *guṇa*, could not possess another *guṇa*. Truth rather looks like a universal and if it were really so it would be like all universals uncaused.

The Naiyāyikas therefore proceed to show that truth is not a universal. There are chiefly three arguments which are advanced to prove that truth is not a true generic universal (*jāti*).[107]

1. Truth and immediacy of perception are involved in *sāṅkarya*, they are overlapping classes. Truth is present while immediate perceptuality is absent in any instance of valid inference. Immediate perceptuality is present while truth is absent in any instance of erroneous perception. Both are again present in right perception. Thus the two characters, though they coexist in some cases, are not related as pervader and pervaded. They are not therefore true generic characters (*jātis*), for *sāṅkarya*, as is well known, is one of the *jātibādhakas*; two *jātis*, if they coexist, must be related to one another as pervader and pervaded.

2. Further, a *jāti* should be *vyāpyavṛtti* (or must have complete occurrence, in the language of Ingalls). It cannot be that a thing is in one part an instance of one *jāti* and in another not.

107. See, amongst others, Udayana's *Pariśuddhi*, pp. 158-159, Gaṅgeśa's *Prāmāṇyavāda*, ch. on *Pramālakṣaṇa*.

If a *jāti* inheres in an individual it must be in it as a whole, and not in parts. But in every instance of error there is an element of truth. Every knowledge, even a case of error, is true insofar as the substantive (*dharmin*) is concerned. Therefore both truth and the absence of truth inhere in the same individual, which is not permissible in the case of a true *jāti*.

3. If truth were a *jāti*, it would always be mentally perceived whenever the appropriate instance is. But that is not always the case, and moreover such a possibility would render any doubt about truth inexplicable. The assumption of truth as a *jāti* is incompatible with the *parataḥ* theory not only with regard to *utpatti* but also with regard to *jñapti*.

It would be by now obvious that these arguments rest on the two highly controversial notions of *sāṅkarya* and *vyāpyavṛttitva*, notions about which even the Naiyāyikas are not in perfect agreement amongst themselves. If *sāṅkarya* is not regarded as a *jātibādhaka* and if the notion of *vyāpyavṛttitva* is suitably defined so as to render truth *vyāpyavṛtti* with regard to that component where it does inhere, then there appears to be no overriding objection against taking truth to be a *jāti*, excepting that such an admission would render the *parataḥ* theory false, at least with regard to the *utpatti* of truth.

The Naiyāyikas may try to save the theory in either of two ways: They may contend that it is not truth with whose origin they are concerned, it is rather the instance of true knowledge. What has *utpatti* is not *pramātva* but *pramā*. This seems to conform to Gaṅgeśa's own formulation of the *utpatti*-thesis: "*Utpadyate'pi pramā parato na tu svato...*". The thesis then is that the causes of a true knowledge are more than the causes of knowledge quâ knowledge: this more that is involved is called '*guṇa*'. The only difficulty about this way out is that it introduces an undesirable cleavage between the *utpatti* and the *jñapti* theses, the former being concerned with truth (*jñānaprāmāṇya*) and the latter with true knowledge (*pramā*). It is certainly desirable that both should pertain to the same thing. But this is not a difficulty that would ruin the theory.

The other way out of the difficulty pointed out earlier is to stick to the contention that truth itself originates. In that case the Naiyāyika would have to say that there is no truth in general, that truth in each case is a different entity, and not being a generic universal it itself originates. Truth in general, namely *tadvati tatprakārakatva* is not itself an entity. It is a dummy schemata containing variables. But *vahnitvavati vahnitvaprakārakatva* is an entity, and it originates with every true knowledge of fire as fire. The Naiyāyika has then to reinforce his arguments for proving that truth (general or specific) is not a *jāti*, and he should make his arguments independent of the controversial notions of *sāṅkarya* and *vyāpyavṛttitva*. But this, it would seem, has not been done satisfactorily enough. There is something deceptive about the thesis that truth, even in the specific sense, originates. A true knowledge considered as an event in time has an origin. Of it surely one may debate whether its origin is *svataḥ* or *parataḥ*. But the same could not be said of its truth. The knowledges of fire as fire may come and go, but *vahnitvavati vahnitvaprakārakatva* is what is common to them all, and surely it is not something which may be said to have an origin in time.

It would seem therefore that the entire *utpatti* thesis about truth (as distinguished from true knowledges regarded as events) is misconceived, and solutions either way—the *svataḥ* or the *papataḥ*—are equally pointless. It must be said though that the *svataḥ* theory at least sees part of the truth, namely that truth does not originate separately. It fails to see at the same time that truth does not originate at all, and in this sense is intrinsic to a knowledge. I think a consistent advocate of the *svataḥ* theory should refuse to admit the very problem of *utpatti*.

Considered in the light of these remarks, the entire controversy about *guṇa* vrs. *doṣābhāva*, namely, whether truth is caused by special excellences or if it is caused by the general causes of knowledge plus mere absence of frustrating circumstances, seems wide of the mark, the arguments and counter-arguments being offered more out of zealous attachment to official dogmas rather than out of any consideration of the facts themselves.

Let us now have a look at those arguments and counter-arguments themselves, not so much to decide whether they are valid or otherwise, but to see their relevance and phenomenological basis.

First, there are the following arguments. If mere absence of *doṣa* were the cause of true knowledge, then, argues the Naiyāyika, it cannot be explained why in the case of the knowledge 'The conchshell is yellow' there should be true apprehension of the conchshell as a conchshell in spite of the presence of *doṣas* like defects in the visual sense-organs. Further, *doṣas* are of an infinite number, and absences of them would be equally numerous. Would it not be more economical if instead of such an array of them we admitted a few *guṇas*?

'But', reply the Mīmāṃsakas, 'it is no better with the *guṇa*-hypothesis. You hold that in perception, the *guṇa* is *bhūyovayav-asannikarṣa* or contact of the senses with the parts of the object. But even if such contacts were there, presence of *doṣas* like defects in the sense-organs frustrates the effect, and produces the wrong perception, e.g., of the conchshell as being yellow. The cause of true knowledge is then not a *guṇa* but absence of such frustrating circumstances. As to the superfluity of assumptions, the *guṇa*-hypothesis is worse off. Absence of *doṣa* has in any case to be admitted, and over and above that you admit a *guṇa*'.

It is interesting to note the peculiar nature of the arguments. It is agreed that a knowledge that is erroneous is only partly so, there being always some qualifier with regard to which the knowledge is true. In the knowledge 'The conchshell is yellow', we have truth with regard to the qualifier 'conchshell-ness' though error with regard to the qualifier 'yellowness'. Now to argue, as the Naiyāyikas do, that if in spite of the presence of *doṣas* the knowledge could be true with regard to one of its qualifiers then the absence of *doṣa* could not be a cause of truth, is to overlook the fact that a *doṣa* is a *doṣa* only in a certain context, that the *doṣa* which distorts colour vision is not usually a *doṣa* with regard to recognition of substances. There is then absence of *doṣa* so far as the perception of the shell is concerned, and understandably there is truth so far. Similarly, what is *guṇa* is so only in a certain context and may not be so in another. What is *guṇa* then insofar as perception of a conchshell as a conchshell is concerned is not a *guṇa*, insofar as it does not guarantee the truth, insofar as colour perception is concerned. One may then point out as against the Mīmāṃsaka that the *guṇa* which could generate a right perception of the colour of the conchshell was really absent, and there were *doṣas* of course in addition; hence the aberration.

The Naiyāyika continues to argue, however. If a true knowledge is caused by absence of *doṣa* plus the generic causes of knowledge, then does not the Mīmāṃsā thesis amount to accepting that the origin of true knowledge is *parataḥ*, for it amounts to introducing an extra factor other than the generic causes of knowledge? But the Mīmāṃsaka replies that it need not be so interpreted. When he denies that there is any extra factor, he is simply denying the agency of any other *positive* factor. Absence of *doṣa* however is a negative factor and so the supposed self-contradiction does not exist. Some Mīmāṃsakas are more cautious. They point out[108] that though there is absence of *doṣa* in the case of a true knowledge this absence is not to be counted as a cause of the true knowledge. Its sole function is to render error impossible; in that case, the true knowldege would arise out of the same conditions as also produce the knowledge itself. They may even go so far as to hold that *guṇas* may also be present, but the function of the *guṇas* is merely to prevent *doṣas* from coming in; in any case neither the *guṇas* nor the absence of *doṣas* could be counted as the causes of the true knowledge.

The Naiyāyika has two replies to all this. He may in the first place say that there is no reason why an absence should not be a cause. Secondly, he may remind the Mīmāṃsaka that sometimes the *doṣa* itself is a negative factor, e.g. absence of light in visual perception. But in that case the absence of the *doṣa*, being the absence of an absence, would be positive so that if it were admitted to be the cause of a true knowledge, truth would be *parataḥ*.

The arguments are again extremely unhelpful, and one is left with the suspicion that if both *guṇas* and absence of *doṣas* are present in the case of a true knowledge it is very much a matter of decision which one of these is to be ranked as the extraordinary cause of it and which one as a merely auxiliary, though necessary factor.

The very concepts of *guṇa* and *doṣa* are riddled with difficulties. The Mīmāṃsakas rigthly insist on the fact that there is no generic character of *guṇatva* i.e. no generic property common to all *guṇas*

108. For a discussion of these views, see Mm. Yogendranāth Tarkatīrtha, *loc. cit.*

by virtue of possessing which they are *guṇas*. But is it any better with the concept of *doṣa*? Does not the Mīmāṃsaka himself admit that *doṣas* cause errors even though he is not able to produce a satisfactory definition of what makes a *doṣa* a *doṣa*? If so, why should he object to the Naiyāyika's contention that *guṇa* is the cause of a true knowledge, even though a satisfactory definition of *guṇa* is similarly lacking?

Gaṅgeśa's strongest argument, the one with which he begins his chapter on the origin of truth, is however this: there is no generic effect which is unaccompanied by specific characters.[109] There is no man in general, there is either an Indian or an Englishman. There is no knowledge in general, there is either true knowledge or false knowledge. Therefore, there is no generic cause as such. The generic cause is always accompanied by the causes of the species. There is no cause of knowledge in general without there being also those specific factors which give rise to either truth or error. Where there is neither *guṇa* nor *doṣa* there is not even the causes of a knowledge. Truth and error are the two species of cognition, therefore there must be a difference in their respective originating conditions. "*Tasmāt pramāpramayor-vaicitryāt guṇadoṣajanyatvam*".

The Mīmāṃsaka agrees that there is either true knowledge or false cognition, so that there is no knowledge in general, no knowledge in other words which is neither true nor false. He also agrees that since true knowledge and false cognition are heterogeneous effects, there must be a difference in their originating conditions. Only he construes the difference in another way. He contends that there is either cause vitiated by defects, or the same cause free from the defects, either *duṣṭakāraṇa* or *doṣara-hitakāraṇa*: in the former case there is error, in the latter case there is truth. There is no quarrel therefore insofar as the principle which Gaṅgeśa uses is concerned, the difference arises in the subsequent application of it. There is however a deeper difference, and this concerns the very conception of knowledge. For the Nyāya, truth and error are two *species* of knowledge. Not so, strictly speaking, for the Mīmāṃsaka. For the *svataḥ* theory, we may say, true knowledge is not a species of knowledge,

109. "*Viśeṣavinākṛtasāmānyakāryābhāvāt*".

it is knowledge in the proper sense. Error is not just another species, it is an aberration, a distortion, caused by the presence of vitiating circumstances. The difference then being deeper down than it would seem at the first sight, the arguments and counter-arguments offered may be regarded as of little value excepting that they *may* suggest to us where exactly the root of the difference lies. If we can lay our finger on that, we may have made substantial gains.

(*b*) The *jñapti* or apprehension of truth:—

It has been said that for us the issue pertaining to the apprehension of truth is more important and also seems more relevant to theory of knowledge as a whole. We may now turn to the arguments advanced by both the sides to the controversy, our aim being to get down to the roots of the matters.

The main argument of the Mīmāṃsaka against the Nyāya theory consists in showing some kind of infinite regress as a consequence of the theory. This may be shown in various ways. It may be argued that if the truth of a knowledge K_1 needs to be verified by another knowledge K_2, then K_2 can do this job only if it itself stands confirmed, and that needs another knowledge K_3. But this process of validation shall have no end, and we shall need K_4, K_5,...*ad infinitum.* In practice however the Naiyāyika stops short of this, and in doing this he is not consistent. He contends, for example, that the knowledge that there is water over there before me is confirmed when I go over there and quench my thirst. But he does not see that the quenching of thirst, which confirms the knowledge of water, needs itself to be validated. Or, the Mīmāṃsaka may argue that unless the person seeing water were certain about the truth of what he knows he would not take the trouble of walking up the distance in order to quench his thirst. Even if in this case he does make an attempt, in cases where the appropriate *pravṛtti* would need great effort a person not certain of the truth of what he knows would not be persuaded to act. He would certainly not act unhesitatingly. There would be no *niṣkampa pravṛtti.* The argument then would be that successful practice cannot confirm the truth of a knowledge, for the very possibility of unwavering practical behaviour presupposes a prior certainty of the truth of the knowledge which provokes the activity.

To all these arguments, the Naiyāyika may reply in various ways. He may concede, as said earlier, that he is not against ascribing some kind of intrinsic truth to the final confirmatory experiences. He might do so in a somewhat weak sense of 'intrinsic', namely in the sense that in their case there is no possibility of error, no occasion for doubt, and hence no need for further confirmation. The process of confirmation would thus come to an end. There would be no infinite regress. This I think is a fairly good reply so far as it goes. The Naiyāyika is not inconsistent in holding this view for he may, as also pointed out earlier, suitably modify his thesis and restrict it only to those cognitions which provoke activity and which have not yet become familiar. In all other cases he may concede an intrinsic truth in rather weak sense.

But a more interesting reply is suggested by Gaṅgeśa (para 52). The Mīmāṃsaka's argument makes two presuppositions. It is assumed that a knowledge cannot give us certainty about its own object unless its own truth is ascertained. It is then argued that K_1 cannot give us certainty about its O unless the truth of K_1 is ascertained which would need another knowledge K_2. But by the same logic K_2 cannot ascertain the truth of K_1 unless its own truth were ascertained by another knowledge K_3. Gaṅgeśa rejects this assumption as unfounded. It assumes more than what is warranted by facts. A knowledge whose truth has not been ascertained may very well give us certainty about its own object. K_2 may confirm K_1 without itself being confirmed. We might very well know an object without knowing that our knowledge of that object is true. To suppose that this is not possible is to assume that every knowledge, to be knowledge, must be known to be true. But this is begging the issue. The Mīmāṃsaka shows an infinite regress in the Nyāya position only because he implicitly assumes the truth of his own position. Given the Nyāya conception of knowledge, the supposed consequences do not follow.

The other presupposition of the Mīmāṃsaka's argument is the belief that a knowledge can give rise to unwavering activity only if the truth of the knowledge has been ascertained. Certainty about the truth of a knowledge is a necessary condition of the possibility of unwavering activity appropriate to that knowledge. Gaṅgeśa again rejects this assumption. He again economises and assumes less than the Mīmāṃsaka. It is not necessary that the knowledge should be known to be true. It is enough that it should not be known to be false. A knowledge causes appropriate activity if the knowledge is not known to be false. It need not be, over and above this, known to be true. This again I think is a positive gain in philosophical insight. Ascertainment of the truth of the knowledge may be necessary if the knowledge is followed by doubt about its truth. The doubt has to be dispelled by a certainty. For this, confirmation is needed. But otherwise we may do without confirmation.

Against this contention of Gaṅgeśa two kinds of objections have been raised.[110] It has been urged in the first place that if truth is not apprehended and if falsity also is not apprehended then there would be doubt and therefore no unwavering activity. But I do not think this objection is tenable. Doubt of course requires amongst other conditions non-perception of the two alternatives (*viśeṣādarśana*), but it does not follow that where there is non-perception of two mutually contradictory properties there would be doubt. It is also necessary that the two alternatives should be remembered. Gaṅgeśa is not contending that the two possibilities of truth and falsity are remembered but neither of them is perceived. He is only saying that a primary knowledge causes appropriate activity if it is not simply known to be false. This does not transform it into a doubt about its own truth! It is also argued that the Naiyāyika is actually exposing himself to an objection which he usually urges against the Prābhākara school of Mīmāṃsā. It is well known that according to the latter error is not a positive cognition but really consists in two different cognitions plus a non-apprehension of their distinction. As against this the Naiyāyikas urge amongst other points that mere non-apprehension of distinction cannot cause *pravṛtti*. What is needed is a positive apprehension of relation. Now however the Naiyāyikas themselves seem to be contending what they have else-

110. See Mahāmahopādhyāya Pandit Yogendranāth Tarkatīrtha, *loc. cit.*, Vol. VII, Pt. II, pp. 140-141.

where regarded as impossible. They now say that *pravṛtti* is caused by mere non-apprehension of falsity! I do not think that this point is worth much, for the analogy between the two cases is not correct. For the Prābhākara the cause of *pravṛtti* is mere non-apprehension. For the Naiyāyika, the cause of *pravṛtti* is a positive knowledge plus a non-apprehension of its falsity, not a mere non-apprehension.

Gaṅgeśa thus effectively answers the charges of the Mīmāṃsaka. But he does more: he turns the table back upon the Mīmāṃsaka and levels the same charge of infinite regress against him (para 52). Without stopping to consider these we may turn to consider the Naiyāyika's arguments against the Mīmāṃsaka.

One common objection against the *svataḥ* theory of apprehension of truth is that if a knowledge were right from the beginning known as true then it could not subsequently be discovered to be false. This objection would have been decisive if it was combined with the *svataḥ* theory of the origination of truth. For if truth did really originate in it, it could not later on turn out to be false. Taken merely as a theory of knowledge of truth, the objection is not tenable. It may be replied that though a knowledge is always at first apprehended to be true, it may, owing either to the discovery of a *doṣa* in the cause or to subsequent contradiction, be afterwards found to be false.

The main argument of Udayana and Gaṅgeśa against the *svataḥ* theory is a special case and a stronger version of this objection, and therefore should be considered separately. Doubt is a kind of *apramā*. The objection now runs as follows: if a knowledge were known for certain to be true right from the beginning, it could not possibly be doubted—soon after the origination of that knowledge—whether the knowledge is true or not. And yet we do sometimes, especially in the case of knowledges of an unfamiliar kind, doubt, immediately after having the knowledge, whether the knowledge is true or not. Such doubts which do undoubtedly take place cannot be accounted for if every knowledge were initially known to be true, i.e. if knowledge of a knowledge always amounted to certainty about its truth. For detailed statement of the argument see Gaṅgeśa's text below, paras 22ff., and our notes thereon. For our present purpose only a few of the salient points of the argument may be stated. In the first place, not all doubt about the truth of the knowledge is claimed to be unexplained in the theory. Of course, doubts which arise later on after the first knowledge of the knowledge has disappeared may well be accounted for, for there remains nothing which may render them impossible. In fact, if the *svataḥ* theory be stated, as it has been by Gaṅgeśa in 7, as maintaining that truth is apprehended by all those knowledges of the knowledge (whose truth is under consideration) which do not apprehend the falsity of the knowledge, then all doubts about the truth of the knowledge would be excluded from the purview of the thesis, and there would remain no inconsistency in maintaining both that truth is known *svataḥ* (in the above sense) and that we may later on doubt or deny it. But the doubt which immediately follows upon the origination of a knowledge raises a special difficulty. It is to be preceded by a knowledge of the knowledge, and the latter yields, according to the *svataḥ* theory, a certainty about truth. Such certainty cannot be *immediately* followed by doubt, for the former is a *pratibandhaka* of the latter. Later on after this certainty disappears in the third moment after its origination (in accordance with the Nyāya metaphysics) there may very well be doubt.

The Mīmāṃsakas, it must be said in all fairness, have given what from their own point of view may be regarded as satisfactory replies to this seemingly formidable objection. The replies may be listed as follows:—

1. The objection presupposes that it is one of the necessary but not sufficient conditions of doubt that the substantive (*dharmi*) of the doubt—the *this*, e.g., in the doubt 'Is this a man or not?'—should be perceived. Now the Mīmāṃsaka may very well deny this assumption. He may contend that all that is necessary is that there should be a contact of the senses with the substantive (*dharmīndriyasannikarṣa*), and provided the other necessary conditions are present there would be doubt without there being a separate knowledge of the substantive. Gaṅgeśa considers this reply but sets it aside in 25 on the ground that unless knowledge of the substantive were a necessary condition of doubt, it cannot be explained why there should be *dharminiyama* and *koṭyutkaṭatva*. As regards '*koṭyutkaṭatva*' it is a highly controversial matter, and not all Naiyāyikas agree that it does characterise doubts. But certainly *dharminiyama* can be accoun-

ted for even on the assumption that doubt is preceded by simply contact of the *dharmi* with the senses and not by a separate knowledge of the *dharmi*. The fact that though the senses are in contact with various objects yet doubt arises only with regard to one of them and not with regard to the others may be explained in the same way in which the Naiyāyika explains the fact that though there is simultaneous contact of the senses with various objects yet only one of them is perceived and not the others. Another knowledge of the object need not intervene between the contact and the resulting doubt. In that case the main backbone of the objection is broken.

Gaṅgeśa however seeks to rescue the argument. The plea that doubt requires sense contact and not a knowledge of it can be advanced only by the Miśra school which believes in an introspective apprehension of knowledge. The Bhāṭṭas certainly cannot take the help of this plea, for on their view knowledge is supersensible. The Prābhākaras also cannot, for they have to accept knowledge of the knowledge which on their view would also amount to knowledge of its truth. Secondly, even if *dharmisannikarṣa* were enough for doubt there would be no way of avoiding further troubles. Gaṅgeśa appeals to the rule (see text para 23, and notes thereon) that if certainty about a thing acts as hindrance to another thing, then the conditions of that certainty would also act as hindrance to the same. If certainty about the truth of a knowledge would hinder the rise of a doubt about the same, then the conditions of that certainty would also serve the same purpose. Now sense contact with the knowledge is a condition of knowing it and so also a condition of certainty about its truth. Therefore, even if no separate knowledge of knowledge is needed, the sense contact with the knowledge would suffice to ward off the said doubt. The Mīmāṃsaka may not however accept the validity of the rule to which Gaṅgeśa appeals, but in that case Gaṅgeśa drives him to swallow unpalatable consequences (see especially note 23.5).

2. The Mīmāṃsaka may then fall back on another reply. He may say that where both the conditions are present, the conditions of doubt and the conditions of certainty, it is the former which, being stronger of the two, would prevail. For Gaṅgeśa's reply, see 23 again. I do not think the argument is of any worth.

The conditions of certainty being present, the conditions of doubt cannot be present. Both the sets of conditions cannot be together present. In the present case, the conditions of certainty of the truth of the knowledge are the first to come into the picture. Therefore there is no ground in suggesting that the conditions of doubt are also present.

3. Another reply is possible exactly on the lines of that given to the generalised Nyāya objection mentioned at the beginning. It may be said that though truth is apprehended yet owing to the presence (or, discovery of) some *doṣa* there again arises doubt about the same. Gaṅgeśa's reply is threefold. First, the case of seeing the conchshell yellow in spite of a prior certainty that it is white is very different from the present one (26.2). Secondly, while a perceptual certainty to the contrary is needed to annul a wrong perceptual belief, yet any prior certainty acts as a hindrance to doubts (26.3). Finally, there are all the difficulties around the notion of *doṣa* (27.1).

4. A more interesting way out is then considered by Gaṅgeśa (27). Let truth be known. But this knowledge of truth itself may come to be doubted. Let the first knowledge be K_1 and its truth T_1. Now suppose T_1 is apprehended by K_2. The problem is, how after this it is possible to have the doubt "Is K_1 true or not?" The present solution is this: We first have doubt about the truth of K_2 Doubt in the truth of a knowledge causes as a rule doubt about the reality of its object. If K_2 is doubted, as a consequence T_1 which is its object would also be doubted, and this is precisely what was to be accounted for. Again, here Gaṅgeśa's objection is effective: The case with K_2 is no better than that with K_1. K_2 is also known to be true *svataḥ*, and it is equally inexplicable how its truth could come to be doubted soon after.

The above discussions show that Gaṅgeśa's argument is strong and offers the Mīmāṃsaka a formidable challenge. But the argument certainly rests on ontological assumptions which weaken its otherwise seemingly unanswerable challenge. Gaṅgeśa assumes that we do have such doubts. No doubt we have some time or other doubts about the truth of some knowledge we had. But any such doubt does not interest Gaṅgeśa. He assumes that we have doubts about the truth of a knowledge immediately after— i.e. in the second, third, and fourth moments after (according as we are dealing with the Prābhākara, Miśra and the Bhāṭṭa views respectively)—the origination of the knowledge. Now that there are such doubts at any one of these moments after the knowledge and not somewhat later, is not an empirically verifiable hypothesis. We may have doubts very soon after. But how to make sure that the doubt arises in the third moment after the origination of the knowledge? The difficulty is due to the peculiar conception of moment. Distinctions of moment are not discernible differences. There is the further metaphysical doctrine that a knowledge has a life history of three moments. Leaving this latter belief aside, the way the argument is made to depend on the supposed fact that there do occur doubts of the said kind in the third (or second, or fourth) moment after the origination of the knowledge makes it vulnerable to attacks from that quarter. It would not do to say that there occur doubts very soon after, for it may always be maintained without the risk of empirical evidences to the contrary that the doubts which occurred very soon after were really several more moments after, let us say, five, six, or seven, and never in the second, third or the fourth moment!

There are two other arguments of the Naiyāyika. Of these two the last one is in our opinion the most important argument. In the first place, it is urged that since truth is a related entity, a *viśiṣṭa* object in which the two components of '*tadvadviśeṣyakatva*' and '*tatprakārakatva*' limit and determine each other, it cannot be apprehended unless the related terms are previously apprehended in precisely those characters in which they are related. It has been said earlier that the Miśras who regard truth as knowable by *anuvyavasāya* understand by 'truth' nothing more than *tadvadviśeṣyakatve sati tatprakārakatva*. Now this is a loose coexistence of two different entities each of which is knowable by *anuvyavasāya* even on the Naiyāyika's view. But this as we have seen is not a good definition of 'truth'. Truth must at least be *tadvadviśeṣyakatvāvacchinnatatprakārakatva*, and this cannot be apprehended unless the component terms '*tadvadviśeṣyakatva*' and '*tatprakārakatva*' are previously known. Now on the *svataḥ* theory truth is known either by the knowledge itself, or by its *anuvyavasāya* or by the inference from *jñātatā*. But none of these is qualified to fulfil the necessary requirements. The *anuvyavasāya* or the self-revealing knowledge itself may apprehend its own '*tadvadviśeṣyakatva*' and '*tatprakārakatva*' but precisely for that reason they are not qualified to apprehend the relatedness of these two entities. This point has been most forcefully and elaborately worked out in the recently published *Prāmāṇyavāda* of Harirama.[111]

The Mīmāṃsakas may avoid this difficulty in either of two ways. They may, like the Prābhākaras, insist that truth is mere '*tatprakārakatva*' and this admittedly is known *svataḥ*. But this is a notion of truth that applies to errors as well and does not serve to distinguish truth from error. It is therefore useless for us. We are investigating that property which distinguishes true knowledges from the false ones and is present in common in all true knowledges. '*Tatprakārakatva*' falls short of this test. It is too wide a definition.

The Mīmāṃsakas may accept the definition of the Naiyāyika and proceed to deny the validity of the rule (on which the Naiyāyika depends) that a knowledge of a related whole presupposes knowledge of the relata separately. But this is too fundamental an issue to be decided here. This concerns one of the central principles of the Nyāya theory of knowledge, the principle on which the Nyāya distinction between *nirvikalpa* and *savikalpa* perceptions is based.

This argument however cannot be a decisive one. For if this were the reason why truth in the Naiyāyika's sense cannot be apprehended by *anuvyavasāya* then one has to allow cases where modifications of the Nyāya position seem quite plausible. Thus Harirama refers to a possible case where one has somehow a prior knowledge of both the relata involved. In that case there is nothing to hinder him from apprehending truth in his first *anuvyavasāya*. One can only add that all that the Nyāya theory implies is that truth is not apprehended *only* by *anuvyavasāya*. But this would be a poor compromise indeed. One has to concede also another case, as Pakṣadhara Miśra does: let the first *anuvyavasāya* apprehend the *tadvadviśeṣyakatva* and the *tatprakārakatva*. If this *anuvyavasāya* is followed by the same knowledge of the same object and then there follows an *anuvyavasāya* of it then

111. "*Evaṃ copadarśitarītyā prāmāṇyaghaṭakībhūtasakalapadārthānāṃ viśṛṅkhalaviṣayitvasiddhāvapi tādṛśavilakṣaṇaviṣayitā tathāvidhavyavasāye asiddhā eveti.*" (*Prāmāṇyavāda*, Sanskrit College, Calcutta, 1964, p. 20).

this second *anuvyavasāya* seems qualified to apprehend truth. Pakṣadhara accepts this possibility[112], and the commentary *Dinakarī* on *Siddhāntamuktāvalī* speaks of it with seeming approval. Harirama however rejects this on the ground that the first *anuvyavasāya* apprehends the qualifiers and the qualificandum of the first primary knowledge whereas the second *anuvyavasāya* can apprehend similar properties in the second primary knowledge. Therefore the fact that the first *anuvyavasāya* apprehended the properties of the first primary knowledge cannot be used to support the claim that the second *anuvyavasāya* apprehends its truth.[113] It may be said then that this view of Pakṣadhara does not represent the main trend of the Nyāya view on the matter.

The argument we have been examining is to the effect that truth being a composite relational entity it cannot be apprehended unless the component relata have been previously apprehended, and that the *svataḥ* theory has no room for this requirement. A variation of this argument is this: a knowledge of the truth of K_1, let us say, would have the form 'K_1 is true'. Such a judgement is possible only if we have a prior acquaintance with K_1 as well as with its truth. It is therefore by no means possible that the first knowledge of K_1 would also be at the same time a knowledge of its truth. This objection in another form threatens the Naiyāyika's account also. The Naiyāyika holds, as is well known, that truth is first apprehended by an inference. But one of the rules of a valid inference is that the *sādhya* must be previously known though it need not be known as belonging to the *pakṣa* of this inference, otherwise there would be the fallacy of *sādhyāprasiddhi*. This fallacy now appears to threaten the Nyāya account. If truth is not known beforehand, if it is ascertained for the first time by the inference then the *sādhya* (which is but the truth of the knowledge concerned) is unknown. Gaṅgeśa makes desperate attempts

112. "*Kiṃca pṛthivījñāne tadanuvyavasāyānantaraṃ punastatraiva viṣaye pṛthivījñāne jāte tadanuvyavasāyānantaramityādivakṣyamāṇaprāmāṇyagraha...*" (*Āloka* on *Prāmāṇyavāda*, Darbhanga edn., p. 64). "*Evaṃ nyāyamate anumiteriva dvitīyānuvyavasāyasyāpi prāmāṇyagrāhakatvam*" (*Dinakarī* on *Muktāvalī* on *Kārikā* 136).

113. "*...prathamānuvyavasāye prathamavyavasāyaniṣṭhaprakāritvādīnāmeva bhānāt, dvitīyavyavasāyavṛttiprakāritvādīnāmanupasthityā tadghaṭitatadīyaprāmāṇyasya bhānāsambhavāt*" (Harirama, *loc. cit.*, p. 74).

to solve this difficulty. For these and for our critical comments thereon, see text paras 36-40 and the notes on them.

We may now turn to the last but at the same time in our opinion the most important argument advanced by the Naiyāyika against the *svataḥ* theory. The argument rests on the rule that mind as an instrument of knowledge is incapable of apprehending outer reality independently (*bahirviṣaye manasorasvātantryāt*). A knowledge is apprehended by the mind, but mind cannot thereby know whether the qualifier of the knowledge really belongs to the object of the knowledge. In other words, the mind is not able to apprehend the *tadvattva* which is a component of '*tadvadviśeṣyakatva*' which again is a component of the notion of truth. In simpler language, I can know my knowledge 'This is silver' to be true only if I know that the object before me is really a silver, i.e. it possesses silverness. But to know this is to know an outer state of affairs, which the mind by itself cannot do. A knowledge of knowledge therefore as such cannot do this. *Anuvyavasāya* at least cannot do this, and as against the Miśra theory the argument is conclusively effective. We have only to ask how far it is effective as against the Prābhākara and the Bhāṭṭa versions of the *svataḥ* theory. Against the Prābhākara theory that a knowledge apprehends its own truth, we may say that though the knowledge 'This is silver' apprehends itself as having the qualifier 'silverness' and also as having the qualificandum 'this' limited by 'thisness', yet it does not apprehend that the qualificandum 'this' possesses silverness. The *this* may in fact possess silverness, but the knowledge does not know itself as having a qualificandum which possesses silverness, and that makes all the difference between the primary knowledge and the knowledge of its truth. As against the Bhāṭṭas we may say with the Naiyāyikas that *jñātatā* could not be a mark of truth, for it serves as a mark of true knowledge and false knowledge alike.

As Gaṅgeśa argues in 33, the form of the *anuvyavasāya* is not 'I know this silver' but 'I have a knowledge of *this* having 'thisness' and 'silverness' as its qualifiers'. For critical remarks on this see notes thereon and also the footnote to 33.1.

We may sum up the matter then by saying that the whole theory of *parataḥprāmāṇya* as advocated by the Naiyāyika, especially by Gaṅgeśa, is based on the conception of truth as what we have called a hybird entity containing both epistemic and ontological components. This nature prevents truth from being readily knowable with knowledge of its focus. One has to take recourse to a process of confirmation and validation. *Pravṛtti* or practical activity however does not wait for a successful outcome of the process of confirmation, unless of course there has been a preliminary doubt to start with.

V. Concluding Remarks

We may now put together the insights we have gained from this critical study. It was said right at the beginning of this introductory study that it was possible to look upon the rival schools insofar as the problem of truth was concerned as in a way supplementing each other. It is likely, we said then, that they are not answering exactly the same questions, that the two points of view do not necessarily clash but may be brought into a happy reconciliation. The apparent contradiction may be due to the fact that they are using the same expressions while in fact giving them different meanings. Both the rival schools are based upon some genuine philosophical insights. Both are appealing to undeniable phenomena. Yet semantic confusions prevail, and where there ought to have been accord of insights there is instead clash of arguments.

We leave aside for the present the ambiguity, equivocation and relativity of the words '*sva*' and '*para*'. Gaṅgeśa has tried his best to remove these and to make their meaning as precise as possible. It goes to his credit to have brought out a common meaning of '*svataḥprāmāṇya*' where there is really a great deal of internal difference amongst the advocates of this theory. But for us the real key words, the words that give shape to the entire controversy we have been examining are two: '*jñāna*' and '*prāmāṇya*', 'knowledge' and 'truth'. The difference between the two theories lies here: they take '*jñāna*' and '*prāmāṇya*' in different senses and as a consequence have to look upon the relation between knowledge and truth also differently.

'*Jñāna*'—The *svataḥ* theory understands 'knowledge' in a strict sense such that the theory becomes an analytic consequence of its conception of knowledge. It understands by 'knowledge' only true knowledge. For it *pramā* and *apramā* are not just co-ordinate species of *jñāna*. If this were so i.e. if true and false cognitions were co-ordinate species of knowledge then Gaṅgeśa's arguments would have successfully exposed the theory. But the theory is invulnerable to these criticisms just because its underlying assumptions are different from those of the *parataḥ* theory. Now this strict sense of 'knowledge' is maintained in either of two ways. Some deny that there is anything called error strictly speaking. Error and doubt are then sought to be resolved into components that are, each taken by itself, true. Others, as shown earlier, accept error and doubt as irreducible forms but do not treat them as forms of knowledge. They are regarded rather as pseudo-knowledges, *jñānābhāsas*. In either of these ways, the strict sense of 'knowledge' is maintained intact in the face of recalcitrant phenomena of error and doubt. No wonder that truth should be taken as intrinsic to knowledge. Error then becomes an aberration, not a species of knowledge.

But it is necessary to point out again even at the cost of repetition that what the *svataḥ* theory is doing *is not a mere linguistic stipulation*, an arbitrary recommendation to use the word 'knowledge' in a certain sense. The theory has a strong support from both phenomena and linguistic usage. It is supported by the usage of 'know' according to which *to know is to know the truth*. It is supported by the phenomenological evidence that error is not knowledge but pretends to be knowledge. Error is error only inasmuch as it can successfully pretend to be knowledge, though its character as error stands exposed along with its pretension.

As contrasted with all this, the *parataḥ* theory takes 'knowledge' in a rather weak sense so as to include within its scope both true knowledge and false knowledge. Even doubt is not excluded. 'Knowledge' then is a generic term which for obvious reasons cannot be defined with reference to what characterises only one species of it. *The word 'belief'*—in spite of all the philosophical difficulties associated with it—*perhaps better expresses this generic knowledge in the weak sense.* No wonder then that in this sense truth cannot be an intrinsic character of all knowledge quâ knowledge. It should also be obvious that a belief *needs confirmation* prior to which it remains a belief, powerful enough to cause appropriate practical response but cognitively still below the rank of true knowledge.

'*Prāmāṇya*'—There are three different *types* of concepts of truth to be met with in the different versions of the *svataḥ* theory. There is on the one hand a *psychological* concept according to which a knowledge is true (and not merely taken to be so) if it is not known to be false, if it has not yet been contradicted. There is next an *epistemological* concept which makes truth a purely epistemological property: it may be defined either simply as *tatprakārakatva* (as by the Prābhākaras who need not distinguish it from error) or as *tadvadviśeṣyakatve sati tatprakārakatva* (as by the Miśras who distinguish truth from error, but do not see that truth must have an ontological reference). There is then the definition of truth as simple *jñānatva* which makes it the generic property of all knowledge quâ knowledge. All these definitions go to make the *svataḥ* theory highly plausible. The last one makes the theory analytically true. The first one makes it psychologically acceptable. The second makes truth knowable by *anuvyavasāya*.

The Naiyāyikas mean something else by truth. It is interesting to note that some advocates of the *svataḥ* theory (like the author of the *Vedāntaparibhāṣā*) explicitly proclaim that the truth which they regard as being *svataḥ* is nothing other than *tadvati tatprakārakatva*. But in fairness it must be said that in further explication of it they must have to part company. Madhusūdana Saraṣvatī clearly says that *tadvati tatprakārakatva* is common to both true and false knowledges. It is obvious that he is explicating it in a sense that is different from the Naiyāyika's.

Both the theories are valid in their own ways, for the word 'true' is predicated of beliefs as well as of knowledge.[114] As predicated of beliefs, the predicate 'true' has a significant opposite i.e. 'false' inasmuch as there are true beliefs and false beliefs. But as predicated of knowledge the predicate 'true' has no significant opposite inasmuch as 'false' is not a predicate of knowledge in the same way as 'true' is.

114. For further elaboration, see Mohanty, "Meaning and Truth", *Visvabharati Journal of Philosophy*, Vol. I, No. 1 (Reprinted in my *Phenomenology and Ontology*, The Hague: M. Nijhoff, 1970).

This way of reconciling the two theories is somewhat fundamentally different from some other attempts to do the same.[115] It has been held by many that what the *svataḥ* theory says is that every knowledge has an intrinsic *claim to truth*, that *prāmāṇya* for this theory is not truth but truth-claim, which has to be accepted unless and until it has been refuted. The Naiyāyikas on the other hand speak of actual truth and not of mere tentative truth-claim. This is indeed a very ingenious device, but I think it is too simple to be true. The *svataḥ* theory, I should think, is talking about truth and not merely of truth-claim. Only it so construes the meaning of 'truth' that the rest of it follows smoothly. Both the theories are concerned with actual truth, though *their notions of truth are different*. It has also been suggested that the *svataḥ* theory is concerned with truth in the unreflective sense, while the *parataḥ* theory with reflective confirmation or validation so that both the theories are correct. There is an unreflective acceptance which does not rule out the need for subsequent validation. I think this way of reconciling the theory fails to account for an important aspect of the *svataḥ* theory, namely for the fact that this theory has no room at all for subsequent validation.

While both the theories are thus in their own ways correct, each of them suffers through confrontation with the other. The dialectics which ensues upon this confrontation tends to distort the original grain of truth in each. Thus the *svataḥ* theory comes to *say* that truth originates from the same conditions as give rise to knowledge quâ knowledge, whereas it ought to have said that truth has no origin at all or that the very question about the origin of truth is nonsensical.

115. For a criticism of my approach to this issue, cp. K. Potter, "Does Indian Epistemology concern Justified True Knowledge", *Journal of Indian Philosophy*, 12, 1984. For my reply to Potter, cp. my "Prāmāṇya and Workability" reprinted as Appendix to this volume.

PRĀMĀṆYAVĀDA: TEXT, TRANSLATION AND NOTES

1. *Atha jagadeva duḥkhapaṅkanimagnamuddidhīrṣuraṣṭādaśa-vidyāsthāneṣvabhyarhitatamāmānvīkṣikīṃ paramakāruṇiko muniḥ praṇināya. Tatra prekṣāvatpravṛttyartham 'pramāṇā-dīnāṃ tattvajñānānniḥśreyasādhigama' ityādāvasūtrayat. Teṣ-vapi (tatra) pramāṇādhīnā sarveṣāṃ vyavasthitiriti pramāṇa-tattvamatra vivicyate.*

Now, the extremely gracious sage composed the Science of Logic[3] which is the most respected amongst all the eighteen sciences,[4] being desirous of raising the world[5] that is immersed in the mud of miseries. Therein, in order that the discerning persons may have interest in studying the work, he laid down the *sūtra*: 'Attainment of the highest good[2] comes from right knowledge of the sources of true knowledge etc....' Of these, all the others rest[7] on the sources of true knowledge. Therefore, the true nature of the sources of true knowledge[6] shall be discussed here.[1]

Notes

1.1. This is a statement of what the author proposes to investigate. Such a statement is called a *pratijñā*. Its purpose is to awaken in the mind of the reader a knowledge of the form 'This is what the author is going to do'. Gaṅgeśa tells us here that his work is concerned with the nature of the sources of true knowledge (*pramāṇas*).

[An author should begin by stating (i) the subject matter (*abhidheya*) and (ii) the purpose (*prayojana*). Further he has to specify the following relations: (a) the relation between the work and its subject matter which is called the *pratipādya-pratipādaka* relation; (b) the relation between the purpose and the subject matter which is a *janya-janaka* relation insofar as the subject matter brings about the fulfilment of the purpose; and (c) the relation between the work and the purpose which is one of means and end (*prayojaka-prayojya*) insofar as the work is the means to the attainment of the purpose.]

1.2. A discerning person would naturally like to know the purpose that would be satisfied by studying this work. It is not enough to say that its study would give us knowledge or clarify our muddles. The only legitimate purpose is either positive satisfaction or cessation of unhappiness, everything else being ancillary to either of these two. Gaṅgeśa therefore states the purpose of his work to consist in its being the means to liberation or the highest good. But instead of stating this point on his own, he prefers to take shelter under the indisputable reputation of Gotama who has said that the highest good is attainable only through right knowledge of the sixteen categories* of being beginning with *pramāṇa*. Gaṅgeśa in fact is giving us an abridged quotation of the very first *sūtra* of Gotama which runs thus: '*Pramāṇa-prameya-saṃśaya-prayojana-dṛṣṭānta-siddhāntāvayava-tarka-nirṇaya-vāda-jalpa-vitaṇḍā- hetvābhāsa-cchala-jāti-nigrahasthānānāṃ tattvajñānniḥśreyasādhigamaḥ*'.

(Although this is the ultimate purpose, the Nyāya is said to be of use in all walks of life and in all the other sciences. Vātsyāyana calls it 'the lamp of all sciences' (*pradīpaḥ sarvavidyānām*) and 'the means to all actions' (*upāyaḥ sarvakarmaṇām*).**

1.3. The name '*Ānvīkṣikī*' is derived from '*anu*' (=after) and '*īkṣ*' (=to know). Thus the word etymologically means the knowledge which comes after some other knowledge. Vātsyāyana explains '*Anvīkṣā*' as 'the critical reflection on what has already been known by perception or verbal testimony' (*pratyakṣāgamābhyāmīkṣitasyānvīkṣaṇamanvīkṣā****). The word '*Anumāna*' has a

* While it is possible, while being controversial to translate the Vāiśeṣika use of '*padārtha*' as 'category', Vātsyāyana's *padārthas* can be called categories only at the risk of serious misunderstanding. My rendering here therefore is misleading.

***Bhāṣya* on *Nyāya Sūtra* 1.1.1.

****Ibid.*

similar derivation from *'anu* and *'māna'*. Vātsyāyana distinguishes it from the Upaniṣads by calling the latter 'spiritual metaphysics' (*adhyātmavidyā*). However, the Nyāya is also *adhyātmavidyā* insofar as it is also concerned with the category of self and aims at imparting knowledge which would bring about liberation.

1.4. Vātsyāyana refers to the fourfold classification of the sciences accepted by Manu into *'trayī'* or the science of sacrifices, rituals etc., *'vārtā'* or the science of agriculture and rural economy, *'daṇḍanīti'* or the science of polity and diplomacy, and *'ānvīkṣikī'* or the science of logic.

1.5. Gadādhara points out that by 'world' is to be meant here the worldly selves, i.e. selves that have not as yet attained liberation; for nothing else, neither the liberated selves nor objects that are not selves, could be said to experience misery.

1.6. The word *'pramāṇa'* may mean either the resulting true knowledge, or the special cause of such knowledge. Accordingly, the word *'pramāṇa-tattva'* may mean either the property of being a true knowledge which is the same as truth (*pramātva*) or the property of being the special cause of true knowledge (*pramākaraṇatva*). The former of these two senses however is the more fundamental of the two, for it is implied in the latter notion. Here, therefore, we shall mean by *'pramāṇatattva'* truth.

1.7. That *pramāṇa* in either of the above senses is the most important of all the categories of being so that in a sense all the others rest upon it is thus stated by Vātsyāyana: *'anyatamāpāye arthasyānupapatteḥ'*.* Nothing else could possibly be posited in the absence of the *pramāṇas*. This priority holds good even though the *pramāṇa* itself is to be included among the objects of true knowledge! The priority however should be construed as logical, which again does not mean that the sources of true knowledge come first in order of knowledge. It only means that no object could be known, proved, established, or even mentioned except through a source of true knowledge.

**Ibid.*

2. *Nanu pramāṇādīnāṃ tattvaṃ pratipādayat śāstram paramparayā niḥśreyasena sambadhyate iti na yuktaṃ, pramāṇatattvāvadhāraṇasyāśakyatvāt, taddhi pramātattvāvadhāraṇādhīnam, tat ca svataḥ parato vā na sambhavati, vakṣyamāṇadūṣaṇagaṇagrāsāt.*

(It might be objected)[1] It is not right to hold that the work which discourses on the nature of the sources of true knowledge etc. is mediately[2] connected with the highest good, for it is not possible to discern the nature of the sources of true knowledge. That would depend upon the apprehension of the nature of truth[3], and this is possible neither intrinsically nor extrinsically[4] because of the host of difficulties to be pointed out in sequence.

Notes

2.1. This is an objection supposedly raised by someone who has no positive contention of his own, whose own position amounts to complete nihilism. Some would ascribe the objection to the Mādhyamikas.

2.2. The scripture is said to be connected with the highest good mediately, for the scripture gives rise to a knowledge which again leads upto the highest good. Thus right knowledge serves as the connecting link.

2.3. The concept 'source of true knowledge' logically involves the concept 'true knowledge'. Determination of the former concept is a *viśiṣṭabuddhi* which presupposes apprehension of the *viśeṣaṇa* which goes into its constitution. Hence a prior determination of the notion of truth is presupposed.

2.4. These two are supposed to be the only possible modes of apprehending truth; between them they leave no room for a third possibility. The terms '*svataḥ*' and '*parataḥ*' would receive their proper elaboration in the subsequent paragraphs. Their translation into 'intrinsic' and 'extrinsic' respectively is adopted here in the absence of any better pair of expressions. The English expressions however fail to convey the original significance of the

Sanskrit terms. But this need not worry us, for the text would explain the terms as fully as possible.

3. *Atha kiṃ prāmāṇyajñānena? Pravṛttimātre tasya vyabhicārāt. Bahuvittavyayāyāsasādhye pravṛttiścāvaśyakārthaniścayādeva.*

Now, why[1] is the apprehension of truth considered to be necessary? There is indeed absence of invariable co-presence between it and activity in general.[2] In the case of something whose achievement involves great expense and enormous trouble activity presupposes a prior certainty about the object.[3]

NOTES

3.1. This is not Gaṅgeśa's own reply to the objection contained in 2. It is to be understood as the suggestion of an outsider who shows a way out. However, it is also obvious that this answer is based on a misconstruction of the original objection.

The original objection was: "The scripture cannot lead upto the highest good, for apprehension of the nature of the sources of true knowledge is not possible".

The present reply construes the objection in a different way, and takes it to consist in the following contention. "One can have incentive to study the scriptures only if one knows for certain that right knowledge leads to the highest good. Since it is not possible to determine the truth of this latter knowledge, i.e. of the so-called *iṣṭasādhanatājñāna*, there cannot be the incentive for studying the scriptures". One could formulate the matter thus: certainty about the conduciveness of the knowledge imparted by the scriptures for the attainment of the highest good is necessary for one's undertaking to study the scriptures, and yet it is from the scriptures that one can have the former certainty.

3.2. Misconstruing the original objection in this manner, the outsider now suggests the following reply. Certainty about the truth of a knowledge, he points out, is not a necessary condition of the appropriate activity. For, we do find men acting even in the absence of the certainty about the conduciveness of the means undertaken for reaching the desired end. Doesn't a patient let himself be treated by a physician even though he is not absolutely certain that the treatment would cure him of his disease? Doesn't a warrior fight a battle even if he is not sure that he is going to win? It would seem therefore that certainty about the effectiveness of the means is not a necessary precondition of acting in the appropriate manner.

3.3. But can it not be said that although in most cases one may and in fact does act in spite of a lack of prior certainty, there are certainly cases where certainty, or absence of doubt, is the indispensable prerequisite for activity? These are cases where attainment of the end involves enormous expense or great difficulties.

Our outsider answers to this possible rejoinder thus. In cases such as these, he points out, what is required for stimulating activity is not certainty about the truth of the knowledge, but certainty about the object of the knowledge. This distinction between '*ārthaniścaya*' and '*prāmāṇyaniścaya*' is a dubious one, but, if granted, it would solve the puzzle. In no case would certainty about the truth of the knowledge be a necessary condition for the ensuing activity. One may therefore quite well begin the scriptures even in the absence of the certainty that a study of the scriptures would lead to the desired end.

4. *Na ca yasya saṃśayavyatirekaniścayau yasya pravṛttipratibandhakau tanniścayastaddhetuḥ—anumitau vyāpteriveti vācyam, tatsandehe satyarthasandehenārthāniścayādevāpravṛttestatra tayorapratibandhakatvād iti cet?*

It is not possible to apply in this case the rule[1] that if with regard to any x it holds good that both[2] the doubt about x and certainty about the absence of x obstruct the origination of another thing y[3], then certainty about such a x is the cause of this y, as for example when x stands for *vyāpti* and y for inferential knowledge.

For, they do not here act as a hindrance.[4] Where there is doubt about truth, there is also doubt about the object, and the absence of activity follows from this latter uncertainty about the object.[5]

NOTES

4.1. An answer to the suggestion contained in 3 is being disposed of. This answer brings to its aid a general rule which could be insightfully apprehended in one single case. It is well known that inferential knowledge is obstructed by doubt about the appropriate *vyāpti* as well as by the certainty that the *vyāpti* does not hold good. Hence both the doubt about the *vyāpti* and the certainty about the absence of the *vyāpti* act as hindrances to inferential knowledge. We also know that certainty about the *vyāpti* is the cause of the inferential knowledge. Now, this single insightful instance, in the absence of any instance to the contrary yields us the general rule that whenever both the doubt about any x and certainty about not-x hinder the origination of any y, then certainty about the x must be the cause of the y.

Let us now apply this general rule to the present case. Substitute 'truth' (of the knowledge that stimulates activity) for x and the resulting activity for y. We find that both the doubt about the truth of the appropriate knowledge as well as certainty about the falsity of it would hinder activity. It should therefore follow that certainty about the truth of knowledge is the cause of the relevant activity. But in that case the difficulty of the original objection stated in 2 stands: in the absence of a prior ascertainment of the truth of the claim that the knowledge imparted is conducive to the highest good, there would be no incentive to study the scriptures.

4.2. Regarding the general rule stated above, it has to be noted that it lays down two conditions both of which must be satisfied. Fulfilment of any one of these alone is not sufficient for the rule to apply. It would not for example suffice to say that if with regard to any x doubt about x hinders the origination of any y, then certainty about the x would be the cause of the y. For, consider 'absence of *vyāpti*' as a value of x, y standing for inferential knowledge (as in the text). It is true that doubt about the absence of *vyāpti* hinders inferential knowledge, though it is false that certainty about the absence of *vyāpti* is the cause of inference. It is easy to show that the other condition demanded by the rule is not satisfied here, for in this case not-x is equivalent to the *vyāpti* itself and certainty about it is far from being a hindrance to the appropriate inference. It could similarly be shown by choosing appropriate values for the variables that if the other condition alone is satisfied the rule does not any more apply.

4.3. Here in the statement of the rule in the text the word '*pravṛtti*' in '*pravṛttipratibandhakau*' seems redundant, for the rule purports to be a general one so that this latter could better be replaced by '*yadutpattipratibandhakau*'.

4.4. To this suggested way out, the outsider who had answered the original objection replies by pointing out that although the general rule may be valid yet it does not apply to the present case. He contends that what hinders activity is not doubt about the truth of the knowledge that induces the activity even if there is such doubt.

4.5. The outsider is again appealing to the distinction between doubt about the truth of a knowledge (*prāmāṇyasaṃśaya*) and doubt about the object of that knowledge (*arthasaṃśaya*). The former has the form 'Is my knowledge that S is p true or not?' The latter has the form 'Is S p or not?' The contention here is that absence of activity is due not to the former but to the latter which always follows upon the former.

5. *Na; prāmāṇyasaṃśayānantaraṃ idaṃ itthamevetyavadhāraṇasya niṣkampapravṛttyaṅgasya prāmāṇyaniścayādhīnatvāt.*

No.[1] For, after there has been doubt about truth, a certainty of the form 'This is such and such'—which certainty is a constituent of unwavering activity[2]—could arise only out of an ascertainment of truth.

NOTES

5.1. Gaṅgeśa now begins to consider the original objection. He starts by rejecting the plea of the preceding attempt to set aside that objection. He agrees with the original objection that a determination of the form 'This is such and such' is a necessary constituent of definite activity. Further, such a determination presupposes ascertainment of the truth of the corresponding knowledge, once there has been previously a doubt about that truth. Gaṅgeśa is not saying that ascertainment of truth is necessary for activity in all cases. He is only making the conditional concession that only when doubt has made its appearance, objective certainty and therefore certainty about the truth are necessary for definitive activity.

5.2. "*niṣkampapravṛtti*" = activity which is free from all hesitation. Only such activity needs a prior ascertainment of truth, and that also when there has been a prior doubt about the truth of the appropriate knowledge.

6. *Nanu svata evāstu tannirūpaṇam?*

Now, let[1] the apprehension of truth be from itself.[2]

Notes

6.1. Though Gaṅgeśa starts by agreeing with the original objection that certainty about truth is an indispensable condition of unhesitating activity, he nevertheless sees no point in the objection that the truth of a knowledge cannot be ascertained. He would of course prove that it can be ascertained. If it can be, then there are only two ways of doing this: either 'from itself' (*svataḥ*), or 'from without' (*parataḥ*). Gaṅgeśa begins by suggesting, "Why not say that truth is ascertained 'from itself'?" It hardly needs to be pointed out that this is not the case on his own view. He begins with this alternative only in order to get rid of it.

6.2. What is the meaning of '*svataḥ*'? The answer to this depends upon what we take the pronoun '*sva*' to stand for. There are two possibilities. '*Sva*' may stand for the truth that is being ascertained: this is suggested by the sentence "*Nanu svata evāstu tannirūpaṇam*", if the demonstrative '*tat*' be taken to be that to which '*sva*' also refers. Or, the '*sva*' may stand for the apprehension of the truth: this is suggested by the first occurrence of '*svataḥ*' i.e. in the sentence "*taddhi pramātvāvadhāraṇādhīnaṃ tacca svataḥ...*", where the '*sva*' refers to '*tat*' and the '*tat*' stands for the apprehension of truth (*pramātvāvadhāraṇaṃ*). In either case, '*svataḥ*' may mean—we may say following *Dīdhiti*—either '*svasmāt*' or '*svakīyāt*'. We will explain these alternatives separately.

A. '*sva*' = truth (*pramātva*):

(α) '*svataḥ*' = '*svasmāt*':—In this case, to say that truth is apprehended *svataḥ* is the same as saying that truth is known by the knowledge whose truth it is. In other words, it would mean that truth is apprehended by the very same knowledge which is its own locus. If the truth in question belongs to K_1, then this truth is known by K_1. This as we shall see is the view of the Prābhākaras.

(β) '*svataḥ*' = '*svakīyāt*':—In this case, to say that the truth of K_1 is known *svataḥ* amounts to saying that the truth of K_1 is apprehended by the knowledge (= let us say, K_2) which apprehends K_1. Under this again there are two possible formulations. (i) If K_2 is an introspective awareness (*anuvyavasāya*) of K_1, then this view may be ascribed to Murāri Miśra. (ii) If on the other hand, K_2 is an inference of the type that is called the *Jñātatā-liṅgaka-anumāna*, then the view is of the Bhāṭṭa school of Mīmāṃsā.

All these three views—(α), β (i), β (ii),—may be expressed together in one formulation according to which truth is apprehended *svataḥ* when it is *svāśrayagrāhakaniyatagrāhya*. The formulation would in effect be explained if we can show that each of the three cases under (A) satisfies it. We may now briefly attempt to do this.

The case (α) would satisfy the definition thus: the truth of K_1 is apprehended—according to the Prābhākaras—by the knowledge which knows K_1. But the Prābhākaras do not in fact believe that K_1 is known by any knowledge other than itself. However, though it is true that according to the Prābhākaras there is no knowledge of K_1 in the ordinary sense yet the word '*grāhaka*' occurring in the definition may be given an extended meaning so as to apply also to the conditions that give rise to K_1. For whenever these causal conditions are present K_1 is not only there but is also at once known (on this theory). Hence, the causal conditions being invariable antecedents of the apprehension of K_1 may also be called the cause of that apprehension.

The case (β) (i) satisfies the definition insofar as according to the Miśra school, the '*svāśrayagrāhaka*' in the definiens stands for the introspective apprehension or *anuvyavasāya* K_2 by which K_1 is subsequently apprehended. It is this K_2 which also apprehends the truth of K_1.

The case (β) (ii) also satisfies the definition. According to the Bhāṭṭas, the '*svāśrayagrāhaka*' in the definiens stands for the so-called *jñātatāliṅgakānumiti* by which K_1 is apprehended and which also apprehends the truth of K_1.

The adjective '*niyata*' in the definiens has the purpose of warding off the possibility of applying the definition to the Naiyāyika's position and thereby of rendering the definition too wide, for it is supposed to be a definition of '*svatogrāhyatva*' of truth and not of '*paratogrāhyatva*'. The Naiyāyikas also admit a case in which the truth of K_1 is apprehended by an inferential knowledge of the form "This knowledge K_1 is true, for ..." Such an inference also apprehends K_1 and therefore may be called '*svāśrayagrāhaka*'. With a view to excluding the possibility of applying the definition to such a case, the definiens is made to contain, besides, the demand that the truth of K_1 must *always* be apprehended by whatever also knows K_1. It goes without saying that such a demand is not acceptable to the Naiyāyikas. *Anuvyavasāya* certainly does not, according to them, apprehend the truth of the primary knowledge.

B. '*sva*' = apprehension of validity (*pramātvāvadhāraṇa*):

(α) '*Svataḥ*' = '*svasmāt*' :—The Prābhākaras in this case may be construed as saying that the apprehension of truth follows from itself. Such an assertion however as such carries no sense and so in order to be made intelligible must be further elaborated as follows.

Let K_1 be the knowledge whose truth is under consideration. The apprehension of its truth is said to be due to itself. This apprehension has for its object both the truth of K_1 and the object of K_1. Suppose K_1 is the knowledge of O. The apprehension of its truth is also apprehension of O. We may then say that this apprehension of truth is caused by those very causal conditions which produce knowledge of O (*svaviṣayajñānasāmagrī*), this latter knowledge being none other than K_1. In other words, the factors which cause K_1 also cause the apprehension of its truth so that '*svatogrāhyatva*' = '*svaviṣayajñānasāmagrījanyatva*'.

(β) *svataḥ*' = '*svakīyāt*' :—

In this case, '*svakīyāt*' means 'from *svaviṣayajñānaprakāśaka-jñānasāmagrī*'. Again, as before, '*sva*' stands for apprehension of the truth of K_1. '*Svaviṣayajñāna*' can be shown as before to be K_1 itself. Now, K_1 is revealed either

(i) by K_2 = *anuvyavasāya* (according to Miśra),
or (ii) by K_2 = *jñātatāliṅgakānumiti* (according to the Bhāṭṭas).

In any case, the apprehension of the truth of K_1 would follow from the conditions producing K_1 and so from *svaviṣayajñāna-prakāśakasāmagrī*.

7. *Tathāhi tatra vipratipattayaḥ* :—*jñānaprāmāṇyaṃ tadaprā-māṇyāgrāhakayāvajjñānagrāhakasāmagrīgrāhyaṃ na vā.*

Then there would be the following alternatives[1]: Is the truth of a knowledge[2] apprehended[3] by all[4] those knowledges which are produced by the same conditions[6] as give rise to the apprehension of that knowledge[5] without producing any apprehension of its falsity? Or, is it not so apprehended?

Notes

7.1. Gaṅgeśa now proceeds to suggest a series of alternative formulations of the issue. The purpose is to state precisely and thereby to clarify both his own position and the *pūrvapakṣa.** A statement of alternative possibilities in this manner is characterised by *Dīdhiti* as being "the source of that doubt without which critical reflection would not be possible" (*vicārāṅgasaṃśaya-jananī*). *Vipratipatti* is a statement in which the alternatives under controversy are presented in an equally strong manner so that the enquirer comes to have doubt, and *vicāra* or critical reflection may ensue. This practice of presenting a series of alternative

*"*Uttaravatpūrva pakṣop pariṣkaraṇīyaḥ*"—Gadādhara.

formulations of both the sides before beginning critical reflection is not found amongst Naiyāyikas before Udayana. Udayana offers such *vipratipattis* in his *Kusumāñjali* and *Ātmatattvaviveka*.

7.2. In '*jñānaprāmāṇya*', '*prāmāṇya*' means not '*pramākaraṇatva*' but '*pramātva*'. Further, '*jñāna*' means not 'instrumental to knowledge' (*jñāyate anena*) but knowledge itself. The commentators Raghunātha and Pakṣadhara Miśra differ in their interpretations of this phrase. The former construes the '*jñāna*' as suggesting that each particular knowledge is to be considered separately, for truth in each case is a different entity. Pakṣadhara interprets '*jñānaprāmāṇya*' to mean '*jñāyamānaprāmāṇya*' i.e. the known truths, for certainly the unknown truths are not apprehended in the manner the proposition states. But Pakṣadhara's point seems to me to be trivial. Of course, only known truths are known, but that need not be made out explicitly being too trivial a matter. It is safe to construe the phrase as meaning the truth of a knowledge, and to exclude the truth—if one can speak of truth in such cases—of desire, etc.

7.3. The proposition that truth is *jñānagrāhakasāmagrīgrāhya* expresses what is common to the three: the Prābhākara, the Bhāṭṭa and the Miśra schools; while the other proposition that it is not so apprehended states the Nyāya view. Thus according to the *svataḥ*-theory, the truth of a knowledge K_1 is apprehended by a knowledge K_2 which is produced by the same conditions which also produce the knowledge of K_1. The *jñānagrāhakasāmagrī* or the conditions producing the knowledge of K_1 are however (i) on the Prābhākara theory, the same as *jñānasāmagrī* or the conditions of K_1 itself; (ii) on the Bhāṭṭa theory, the same as the *jñātatāliṅgakānumitisāmagrī* or the conditions of the inference having *jñātatā* or knownness for its mark; and (iii) on the Miśra theory, the same as the *anuvyavasāyasāmagrī* or the conditions of the introspective awareness of K_1.

7.4. The word '*yāvat*' is meant to qualify the term '*graha*' or knowledge which is a constituent of the term '*grāhya*'. Actually '*jñānagrāhakasāmagrīgrāhya*' means *jñānagrāhakasāmagrījanyajñānaviṣaya* or the object of such knowledge K^1_2 which is caused by the same conditions as also produce the knowledge K_2 of the original knowledge K_1. Now *yāvat* may be construed as qualifying K^1_2. In that case, '*yāvajjñānagrāhakasāmagrīgrāhyam*' would be equivalent to '*jñānagrāhakasāmagrījanyayāvajjñānaviṣayam*'. In other words, the truth of K_1 would be said to be *svataḥ* if it is the object of all K^1_2s. This interpretation follows Raghunātha.

The insertion of '*yāvat*' as just explained is necessary in order to ward off two difficulties which would otherwise arise: (i) The Nyāya also admits that sometimes the truth of K_1 is known by an inference of the form "K_1 is true, because..." This inferential knowledge has for its object the knowledge K_1 whose truth is being thereby apprehended. Such an inference may then be taken as *jñānagrāhaka* i.e. as a K_2. In such a case the truth of K_1 may be taken even on the Nyāya view as being *jñānagrāhakasāmagrījanyajñānaviṣaya*. Now, if the Nyāya also assents to the first i.e. the affirmative alternative, then the negative alternative becomes vacuous inasmuch as none, not even the Nyāya, would assent to it. (ii) Further, if the Nyāya assents to the affirmative alternative there would be no point in the Mīmāṃsaka's trying to establish a thesis which is not challenged by anyone.

These two difficulties are avoided by adding '*yāvat*' as explained before. For, what the *svataḥ*-theory then would mean is that *all* K^1_2s should have the truth of K_1 for their object: to this the Nyāya would not in any case give its assent. It is only one kind of K^1_2 which according to the Nyāya apprehends the truth of K_1, and this is the above-mentioned sort of inference. But other K^1_2s do not. The *anuvyavasāya* of K_1 for example does not.

7.5 The clause '*tadaprāmāṇyāgrāhaka*' is inserted with a view to avoiding the following difficulty:

Now that the *svataḥ*-theory contends that truth should be the object of all K^1_2s, consider the inferential knowledge of the form "K_1 is false, because..." This inference has K_1 for its object, therefore it also may be regarded as a K_2. The corresponding K^1_2 has not however by any means the truth of K_1 for its object, hence it cannot be said that all K^1_2s have for their object the truth of K_1. As a consequence, the affirmative alternative attributed to the Mīmāṃsaka is rendered pointless for no one could give it an unconditional assent.

This difficulty would be warded off if the clause '*tadaprāmā-*

ṇyāgrāhaka' be inserted and made to qualify the term '*sāmagrī*'. In that case, the conditions producing K_2 should be such as do not also produce any apprehension of the falsity of K_1. Hence we are to exclude from the purview of the proposition any inference of the falsity of K_1 as also all doubt about its truth or falsity (for such doubt must have its falsity as one of its objects).

7.6. What however is the purpose of inserting the term '*sāmagrī*'? Is it not enough to say that the truth of K_1 is apprehended *svataḥ* when it is the object of all knowledges that are caused by whatever apprehends K_1 but does not apprehend the falsity of K_1 (*tadaprāmāṇyāgrāhakajñānagrāhakajanyayāvajjñānaviṣaya*)? That this would not do would be clear from the following consideration. Consider the self of the knower as that which apprehends K_1 i.e. as *jñānagrāhaka*; in that case all knowledges belonging to the same self may be regarded as *jñānagrāhakajanyajñāna* insofar as the self is one of the causes of all its knowledges. But all knowledges do not apprehend the truth of K_1. According to the Bhāṭṭa and the Miśra schools it is only the *jñātatāliṅgakānumiti* and the *anuvyavasāya* of the primary knowledge that apprehend the truth of the primary knowledge. Even according to the Prābhākara, the truth of K_1 is not apprehended by any knowledge K_i, when $i > l$.

The insertion of the word '*sāmagrī*' fulfils the purpose of warding off this difficulty. For now we have to consider *all* the conditions which gave rise to K_2. In fact Raghunātha means by '*sāmgarī*' all the conditions taken together. Now all those conditions taken together cannot produce any knowledge other than K_2. Hence the expression '*jñānagrāhakasāmagrījanyayāvajjñāna*' cannot stand for any knowledge other than K_2.

Some commentators including Pakṣadhara Miśra construe '*yāvat*' as qualifying the '*graha*' or apprehension which is a component of the word '*grāhaka*'. On this view then truth of K_1 is *svataḥ* if and only if it is apprehended by a knowledge that is caused by the conditions of all K_2s. But consider the following difficulty. There are many knowledges which apprehend K_1, and which therefore may be reckoned as *jñānagrāhaka*. Apart from many others which are non-controversial, there is the usual introspection, there is the *jñātatāliṅgakānumiti* of the Bhāṭṭas, and there is the inference of truth of the Naiyāyikas. Now each of these has its own separate set of conditions. But the conditions of all such knowledges taken together do not produce any knowledge. Hence the entity being referred to by '*jñānayāvadgrāhakasāmagrījanyajñāna*' is nonexistent, and the two alternatives become pointless. It is better therefore to construe '*yāvat*' as qualifying '*sāmagrī*' and not '*grāhaka*', so that we are required to reckon with all the conditions of each K_2 separately and not with all the conditions of all K_2s, taken together.

8. *Tajjñānaviṣayakajñānājanyajñanagrāhyaṃ na vā.*

Is[1] the truth of a knowledge apprehended by a knowledge[3] which is not produced by any knowledge[2] which has the first knowledge for its object? Or, is it not?[4]

Notes

8.1. This is the second statement of the two alternative and mutually incompatible theories. The positive alternative, here as in the just preceding statement, represents a position which would be acceptable in common to all the three advocates of the *svataḥ*-theory while the negative alternative represents the standpoint of the Naiyāyikas.

8.2. Let the original knowledge whose truth is under consideration be, as before, K_1. The knowledge K_2 which has K_1 for its object is different in the three different formulations of the *svataḥ*-theory. According to the Prābhākaras, $K_2 = K_1$, for K_1 is self-illuminating. According to the Miśras, K_2 is the *anuvyavasāya* or introspective apprehension of K_1. According to the Bhāṭṭas, K_2 is the supposed inference having knownness for its mark (*jñātatāliṅgakānumiti*).

8.3. The *svataḥ*-theory holds, according to Gaṅgeśa, that truth is apprehended by a knowledge which is not caused by K_2. Certainly amongst all such knowledges which are not caused by K_2, K_2 itself is one (for it is not caused by itself). There are of course knowledges other than K_2 which are not caused by K_2 and which do not apprehend the truth of K_1, but that does not affect the validity of Gaṅgeśa's formulation of the theory, for the theory does not hold that all such knowledges have the truth of K_1 for their object.

8.4. The negative alternative representing the Nyāya point of view however makes a universal negative statement. In other words, according to the Nyāya no such knowledge, namely no knowledge that is not caused by K_2 could apprehend the truth of K_1. Certainly, neither K_1 itself, nor its *anuvyavasāya*, nor the supposed inference having knownness for its mark apprehends, on the Nyāya view, the truth of K_1. It is apprehended only subsequently as a consequence of successful practice and through an inference of the form 'This K_1 is true, for...' It is obvious that this inference presupposes, and is caused by, the *anuvyavasāya* which according to the Nyāya is the K_2. It follows that on the Nyāya view, the truth of K_1 is apprehended only by a knowledge which *is* caused by a knowledge of K_1.

9. *Parataḥ pakṣe jñāta eva jñāne prāmāṇyagrahaḥ, svatastve prāmāṇyavata eva jñānasya grahāt.*

On the *parataḥ*-theory, truth is apprehended only after the knowledge is known. On the *svataḥ*-theory, knowledge is apprehended as possessing truth.[1]

Notes

9.1. Curiously enough, Gaṅgeśa adds this general remark only after the second *vipratipatti*. His meaning is clear. According to the one theory a knowledge is first apprehended and only subsequently its truth is known. According to the other theory a knowledge and its truth are apprehended simultaneously so that the knowledge is always apprehended as true.

10. *Svāśrayagrāhakeṇa gṛhyata eve na vā.*

Is truth apprehended[2] by all those knowledges[3] which (also) apprehend the locus of that [1] truth? Or, is it not?

NOTES

10.1. The word '*sva*' in the text stands for the truth under consideration. '*Svāśraya*' then means the knowledge whose truth it is.

10.2. According to the *svataḥ*-theory the truth of a knowledge K_1 is apprehended by the same knowledge which also apprehends K_1. The knowledge K_2 is, as is well known by now, *anuvyavsāya* according to the Miśra, and the inference having knownness for its mark according to the Bhāṭṭas. On the Prābhākara view however $K_2 = K_1$.

Mathurānātha first takes this as a statement, like the preceding two statements, of what is common to all the three. But subsequently he interprets it as being a statement only of the Miśra view.* But in that case, '*svāśrayagrāhakeṇa*' is to be taken as '*svāśrayaviṣayakasākṣātkāreṇa*'. K_2 must be taken to be a perceptual apprehension of K_1.

10.3. Mathurānātha points out that the '*eva*' in the text must be taken to mean 'all' (*yāvat*), for otherwise—that is to say, unless we take 'all those knowledges which apprehend K_1'—the affirmative alternative would be acceptable to the Naiyāyikas so that the Mīmāṃsaka's attempt to defend it would be rendered pointless. This would happen in the following way. The Naiyāyikas would admit cases where the truth of K_1 (the like of which is known to be true before) is apprehended by the introspection of it. In such cases the apprehension of truth is mediated by memory of the truth earlier apprehended in a similar knowledge and hence is a case of *jñānalakṣaṇasannikarṣa*.** In cases such as these the truth is apprehended by a *svāśrayagrāhaka* even on the Nyāya view. But not every *anuvyavasāya* apprehends the truth of its corresponding primary knowledge, so that the in-

*Thus *Māthurī*: "*Vastutastu na hi ekadā tribhirdvābhyām vā vivādaḥ, ataḥ pratyekamatamātrasādhāraṇaṃ vipratipattidvayamāha, idantu miśramate*". As mentioned before, the statement may also be interpreted as giving us what is common to both the Bhāṭṭas and the Miśras.

**It may be noted here that this is said to be *alaukika* or extraordinary in a very technical sense. Contrast with this the case mentioned in 12.2b.

sertion of the word '*yāvat*' would seıve to distinguish the Mīmāṃsā view from the Nyāya. For the Miśra school, every *anuvyavasāya* apprehends the truth of the corresponding primary knowledge.

The same purpose may be served by specifying that the apprehension of truth is intended here to be an ordinary or *laukika* one. The hypothetical case of apprehension of truth through *jñānalakṣaṇasannikarṣa* is a case of extraordinary or *alaukika* perception. Taking this into consideration, the affirmative alternative may be restated thus: the truth under consideration, according to the Miśra view, possesses *svāśrayaviṣayakajñānīyalaukikaviṣayatā*, or what amounts to the same, it is the object of an ordinary apprehension of its own locus.

Complications however do not end here. There are cases where due to some hindrance (*pratibandhaka*) or other the *anuvyavasāya* of K_1 fails to apprehend its truth. This may happen, for example, in those cases where the K_2 takes the form 'This knowledge has no *prakāra*'. Such a K_2 would naturally be false (for, *anuvyavasāya* of a non-predicative knowledge is ruled out as impossible by the Nyāya) but once it is there the same introspection cannot apprehend the truth of K_1 (for, truth is defined, as we shall subsequently see, in terms of *prakāra*). In order to avoid such cases, we are to further modify the statement so that the *svāśrayaviṣayakasākṣātkāra* is taken to be *tatprāmāṇyagrahapratibandhakāsamavahita*. In other words, the perception of the locus of the truth—if it is to apprehend the truth as well—must be unaccompanied by any thing which hinders the apprehension of that truth.

Further, not all primary knowledge is capable of being apprehended subsequently. Two such cases may be mentioned here. Consider the primary knowledge which is immediately followed by a state of unconsciousness, so that the introspection does not take place. Or, consider a serial knowledge (where the same knowledge i.e. knowledge of the same object is repeated through several consecutive moments) in which case each primary knowledge being succeeded by another there is no room left for introspection of each one of them. It is only the last member of the series which can be introspected. The earlier members go without any. In view of such possibilities, Mathurānātha adds that the *pakṣa* should be taken to mean such truth as belongs only to those knowledges that *can* be objects of *anuvyavasāya,* otherwise the *svāśrayagrāhaka* would be nonexistent in some cases.

11. *Svāśrayeṇa gṛhyata eva na veti pratyekameva vā.*

Truth is[1] apprehended by its own substratum[2], or it is not so apprehended. So in each of the cases[3].

Notes

11.1. Just as the preceding *vipratipatti* stated the view of the Miśra school, so the present one states the view of the Prābhākaras alone. Raghunātha explains this procedure of Gaṅgeśa as being due to the fact that one cannot quarrel with all the three at a time (*"na hi tribhirekadā vivāda ityabhipretya"*) so that—as Gadādhara comments—a statement of what is common to all the three would be useless (*"matatrayasādhāraṇavidhikoṭiprayāso' narthaḥ"*).

11.2. The word *'sva'* stands as before for the truth in question. *'Svāśraya'* then stands for that knowledge whose truth is under consideration. According to the Prābhākaras, a truth is apprehended by the knowledge whose truth it is.

11.3. The significance of Gaṅgeśa's text *"pratyekameva vā"* is thus brought out by Gadādhara: Gaṅgeśa's text would suffer in importance if it did not also apply to the Miśra and the Bhāṭṭa views (*"Miśramate Bhāṭṭamate ca vipratipatterapradarśanena mūlasya nyūnatā syāt iti"*). Hence Raghunātha himself shows how Gaṅgeśa's statement would have to be reformulated if it were to apply to these two views. In order to apply to the Miśra view it should be reformulated thus: *"svāśrayānuvyavasāyena grāhyaṃ na veti"*. On the Bhāṭṭa view we should say, *"svāśrayagrāhakajñātatāliṅgakānumityā gṛhyate na vā'*. But there would be a fresh difficulty. The Naiyāyika does not recognise any such entity as *jñātatā*, so that for him the so-called *jñātatāliṅgakānumiti* is a fiction. As a consequence, the corresponding negative alternative is reduced to something that is not at all admitted by him. To avoid this difficulty we should rather say: *'svāśrayagrāhakānu-*

mityā gṛhyate na vā'. But since the Naiyāyika also recognises an inferential knowledge which apprehends both a knowledge and its truth, the Bhāṭṭa view—as also the corresponding Nyāya contention—should be further restated thus: '*svāśrayagrāhakayāvadanumityā gṛhyate na vā'*. The Naiyāyika of course does not believe that all those inferences which have a knowledge for their object also apprehend the truth of that knowledge.

12. *Yattu yogajadharmasāmānyalakṣaṇapratyāsattyā svāśrayaprāmāṇyaṃ tenaiva gṛhyata ityaṃśatassiddhasādhanamato yogajadharmādyajanyatvaṃ viśeṣaṇamiti, tanna, paraṃ pratyasiddheḥ. Prāmāṇyamātrapakṣatve prāmāṇyaṃ svāśrayeṇa gṛhyata eveti uddeśyapratīterasiddheśca nāṃśatassiddhasādhanam.*

If[1] it be said that the adjective 'being other than what is caused by yogic power etc.' should be inserted as there is partial *siddhasādhana*[5] owing to the fact that[2] the truth of a knowledge is apprehended by that knowledge itself either through yogic power[2a] or by extraordinary contact through a universal[2b]; (we reply) this is not (necessary). For, these are not admitted by the others[3]; (further,) since truth in general has been made the *pakṣa*[4], the intended conclusion that truth is apprehended by its own substratum remains unestablished, and so there is no partial *siddhasādhana*[5].

Notes

12.1. This suggestion may be attributed to some Naiyāyikas. Gaṅgeśa mentions it only to reject it.

12.2. It has been said before that according to the Mīmāṃsakas the truth of a knowledge is apprehended by that knowledge itself (*svāśrayeṇa*) or by the knowledge which apprehends that knowledge (*svāśrayagrāhakeṇa*). At this stage, the Naiyāyika may suggest that he also admits this in some cases so that the Mīmāṃsaka's attempt to prove his thesis would be guilty of the fallacy of trying to prove what is partially conceded by the other party to the controversy. Now what are those cases in which even the Naiyāyika admits that the truth of a knowledge is apprehended either by that knowledge itself or by the knowledge which apprehends that knowledge? Two such cases are suggested here.

12.2a. The Naiyāyika admits the possibility of a type of extraordinary perception called yogic perception in which everything is all at once presented. Since everything is all at once given to such extraordinary perception, the truth of such a perception is also simultaneously apprehended by the yogin, in which case the Naiyāyika also has to admit the *svataḥ*-theory at least partially.

12.2b. The truth of a knowledge may be, even according to the Naiyāyikas, in some cases apprehended by the corresponding introspective awareness. This happens when similar knowledges have been known to be true before, so that the generic feature of truth is already known. The truth of the present knowledge may then come to be apprehended in the extraordinary mode known as *sāmānyalakṣaṇā pratyāsatti.**

In view of such possibilities, it is now suggested that the *pakṣa* which is mere 'truth of a knowledge' (*jñānaprāmāṇya*) should be further limited by the adjective 'being other than what is caused by yogic power etc.' (*yogajadharmādyajanyatvam*) so that the *svataḥ*-theory may be intended to hold good only of the truth of such knowledges as are not caused by yogic power etc.

But, if the adjective 'being other than what is produced by yogic power etc.' is made to limit the *pakṣa*, does this help us to exclude the case explained just above? Certainly when according to the Naiyāyika introspection apprehends the truth of a primary knowledge (in the extraordinary manner mentioned above), the primary knowledge (as also its truth) is uncaused by yogic power etc. It may therefore be better to let the adjective qualify also the knowledge which is said to apprehend the truth, be it the primary knowledge itself or its introspection. In the present case, the introspection is caused (and so is not uncaused)

*This is the perception of all members of a class, made possible by perceiving the class character in any one member which is presented to the senses in the ordinary (*laukika*) manner.

by an extraordinary sort of contact, so that insertion of the adjective would serve to exclude such cases.

12.3 After having stated this suggestion for modifying his own formulation of the Mīmāṃsā point of view, Gaṅgeśa goes on to show reasons for rejecting the suggestion. He offers two reasons why the suggestion cannot be accepted. In the first place, not everyone admits such modes of extraordinary perception. The Mīmāṃsaka does not, and so he is not obliged to modify the statement of his position in the light of such cases which he is very likely to dismiss as being fictitious.

12.4. Even if we do admit that such cases occur, Gaṅgeśa gives a second reason for rejecting the suggested modification. Now, each alternative of a *vipratipatti* may be understood as a *pratijñā** of an inference, for when *vicāra* begins each party tries to prove its own contention. The Mīmāṃsaka would thus try to prove that the truth of a knowledge is apprehended either by that knowledge itself or by the knowledge which apprehends that knowledge. If the Naiyāyika concedes that in some cases this may be so, then the Mīmāṃsaka's thesis would be partially established and there would be no point in further proving it. It was therefore suggested that the *pakṣa* in the Mīmāṃsaka's inference should be delimited so as to exclude the cases conceded by the opponent. To this Gaṅgeśa replies as follows: the Mīmāṃsaka's contention is a universal proposition; he seeks to establish the *svataḥ*-theory in all cases of knowledge. Even if it be conceded that the *svataḥ*-theory is true in some cases, the Mīmāṃsaka's intended thesis nevertheless remains unproved and controversial so that the partial *siddhasādhana* to which attention was drawn ceases to be a fault. Gaṅgeśa is in fact making use of a more general point. An inference may prove that the *sādhya* is present in all cases of *pakṣa*, or it may simply prove that it is present in some cases of *pakṣa*. The former is called '*pakṣatāvacchedakāvacchedena sādhyānumiti*', the latter is called '*pakṣatāvacchedakasāmānādhikaraṇyasaṃsargeṇa sādhyānumiti*'. The Mīmāṃsaka's inference of the *svataḥ*-theory is intended to be one of the

*'*Pratijñā*' is the unasserted proposition which is to be proved and which is stated first in the Nyāya 5-membered syllogism.

first kind. Now, as a rule, partial *siddhasādhana* is not a fault in the case of such inferences. For even if it be already known that the *sādhya* is present in some cases of *pakṣa*, it yet remains to be proved that it is true in all cases.

12.5. The fallacy of *siddhasādhana* arises when one seeks to prove a thesis which is admitted by the opponent. It is trying to prove what is beyond dispute.

13. *Yadvā ghaṭo'yamiti jñānaprāmāṇyametajjñānagrāhyaṃ na vā, etajjñānagrāhakamātragrāhyaṃ na veti.*

Or (it may be like this): the truth of the knowledge 'This is a jar' is either apprehended by this knowledge itself or not; it is either apprehended by the knowledge which apprehends this knowledge or it is not so apprehended.[1]

Notes

13.1. This is the last one of the five *vipratipattis*. Gaṅgeśa's purpose in adding this one to the list seems to be that all the preceding ones concerned truth in general. The present one however specifies the knowledge and as a consequence also specifies the truth. The first part of the *vipratipatti* contrasts the Prābhākara view with the Nyāya; the second part contrasts what is common to the Miśra and the Bhāṭṭa views with the Nyāya. The word '*mātra*' is to be understood as meaning *yāvat* and is inserted to ward off difficulties mentioned in earlier sections.

14. *Tatra yadyapi viśeṣyāvṛttyaprakārakatvamagṛhītagrāhitvaṃ vā, sarvadhīyathārthatvapakṣe'nubhavatvajāterabhāvena smaraṇānyajñānatvaṃ viśiṣṭajñānatvaṃ vā prāmāṇyaṃ svasya na tenaiva na vā anuvyavasāyena grahaṇayogyaṃ; viśeṣyāvṛttyaprakārakatvāderviśeṣaṇasya prāganupasthitau tadvaiśiṣṭyasya jñātumaśakyatvāt. Nāpi jñānātīndriyatve jñānānumityā tadgṛhyate, jñanamātraliṅgasya prākaṭyādestadvyabhicārāt. Nāpi pramāhitajñātatāviśeṣāt, tasya prathamaṃ durnirūpatvāt. Anyathā apramāhitajñātatayā aprāmāṇyasyāpi svatograhāpattiriti.*

Although[1] truth taken either as 'the property of not having a qualifier that is absent in the qualificandum'[2], or as 'the property of being an apprehension of what has not already been apprehended'[3], or—on the theory of those[4] who regard all knowledge as valid and do not regard *anubhavatva* as a *jāti*[5]—as 'the property of being a knowledge other than memory'[6], or as 'the property of being a qualified knowledge'[7], is not in any case capable of being apprehended either by that knowledge (whose truth it is) or by its introspection, yet, the adjectives beginning with 'the property of having a qualifier that is absent in the qualificandum', not being presented beforehand, the fact that anything is qualified by them could not possibly be apprehended[8]. It cannot be said that it is apprehended—on the theory of those who take knowledge to be supersensible[9]—by the inference which apprehends the knowledge, for the sign of mere knowledge, namely manifestedness, has no relation of pervasion with it[10]. It cannot be contended that the inference can be made from that special sort of manifestedness which is exhausted by a true knowledge, for in the first place such a manifestedness cannot be ascertained. But again (if it could be determined) falsity should also be regarded as apprehended *svataḥ* with the help of that special sort of manifestedness which is exhausted by false knowledge.[11]

NOTES

14.1. Gaṅgeśa now proceeds to make precise the sense of '*pramātva*' in which truth is, according to the Mīmāṃsaka, *svataḥ*. This is necessary before critical consideration of the theory could begin. He gives us a list of different meanings of '*pramātva*', and adds that in none of these senses truth is or can be regarded as *svataḥ*. The only sense in which it can be so regarded is stated in the following paragraph beginning with '*tathāpi*' (which is intended as a rejoinder to the present text beginning with '*yadyapi*').

14.2. A true knowledge is not one whose qualifier is absent in its qualificandum. A false cognition on the other hand has some qualifier which is not present in its qualificandum. When a rope is falsely regarded as a snake, the judgment 'This is a snake' has as one of its qualifiers 'snakehood' which is absent in the qualificandum, namely the rope. This is not the case with true knowledge.

14.3. The Mīmāṃsakas lay it down that a *pramā* is not to be a knowledge of what is already known. A knowledge which knows what is already known is mere *anuvāda* or 'repetition', It should be noted that in advancing this claim the Mīmāṃsaka is not merely explicating the ordinary notion of truth but is adding his own recommendation. He is in factsuggesting what ought to be called true knowledge. '*Pramā*' becomes thereby a technical term and not the same as it is in ordinary use. In this sense, truth is the property of apperehending what has not been previously apprehended.

14.4. Gaṅgeśa is here referring to the Prābhākaras who regard all knowledge as true. What is usually called error is on this view not one unitary knowledge, it consists in fact of two distinct cognitions, one apprehension and another memory, each one of which is true taken in itself but which are left undistinguished owing to the presenceof some *doṣa* or vitiating circumstance.

14.5. According to the Prābhākaras then knowledge as knowledge is true. Truth may accordingly be defined as the property of being a knowledge other than memory (memory being awareness of what is already known). Truth cannot however be defined as *anubhavatva* i.e. the property of being *anubhava*, for the Prābhākaras do not recognise *anubhavatva* as a *jāti*. This though is a minor point and does not affect the main contention. The Prābhākaras think that only substances or *dravyas* possess *jāti*. Knowledge being a *guṇa* is then said to have no corresponding *jāti*.

14.6. Truth on the Prābhākara theory may then be defined as 'the property of being a knowledge other than memory'. Any knowledge other than memory is true.

14.7.,The Prābhākaras may also define truth simply as 'the property of being a qualified knowledge' (*viśiṣṭajñānatvam*). Error, on this theory, is not one unified knowledge in which terms are apprehended as related to or as qualifying each other; it consists simply in the non-apprehension of non-relatedness of the terms involved. In true knowledge on the other hand there is a genuine apprehension of relatedness or of the terms qualifying each other. This then may be regarded as a distinguishing property of all true knowledge as such. It may be remembered however that neither 'the property of being a knowledge other than memory' nor 'the property of being a qualified knowledge or of being a knowledge of relatedness' is, strictly speaking on the Nyāya theory, a *jāti*; they are what is called in the system *akhaṇḍopādhi*. Into the tenability of the distinction between *jāti* and *akhaṇḍopādhi* we need not enter here as that does not affect the main trend of the argument. For this see Ingalls, pp. 40-42.

14.8. In none of these senses of 'truth' is truth apprehended either by the knowledge whose truth it is, or by the knowledge which apprehends that knowledge. The reason adduced for this contention is that each of these is a determinate or qualified entity. Now as a rule apprehension of a qualified entity presupposes a prior apprehension of the qualifiers involved in it. Or, what amounts to the same, apprehension of relatedness presupposes apprehension of the terms related. In the present case the qualifiers are certainly not apprehended in the very same knowledge whose truth is in question. Therefore the qualified entities which are called 'truth' could not possibly be apprehended either by that knowledge or by the knowledge of that knowledge.

14.9. A Bhāṭṭa might—but need not—internvene and suggest a way out. The Bhāṭṭas, as is well known, regard knowledge as something supersensible, our only knowledge of it being according to them inferential. The most important of these inferences—that by virtue of which we always come to know that we know—is one in which certain objective property called 'knownness' in the object serves as the sign or *hetu*. The Bhāṭṭa may now suggest that features like those enumerated above might as well be apprehended by the very same inference (namely by the inference from knownness) which also apprehends the knowledge to which they belong.

14.10. Gaṅgeśa rejects the Bhāṭṭa suggestion on the following ground. Taking for granted that there is such an objective property as 'knownness' which could serve as a sign for the presence of knowledge, it may yet be argued that this knownness is a sign only for knowledge quâ knowledge and certainly not for a knowledge as possessing truth in any of the above senses of 'truth'. In other words, knownness may be there without the knowledge being true. The supposed inference of the truth of the knowledge would therefore be fallacious, the *hetu* would not be a genuine *hetu*.

14.10. The Bhāṭṭa may not give up and may continue his argument further. He may insist that the knownness which is produced by a true knowledge carries on itself a stamp of its distinctive origin. The knownness which owes its origin to true knowledge would serve validly as a sign of true knowledge. Gaṅgeśa has two replies to this. In the first place it is not possible to determine which knownness is produced by true knowledge and which is not. And, secondly, if a knownness always bears upon itself the stamp of its distinctive origin, then a knownness which owes its origin to a false knowledge would be directly recognised as such, and therefore could serve as a valid sign for the fact that the knowledge causing it is false, in which case falsity also—contrary to the theory of the Bhāṭṭa—would be apprehended *svataḥ*.

Therefore, the attempt has to be given up and it has to be conceded that in none of the senses enumerated in this paragraph truth, according to the Mīmāṃsaka, is apprehended *svntaḥ*.

15. *Tathāpi tadvati tatprakārakajñānatvaṃ tadvati tadvaiśiṣṭyajñānatvaṃ vā prāmāṇyaṃ, tanniścayādeva niṣkampavyavahārāt lāghavāt. Nānyadgauravāt. Tacca jñānagrāhakasāmagrīgrāhyameva.*

Nevertheless[1], truth is (to be taken as) 'the property of being a knowledge whose qualifier (really) belongs to the qualificandum'[2] or 'the property of being a knowledge of the relatedness which belongs to the qualificandum'[3]. It is truth in this sense from whose ascertainment unhesitating behaviour follows. There is (also) economy. Any other assumption has to be rejected on the ground of superfluity[4]. This again is apprehended by a knowledge which is produced by the same conditions which produce the apprehension of that knowledge (whose truth is under consideration).[5]

Notes

15.1. Although truth in none of the above senses can be shown to be apprehended *svataḥ*, yet there is a sense in which it may be said to be so apprehended. Indeed when the Mīmāṃsakas consider truth to be apprehended *svataḥ*, they mean by 'truth' either of two things: truth is either *tadvati-tatprakārakatvam* or *tadvati-tadvaiśiṣṭyajñānatvam*.

15.2. For a fuller explanation of this definition of truth as *tadvati-tatprakārakajñānatvam*, see pp. 39-41 of the Introduction. It should be borne in mind that the definition gives a general formula containing variables, and once the variables are replaced by constants we get the definite property which truth in the case of a particular knowledge is. Thus if the true knowledge is 'This is silver', its truth is nothing other than 'the property of being a knowledge which has silverness for a predicate and whose qualificandum really possesses silverness'. For further improvements on this definition, see Introduction. In general, a knowledge 'S is p' is true when p really belongs to S, i.e. when S (p) is known as p. In the case of error, on the other hand, S is known as p no doubt, but the subject is not S (p), but rather S (-p). In the case of a false cognition of the same judgmental form as above viz. 'This is silver', the cognition is no doubt one having silverness for its predicate, but in that case the *this* does not possess silverness, for it is really something which merely looks like a silver.

15.3. This second definition of truth is not quite the same as the first one. Whereas according to the first one, a knowledge of S as qualified by p is true when p really belongs to S, according to the present one a knowledge of S as related to p is true when it is in fact so related. In general Srp (or, S has the relation r to p) is true when S = S (rp).

It may be that whereas the first definition applies only to proposition of the subject-predicate type, the second one applies to relational propositions (like 'Brutus killed Cæsar') and may of course be extended to cover other cases as well.

15.4. Truth in any of these two senses is a less complex entity than truth in any of the other senses mentioned in paragraph 14. Therefore, if it can be shown that truth in any of these two senses suffices for unwavering practice and that it is apprehended *svataḥ*, then the Mīmāṃsaka would have proved his case in the most economical manner.

15.5. Truth taken in either of these two senses is apprehended *svataḥ*, i.e. it is apprehended by the same knowledge which also apprehends the knowledge whose truth is under consideration. The next para gives some reasons for the Mīmāṃsaka contention.

16. *Tathā hi viśeṣye taddharmavattvaṃ taddharmaprakārakatvañca vyavasāyasyānuvyavasāyenānumityā svaprakāśena vā gṛhyate, viṣayanirūpyaṃ hi jñānam, ato jñānavittivedyo viṣaya iti vyavasāye bhāsamāne dharmadharmivat tadvaiśiṣṭyamapi viṣayaḥ, vyavasāyarūpapratyāsattestulyatvāt; sambandhitāvacchedakarūpavattayā jñāyamāne sambandhini sasambandhikapadārthanirūpaṇamityanuvyavasāyasya rajatatvāvacchinnatvena purovartiviṣayatvācca. Anyathā purovartinaṃ rajataṃ ca jānāmīti tadākāraḥ syāt, na tu rajatatvena purovartinamiti.*

Thus, that the qualificandum has the property of possessing that quality and that the primary knowledge has that qualifier[1] are apprehended either by the *anuvyavasāya* or by the inference with knownness as its mark, or by the self-revealing knowledge itself. (For) Knowledge is determined by (its) object.[2] Therefore, the object is apprehended by the knowledge of knowledge. As the primary knowledge is revealed, like the substantive and the quality their relatedness also becomes the object[3], for the contact through the primary knowledge[4] is the same. (And also because) Since a relative entity is perceived if its co-relative entity is apprehended as qualified by the property which limits the relatedness[5], the *anuvyavasāya* must have for its object the yonder object as determined by 'silverness'. Otherwise, it would have the form 'I know the yonder object *and* the silver', but not the form '(I know) the yonder object as (qualified by) silverness'.

NOTES

16.1. With a view to stating precisely and also defending the Mīmāṃsaka's view, Gaṅgeśa again formulates what he thinks to be common to all the three schools of Mīmāṃsā. The primary knowledge apprehends its qualificandum as possessing such and such qualification. The *anuvyavasāya* is then said to apprehend two facts: first, that the qualificandum of the primary knowledge possesses such and such property (e.g. the *this* possesses silverness), and secondly that the primary knowledge has such and such qualifier (e.g. that it has 'silverness' for its qualifier). In other words, it apprehends (i) the fact that silverness belongs to the *this*, and (ii) also the fact that 'silverness' is a qualifier of the knowledge. But it may still be asked, does *anuvyavasāya* apprehend the unity of (i) and (ii)? In other words, does it also apprehend the fact that the fact (ii) is limited by the fact (i)? Unless this unity of (i) and (ii) is apprehended we cannot say that truth is apprehended. For reply to this see note 16.5 below. Now these two facts (i) and (ii) are apprehended on the Miśra theory by the *anuvyavasāya*, on the Bhāṭṭa theory by the inference from *jñātatā*, and on the Prābhākara theory by the self-revealing primary knowledge itself.

16.2. Now taking up the Miśra view, Gaṅgeśa tries to prove that the *anuvyavasāya* does apprehend the truth of the primary knowledge. For this purpose he uses as his premise the rule that a knowledge owes its determinations to its object. According to the Naiyāyika, knowledge has no shape or form (*ākāra*) of its own. Whatever determinateness a knowledge has it owes it to the object.* It follows that a knowledge is never known *perceptually* by a knowledge which does not also know the object of that knowledge (*viṣaya-aviṣayakapratyakṣāviṣaya ityarthaḥ***). It is the object therefore which makes it possible for us to ascertain the nature of the knowledge. Now, since the *anuvyavasāya* apprehends the primary knowledge, it should also apprehend the primary knowledge as being knowledge of such and such object. In that case, all the features of the object which were apprehended in the primary knowledge would also be apprehended in the *anuvyavasāya*. Raghunātha adds that this holds good only in the case of a perceptual knowledge of a knowledge, for, as Gadādhara explains, an inferential knowledge of a knowledge does not apprehend all the features of the object of the first knowledge.

Raghunātha points out that the Mīmāṃsaka depends on a rule, namely, that a knowledge is determined by its object, which the Nyāya also admits. But the Nyāya does not hold that all the features in the object determine its knowledge. Consequently, a secondary knowledge knowing the primary knowledge 'This is silver' does apprehend that the knowledge has 'silverness' for its qualifier and also that silverness belongs to the qualificandum of the knowledge, but it need not apprehend the sort of unity of these two facts implied by the notion of truth. In other words, it may not apprehend the objective relatedness of the *this* and the silverness.*** The Mīmāṃsaka replies to this by saying that since all the conditions for the apprehension of objective relatedness are present the secondary knowledge cannot but apprehend the same.

16.3. In primary knowledge three things are given: the substantive (*dharmi*), the quality (*dharma*) as well as their relatedness (*vaiśiṣṭya*). In the primary knowledge 'This is silver', we apprehend not only the *this* and the silver (or, silverness) but also their relatedness, no matter whether the knowledge is true or false.

*Thus writes Udayana: *Arthenaiva viśeṣo hi nirākāratayā dhiyām*" (*Nyāyakusumāñjali*, Stabaka 4).

***Dinakarī* on *Siddhāntamuktāvalī*, Kārikā 136.

***Thus Raghunātha : *viṣayanirūpyatve'pi yāvadviṣayanirūpyatvāsiddhau na vaiśiṣṭyaviṣayatāsiddhirata āha*. (*Dīdhiti* on *Prāmāṇyavāda*).

The same relatedness must therefore be apprehended in the *anuvyavasāya* as well—argues the Mīmāṃsaka—which would mean that *anuvyavasāya* would apprehend the truth of the primary knowledge.

16.4. It has been said above that the secondary knowledge K_2 apprehends not only the primary knowledge K_1, but also the latter's object O. It may now be asked, how could K_2 (which, let us suppose, is an inner perception of K_1) apprehend an external object O? Inner perception admittedly has not the capacity of apprehending an outer object. The Naiyāyika therefore holds that although K_2 is an ordinary (*laukika*) perception of K_1, yet it is an extraordinary perception (*alaukika-pratyakṣa*) of O. The extraordinary contact is supposed to have been made possible through K_1 (*vyavasāyapratyāsatti*). The original question was: could K_2 apprehend the objective relatedness which was apprehended by K_1? The Mīmāṃsaka now replies that if the substantive and the quality could be apprehended there is no reason why their relatedness also should not be, for the nature of the contact i.e. the extraordinary contact through K_1 is the same in all the three cases.

16.5. Against the Mīmāṃsaka's argument that *dharmadharmivat tadvaiśiṣṭyamapi viṣayaḥ*, it might be replied in the following manner: "Let it be granted that the *this*, the silverness and their objective relatedness are all given in K_2, but it is still possible that these three are apprehended separately in one collective awareness of what is called the *samūhālambana* type. In that case K_2 would not apprehend the truth of K_1." Anticipating this objection, Gaṅgeśa defends the Mīmāṃsaka thus.

Gaṅgeśa again takes the help of a general rule. If a term, say A, is relative to another term B, then that term A cannot be perceived unless B is apprehended in its character B-ness (which, let us assume, is the property limiting its correlativity to A). In the present case, A is knowledge of silver, and B is silver. An apprehension of the knowledge of silver is not possible unless the silver itself is apprehended as qualified by silverness. From this it should follow that the *anuvyavasāya* of the knowledge 'This is silver' must apprehend the yonder object as qualified by silverness. This would amount to saying that the *anuvyavasāya* apprehends the truth of the primary knowledge.

Another interpretation of this passage beginning with '*sambandhitāvacchedakarūpavattayā*' is possible. By the '*sasambandhikapadārtha*' may be meant the relatedness or *vaiśiṣṭya* under consideration. The rule in that case is to the effect that this relatedness cannot be apprehended unless the two relata are known precisely in those very characters in which they constitute this relatedness. If that be so then an awareness of the relatedness would be inseparable from the apprehension of the substantive and the quality. It would follow that the possibility of a bare collective knowledge of the type apprehended in the objection is ruled out. Consequently, what the secondary knowledge apprehends would not fall short of the truth of the primary knowledge.

17. *Ata evāpramāpi pramā ityeva gṛhyate, anuvyavasāyasya bhramaviṣayavaiśiṣṭyaviṣayatvāt. Na ca na prāmāṇyaṃ prathamato jñātamiti na tadāropaḥ syāditi vācyaṃ,—prāmāṇyasya jñānagrāhakasāmagrīgrāhyatvena jñānavittivedyatvāt abhāvapratītau pratiyogitvābhāvatvayoriva.*

Therefore even a false knowledge is apprehended as true[1], for the *anuvyavasāya* apprehends the relatedness of the object of error. It cannot be said that since truth is not at first apprehended it cannot therefore be subsequently imposed[2]; for, truth being the object of (all) knowledges that are produced by the same conditions as give rise to the apprehension of the knowledge (whose truth is under consideration) is apprehended by the knowledge that knows (that) knowledge, as are counter-positiveness and absence-ness in the case of apprehension of absence.[3]

Notes

17.1. It follows from the Mīmāṃsaka's position that even false cognitions are initially apprehended as true. For (Gaṅgeśa here refers to the Miśra theory though he could have equally well said the same of the Bhāṭṭa also) the *anuvyavasāya* of the primary false cognition 'This is silver' has for its object the relatedness of the silver and the *this*. The *this* is apprehended as silver. There is in fact no difference between the secondary knowledge of the knowledge 'This is silver' when the latter is true and the secondary knowledge of it when it is false.

17.2. It might be objected against the Mīmāṃsaka's theory that since truth is not apprehended in the primary knowledge, the secondary knowledge could not be of the form 'This knowledge is true'. For there is a general rule to the effect that a knowledge of a thing as qualified presupposes prior knowledge of the qualifiers themselves. Unless therefore truth is apprehended in the primary knowledge, the secondary knowledge of it could not apprehend the knowledge as qualified by truth.

17.3. In defending the Mīmāṃsaka against this somewhat pertinent objection, Gaṅgeśa waives the application of the general rule in this case, which fortunately is not the only permissible exception. When we apprehend an absence, we also apprehend the counterpositiveness (of the counterpositive) and the absenceness of the absence. We apprehend the absence as being qualified by such and such counterpositiveness and also as being an absence. But in this case we cannot say that the qualifiers like counterpositiveness and absenceness were apprehended in an indeterminate perception. The Naiyāyika cannot say this insofar as he does not accept an indeterminate perception of an absence as an absence. The same may be said to be true in the case of the *anuvyavasāya* of the form 'This knowledge is true'.

18. *Tadabhāvavati tatprakārakajñānatvamaprāmāṇyaṃ parato jñāyate, tadabhāvavattvasya bhramānullikhitatvenānuvyavasāyāviṣayatvāt. Na caivamanuvyavasāyasya yāvadvyavasāyaviṣayaviṣayakatve bhrāntabhrāntijñasaṅkara iti vācyaṃ,—bādhānavatāradaśāyāṃ tasyeṣṭatvāt, tadavatāre tasyaiva pratibandhakatvāt, upanāyakabhrānterabhāvācca. Ata evānyabhrāntijñasya na bhramaḥ.*

Falsity which is the property of being a knowledge whose qualifier is absent in the qualificandum is apprehended extrinsically, for, the fact that the qualifier is (so) absent is not mentioned in the (judgment of) error and hence is (also) not apprehended in the *anuvyavasāya*.[1] It cannot be said that since *anuvyavasāya* apprehends all that is apprehended in the primary knowledge there would be fallacy of the same person being in error and yet knowing that it is an error[2]; for, this is admitted so long as the contradiction has not set in. When, however, contradiction does set in that (contradiction) itself would function as a hindrance[3] (against the knower of error being also in error). Further, there is absence of (an entirely) *upanāyaka* error.[4] If (again) the knower of error is another person, then he is not in error.

NOTES

18.1. The primary knowledge even when it is erroneous has the form 'This is silver'. Nowhere in it is there mention of the fact that silverness is absent in the *this*. What is not so mentioned is not also apprehended by the knowledge expressed by the judgment. What is not apprehended in the primary knowledge cannot be apprehended by the secondary knowledge. The *anuvyavasāya* cannot therefore apprehend the falsity of the primary knowledge.

18.2. An objection is now anticipated and then disposed of. Let the primary knowledge 'This is silver' be erroneous. The *anuvyavasāya* apprehends as a rule all that was apprehended primarily. It has the form 'I know that this is silver'. This implies on the one hand that the *anuvyavasāya* also apprehends the *this* as silver, and insofar is itself in error and on the other hand that the *anuvyavasāya* apprehends the primary one which is the error. From above it follows that the apprehension of error may be itself in error, which is absurd, for, one who apprehends an error is not himself in error.

18.3. Gaṅgeśa defends the Mīmāṃsaka against the above objection in two ways. In the first place, he concedes that so long as the error has not been contradicted such a paradox is unavoidable: the person in error also knows the error, though of course he does *not* know the error as an error. As soon as the error is contradicted, the contradiction wards off any such paradoxical situation. For after the contradiction the person knows his error as an error, and so is not any longer in error.

18.4. The Mīmāṃsaka may also give another reply. Of course, according to the Naiyāyika, all error is due to the sort of extraordinary contact called *jñānalakṣaṇā*. The object of false apprehension is presented through past knowledge (of it); it is thus *upanīta*. Such a presentation is called *upanītabhāna*. Now in the case of *anuvyavasāya*, as is well known, there is on the one hand an ordinary mental perception of the primary knowledge and on the other an extraordinary presentation through past knowledge of the object of the primary knowledge. If the primary knowledge is 'This is silver', the *anuvyavasāya* is 'I have a knowledge whose qualificandum is 'this' and whose qualifier is 'silverness'' (*Idaṃviśeṣyakarajatatvaprakārakajñānavānaham*). Now it might be argued that there is nothing erroneous in this, for all that it amounts to is that both 'this' and 'silverness' have appeared as qualifying my *knowledge* but nothing is being asserted in this *anuvyavasāya* about the (ontological) relation between the *this* and the *silverness* themselves. Therefore the *anuvyavasāya* is valid so far as it goes. The same situation may now be put in another way. The primary knowledge may err, for its apprehension of the object is not entirely extraordinary: the *this* is ordinarily perceived though the silver is extraordinarily presented. In the *anuvyavasāya* however the entire object (of the primary knowledge) is presented extraordinarily through *jñānalakṣaṇā* so that here there can be no error about *that* object. The rule seems to be that there can be no error in a knowledge which in its entirety is extraordinary. Of course, the *anuvyavasāya* is not so, for it is mainly an ordinary perception of the primary knowledge. But insofar as the objects of the primary knowledge, i.e. the *this* and the silver are concerned, the *anuvyavasāya* has only an extraordinary perception of them and so it cannot err with regard to them. This shows that there is really no possibility of the same person being in error and knowing the error.

19. *Atha tadvattvaṃ na dharmadharmivaiśiṣṭyamātraṃ, kintu*

tasya viśeṣaṇatāviśeṣaḥ, sa ca vyavasāye bhāsate, nānuvyavasāye, manaso bahirasvātantryāditi cenna; vyavasāyopanītatvena viśeṣaṇaviśeṣyayoriva viśeṣaṇatāviśeṣasyāpi tadviṣayatvāt, viśeṣaṇatāyā nirākariṣyamāṇatvācca

'If it be said that the '*tadvattvam*' (in the definition of truth given in para 15) is not mere relatedness of the adjective and the substantive but is a special sort of qualifying relation[1] and that this is apprehended in the primary knowledge but not in the *anuvyavasāya* as the mind has no independent ability to apprehend outer objects,

then (we say) this would not do. The special sort of qualifying relation can be the object of *anuvyavasāya* being presented through the primary knowledge, as much as the quality and the qualificandum are.[2] Further, we shall in future reject (the theory of) any such (special) qualifying relation.[3]

Notes

19.1. Another possible objection against the Mīmāṃsā theory that the *anuvyavasāya* apprehends the truth of *tadvati tatprakārakatva* of the primary knowledge is taken up. It may be that the '*tadvattva*' (or the property of possessing that—the 'that' referring to the qualifier of the knowledge) involved in the concept of truth is more than the simple relatedness of 'this' and 'silverness'. What is necessary is that 'silverness' must qualify the 'this' in some special manner. Now, although the *anuvyavasāya* does apprehend the substantive, the adjective as well as their relatedness—all of which are given in the primary knowledge—it may yet be maintained that the special qualifying relation apprehended in the primary knowledge is not given in the *anuvyavasāya*, so that the latter does not, strictly speaking, apprehend the truth of the primary knowledge, though it apprehends only the latter's '*tatprakārakatva*'. The objection is based upon the argument that the *anuvyavasāya* being a mental perception has no independent capacity to apprehend outer objects.

19.2. This objection is immediately disposed of in the following manner. It is only too obvious that if the *anuvyavasāya* apprehends all the other three—the substantive, the adjective and their relatedness—there ought to be no reason why some special sort of qualifying relation given in the primary knowledge should be beyond its power of apprehension. In all cases the mode of presentation, as said before, remains the same, namely, presentation through previous knowledge.

19.3. Gaṅgeśa of course suggests a more radical answer to the objector, namely, that there is no such special qualifying relation at all.

20. *Etenāsvaprakāśe na svataḥ prāmāṇyagrahaḥ, dharmyagrahe taddharmāgrahāt; śabdagandhavat yogyatvāt tadgrahepi jñānaṃ pramāṇamiti dhīrna syāt. Svaprakāśepi svamātrasākṣiṇaḥ svadharmagrahe'sāmarthyāt; sāmarthye vā aprāmāṇyamapi gṛhṇīyāt. Paraprakāśe liṅgena manasā vā jāyamānaṃ jñānaṃ na bhramavyāvṛttaṃ prāmāṇyaṃ gṛhṇīyāt, vyabhicārāt. Na ca yatra yadasti tatra tadgṛhyate, aprāmāṇyasyāpi svato grahāpatteḥ. Anuvyavasāyasyānumitervā viṣayājanyatvācceti nirastam.*

With this are set aside (all the following objections):—

On the theory that knowledge is not self-revealing, truth cannot be intrinsically apprehended, for a property cannot be apprehended if its substantive is not. Even if there be the capacity for apprehending truth, as there is for apprehending sound and smell, there cannot be a knowledge of the form 'The knowledge is true'[1]. If knowledge is self-revealing, it is witness only to itself but has no capacity to apprehend a property belonging to itself. If however it has this capacity then it should also apprehend (its own) falsity.[2] If knowledge is revealed by another, then the knowledge arising either through a mark or through the mind cannot apprehend truth *as distinguished from* error, for there is instance to the contrary.[3] Nor can it be said that what is there is apprehended there, for in that case even falsity ought to be apprehended intrinsically; and also because the *anuvyavasāya* and the inference are not caused by the object.[4]

NOTES

20.1. Four more objections are suggested against the Mīmāṃsaka's theory, but only to be set aside before the final onslaught by Gaṅgeśa begins. As is well known by now, there are two varieties of the *svataḥprāmāṇya* theory, one combined with the theory that knowledge is self-revealing, and the other combined with the theory that knowledge is not self-revealing. Criticisms are now offered against both these varieties of the theory. First, any theory which does not regard knowledge as self-revealing cannot at the same time consider the truth of knowledge to be *svataḥ*. For, truth is a property of knowledge, and if knowledge itself is not apprehended, none of its properties can be. A property cannot be known when that whose property it is is unknown. It may be replied to the above that just as a knowledge has the ability to apprehend many other objects like sound and smell etc., so also it may possess the ability to apprehend its own truth. To this however one may reply that even if such ability be there, an actual knowledge of the form 'This knowledge is true' cannot arise when the substantive, the knowledge itself, is yet unknown.*

20.2. Secondly, the theory when combined with the theory that knowledge is self-revealing fares no better. For the character of being self-revealing confers on a knowledge the privilege of being a witness to itself, but it does not thereby come to acquire the privilege of apprehending all properties belonging to itself. Thus from the mere fact that knowledge is self-revealing it does not necessarily follow that a knowledge should apprehend its own truth. If however it be expected that being self-revealing a knowledge should also apprehend all its properties, then of course the falsity of a false knowledge out to be, like the truth of a true knowledge, self-revealing,—a consequence that is not acceptable to the Mīmāṃsaka.

*Compare Udayana in *Pariśuddhi*: "*Yo hi yadgṛhṇāti sa taddharmamapi gṛhṇīyāditi sambhāvyetāpi, yastu dharmiṇameva nākalayati tasya dharmagrahaṇavārtāpi kva. Yadyapi śabdagandhādayo vyomabhūmyādyagrahe'pi gṛhyante, tathāpi na taddharmatayā ityarthaḥ*" (Asiatic Society edn., p. 48). Vardhamāna comments that although the property may be apprehended yet *jñānaṃ pramā iti jñānaviśeṣyapramitirna syāt*.

20.3. Coming back again to those who do not believe that knowledge is self-revealing, we know that according to them a knowledge is apprehended either through *anuvyavasāya* or through the special inferential process admitted by the Bhāṭṭas. But neither of these two could apprehend in the primary knowledge such truth as serves to distinguish right knowledge from error. For where either the *anuvyavasāya* or the inference from *jñātatā* does apprehend truth in some sense, the knowledge may and often does subsequently turn out to be false, so that the truth apprehended fails to distinguish right knowledge from error: such cases are referred to in the text as cases of *vyabhicāra*.

20.4. The Mīmāṃsaka might offer a very general argument in self-defence: whatever is, is apprehended where it is. If truth is present in a knowledge, there is no reason why it should not be apprehended therein. But such an argument is suicidal. For it would render falsity also capable of being apprehended *svataḥ*. What is more important is this: the rule that whatever is, is apprehended where it is, is not always correct; it might at most apply only to those knowledges that are produced directly by the object. Secondary knowledges, whether *anuvyavasāya* or inference from *jñātatā*, are not directly caused by the object; they are rather caused by the primary knowledge of the object; they are thus *viṣayājanya*. The *tadvattva* of the object, the fact that the object really possesses that, would not be manifested through them.

The words '*etena*' and '*nirastam*' mean that all these arguments are rejected.

21. *Tadvati tatprakārakajñānatvam tadvati tadvaiśiṣṭyajñānatvaṃ vā prāmāṇyaṃ vyavasāyasya svenānuvyavasāyenānumityā vā tadgrahāt, tadviṣayatvasya tatprakārakatvasya ca jñānagrāhakasāmagrīgrāhyatvāt. Yadi ca prāmāṇyaṃ parato jñāyeta, tadā aprāmāṇyajñāne api tadanumāpakaliṅgapakṣavyāptyādijñāneṣu ca svaviṣayaniścayārthaṃ prāmāṇyasya parato jñeyatve phalamukhī kāraṇamukhī cānavasthā syāditi prāmāṇyaṃ na jñāyeta eveti pariśeṣādapi svataḥ prāmāṇyagrahaḥ iti pūrvapakṣaḥ.*

(For) The truth of the primary knowledge, (taken) either (as) *tad-*

vati tatprakārakajñānatva or (as) *tadvati tadvaiśiṣṭyajñānatva* is apprehended either by itself or by *anuvyavasāya* or by inference; for, both the property of having that as its object and the property of having that as the qualifier are apprehended by the same conditions which also apprehend the knowledge.[1] If again truth is apprehended extrinsically, then in case of (subsequent) knowledge of falsity as also in cases of knowledge of the mark, *pakṣa* and *vyāpti* etc. which support that knowledge (of falsity) there must ensue an infinite regress[2]—both in the direction of the cause and in the direction of the effect—in course of (our) attempt to ascertain their (respective) objects, since truth is apprehended extrinsically. Truth in that case would never come to be ascertained. Therefore, in the absence of any other alternative recourse, (we have to conclude that) the apprehension of truth is intrinsic.

Thus ends the pūrvapakṣa.

Notes

21.1. Gaṅgeśa now gives his final defence of the Mīmāṃsaka position. No point by point reply is given to the objections listed in the preceding paragraph. It is pointed out that truth in the sense of either *tadvati tatprakārakajñānatva* or *tadvati tadvaiśiṣṭyajñānatva* is apprehended in the secondary knowledge. The reason now given—in addition to those adduced on earlier occasions—is only that the two component entities, 'the property of having that as its object' and 'the property of having that for its qualifier', are apprehended in the secondary knowledge. In other words, it is claimed that the secondary knowledge does apprehend the primary one as having for its object, to take the familiar example, what possesses silverness and also as having silverness as a qualifier: in that case the primary knowledge is *ipso facto* known to be true.

21.2. The Mīmāṃsaka reserves to the end the fallacy of infinite regress which is his strongest charge against the *parataḥ* theory. There is however a slight deviation in Gaṅgeśa's formulation of this charge—a deviation which certainly adds to its effectiveness.

In its usual form, the argument is, if the ascertainment of the truth of a knowledge depends upon some other knowledge, then that other knowledge is in need of being validated before it could validate the first knowledge—a process which would give rise to infinite regress. Gaṅgeśa takes up the ascertainment of the falsity of the primary knowledge. On both views, falsity is apprehended *parataḥ*. This ascertainment would be of the form 'This knowledge is false'. This last mentioned knowledge itself needs to be known as being true, but truth of any knowledge being capable of being known only *parataḥ*, we are landed in an infinite regress. Further, in inferring falsity (as we do, according to the Mīmāṃsaka and the Naiyāyika, both) we have to fall back—as in case of all inferences—on perception of a mark and (in this case) memory of the *pakṣa* as well as on a prior knowledge of *vyāpti* between the mark and the truth. All these knowledges themselves require to be apprehended as true. But if truth is apprehended *parataḥ*, we are already within the grips of an infinite regress. Thus there remains no other alternative except admitting that the apprehension of truth accompanies the first apprehension of the knowledge whose truth it is.*

*There is a variant reading of the text which is '*Yadi ca prāmāṇyaṃ parato jñāyeta tadā prāmāṇyajñāne api tadanumāpaka....*' which would imply the usual form of the charge of infinite regress stated above. This reading is given in the Darbhanga edition of *Prāmāṇyavāda*, whereas the text we have used is in conformity with the Kanchi edition.

ATHA SIDDHĀNTAḤ

22. *Siddhāntastu prāmāṇyasya svato grahe'nabhyāsadaśotpanna-jñāne tatsaṃśayo na syāt, jñānagrahe prāmāṇyaniścayāt. Aniścaye vā na svataḥ prāmāṇyagrahaḥ. Jñānāgrahe dharmijñānābhāvāt na saṃśayaḥ.*

The author's standpoint is this: if truth were apprehended intrinsically, then in case of knowledges that arise in unfamiliar circumstances there ought not to be doubt about it. For, with the apprehension of knowledge truth would be ascertained. If on the other hand truth is not ascertained, then the apprehension of truth is not intrinsic. If the knowledge is not apprehended, then in the absence of knowledge of the substantive there would be no doubt.[1]

NOTES

22.1. Gaṅgeśa now undertakes to give his own refutation of the Mīmāṃsā theory whose defence he had so long tried to build up. The central point of Gaṅgeśa's attack is the fact that often soon after we have a knowledge we also ask ourselves, 'Is this knowledge true or not ?' This is more often so in cases of unfamiliar knowledges, for where a knowledge belongs to a familiar type previous experience acts as assurance that the present one, being like the previous ones in other respects, is also true.* Gaṅgeśa would soon make it clear that when he says the Mīmāṃsā theory cannot account for doubts about truth which we often have immediately after we have a knowledge, he means by 'immediately after' something very precise. He means 'in the third moment after the origination of the knowledge'. It is only the possibility of doubt in this third moment after the origination of a knowledge which, according to Gaṅgeśa, cannot be accounted for on the Mīmāṃsā theory. He is not claiming, so I presume, that the

*Thus Vācaspati: "*Abhyāsadaśāpannasya tajjātīyatvena prāmāṇyānumānam*" (*Tātparyyaṭīkā*, p. 10).

Mīmāṃsaka cannot explain any other later doubt. (This shows, as has been argued in the introductory study, that the validity of Gaṅgeśa's argument would depend upon the tenability of his conception of a 'moment' and the Nyāya conception of a knowledge as passing through a lifetime of three moments, one each for origination, existence and destruction.)

Now, doubt presupposes (a) knowledge of the substantive (*dharmi*), (b) remembrance of two, mutually contradictory, alternative qualifiers, and (c) absence of the perception of any of those specific properties with which either of the alternative qualifiers is universally concomitant.*

There often takes place, soon after a knowledge arises, namely, in the third moment after the knowledge originates, doubt of the form 'Is this knowledge true or not?' This doubt presupposes (a) knowledge of the substantive which in the present case is the knowledge whose truth or falsity is being doubted; (b) remembrance of the two, mutually contradictory alternative qualifiers 'truth' and 'falsity' (both understood in those specific and determinate senses which arise as soon as the variables in the definitions of 'truth' and 'falsity' are replaced by appropriate constants); and (c) absence of the perception of any such specific character which would establish one of the alternatives to the exclusion of the other.

Now, since according to (a) above the knowledge itself must be apprehended, and since according to the Mīmāṃsaka's theory a knowledge is apprehended together with its truth, the possibility of doubt about its truth is at once excluded, for prior certainty about one of the alternative qualifiers excludes doubt about the same. It is necessary to bear in mind that this initial certainty about truth can serve to exclude doubt only in the immediately succeeding moment, though there may arise doubt later on. The situation may be represented thus:—

*Thus Gotama: "*Samānānekadharmopapattervipratipatterupalabdhyanupalabdhyavyavasthātaśca viśeṣāpekṣo vimarśaḥ saṃśayaḥ*" (*Nyāya Sūtra* 1.1.23). For an account of the Nyāya theory of doubt, see Mohanty, "Nyāya Theory of Doubt" in Mohanty, *Phenomenology and Ontology*, The Hague: Martinus Nijhoff, 1970.

Moment 1	*Moment* 2	*Moment* 3
The knowledge K_1 originates.	K_1 persists. K_2 = knowledge of K_1 originates. Certainty about the truth of K_1.	K_1 perishes. K_2 persists. Certainty about the truth of K_1 persists. Doubt about the truth of K_1 is not possible.

Either K_1 is apprehended and along with it its truth, or K_1 is apprehended without its truth, or K_1 is not apprehended at all. In the first case, as we have shown, doubt is not possible; in the second case, the *svataḥ* theory has to be given up; and in the third case doubt is not also possible, the substantive being unknown.

23. *Nanu koṭismaraṇādinā saṃśayapūrvakṣaṇe vyavasāyavināśānna tadviśeṣyako mānasaḥ saṃśaya iti cet—na. Jñānopanīte vyavasāye prāmāṇyasaṃśayāt. Nanu—dharmijñānaṃ na saṃśayahetuḥ koṭijñānaviśeṣādarśanadharmīndriyasannikarṣāt prāmāṇyasaṃśayarūpa eva jñānagraha utpadyata iti cet—na. Jñānātīndriyatve tajjñānaṃ vinā taddharmikamānasasaṃśayānupapatteḥ, liṅgaṃca na saṃśayajanakam, tasya niścāyakatvāt. Jñānasya mānasatve ca prāmāṇyajñānavat tatsāmagryapi saṃśayapratibandhikā, tanniścāyakatvāt. Anyathā viśeṣadarśanakāle'pi saṃśayāpatteḥ.*

If it be said that after the remembrance of the alternatives etc. (and) at the moment (just) preceding the doubt the primary knowledge is destroyed, so that there cannot be mental doubt about it, then, (we say) no. For, doubt about truth is possible in the primary knowledge as presented through (its past) knowledge.[1] Nor can it be said that knowledge of the substantive is not a cause of doubt and that (therefore) the apprehension of the knowledge takes place in the form of doubt regarding (its) truth, (arising) through knowledge of the alternatives, non-perception of the specific characters and contact of the sense with the substantive.[2] For, if knowledge is supersensible, mental doubt with a knowledge as its substantive is not possible in case that knowledge is not known. The mark again cannot cause doubt, for it causes certainty.[3] If on the other hand knowledge is an object of mental perception, the conditions of the apprehension of truth function, like the apprehension of truth itself, as hindrance to doubt, because they give rise to certainty about that.[4] Otherwise, there should be doubt even when there is perception of specific characters.[5]

NOTES

23.1. It has been said that often a knowledge may be soon followed by doubt about its truth. But doubt, we have seen, requires some conditions to be fulfilled. In the present case at least two intermediate steps are needed: apprehension of the substantive namely the primary knowledge, and remembrance of the alternatives. Each of these would take a moment. Can it now be said that by the time one has gone through these steps the original primary knowledge must have been dead and gone? How can there be doubt in that case about that knowledge which is not being perceived any more? This is a minor objection, and it suffices to point out that there can be doubt about a remembered knowledge, or about a knowledge that is extraordinarily presented through memory.

23.2. Gaṅgeśa's point rests on two propositions. First, there undeniably are such cases of doubt. Secondly, doubt presupposes knowledge of the substantive (which in such cases would be the primary knowledge concerned). Is it not possible to deny the second proposition? If this condition could be waived, then the following possibility may be imagined. First, there occurs remembrance of the alternatives. This is followed by a knowledge. As soon as the knowledge is there, there automatically takes place the mind's contact with it. As a consequence, there arises in the next moment doubt about its truth, this doubt *being at the same time* apprehension of that knowledge. It cannot be said since this also is an apprehension of a knowledge it should, on the *svataḥ* theory, apprehend the truth of that knowledge and so exclude the possibility of the doubt; for, only those knowledges of a knowledge apprehend its truth which—as has been said before—do not apprehend its falsity (*aprāmāṇyāgrāhaka*). The present one being also a case of doubt apprehends falsity (which is one of the qualifiers) and therefore would not apprehend the truth as well.

23.3. Gaṅgeśa refutes this objection in two stages. He argues first that on the Bhāṭṭa theory since knowledge is supersensible there can be no doubt about its truth unless that knowledge itself were known. The mark of knowledge, namely, knownness (*jñātatā*) cannot possibly give rise to a doubt, for it is the function of a mark as a mark to give rise to certainty through inference.

23.4. Similarly, on the Miśra theory, even if we suppose that the actual knowledge of the primary knowledge does not precede doubt about its truth yet the conditions of *anuvyavasāya* are all present, and these very conditions, Gaṅgeśa insists, are as much hindrances to the possibility of doubt as is the actual *anuvyavasāya* itself. Gaṅgeśa's contention is based on a general rule which Raghunātha formulates as: 'If certainty of x is a hindrance to y, then the conditions of that certainty are also hindrances to y' ("*Yanniścayasya yatra pratibandhakatvaṃ tanniścayasāmagryāstatra pratibandhakatvam*"). Certainly, certainty about truth is a hindrance to doubt about that truth. It follows that the conditions of certainty about truth would also hinder the rise of that doubt. On the *svataḥ* theory, the conditions of the apprehension of a knowledge are also the conditions of the apprehension of the truth of that knowledge. Therefore, the conditions of the apprehension of a knowledge being present, any doubt about the truth of that knowledge would be impossible.

23.5. If the Mīmāṃsaka does not accept the above general rule, then—Gaṅgeśa reminds him—he would have to swallow unpalatable consequences. For example, he would have to concede that a doubt can arise precisely when one is perceiving the specific characters. Perception of the specific characters (i.e. of characters which are marks of any one of the remembered alternatives) is well known to be a hindrance to doubt. If the general rule mentioned above is not accepted, then the conditions of the perception of specific characters would not obstruct doubt, so that doubt about an alternative and perception of the specific marks of that alternative might very well take place together, which is manifestly absurd.

Or, better still, imagine the following possibility. It may very well be that first a doubt arises, which is followed by perception of the specific marks of one of the alternatives (of the doubt). Such perception should as a rule destroy the doubt and establish perceptual certainty with regard to that alternative qualifier whose marks have been perceived. According to the rule formulated by Raghunātha, since perceptual certainty is a hindrance to doubt, the conditions of that certainty also should function as hindrance to the same doubt. In the present case, the condition of perceptual certainty of one of the alternatives is none other than perception of the specific marks of that alternative. Hence, perception of specific marks also should hinder doubt. If however the rule is not accepted, then perception of specific marks, coming after a doubt, would not suppress the doubt and we would be left with the unpalatable consequence that doubt would re-emerge after, or simultaneously with, perceptual certainty regarding one of the alternative qualifiers of the doubt.

24. *Atha dharmiṇi viśeṣādarśanadaśāyāmekakoṭismaraṇe tadāropaḥ koṭidvayasmaraṇe saṃśaya iti niścayasāmagrītassaṃśayasāmagrī balavatīti koṭidvayasmaraṇe saṃśaya eva syāt na tu niścaya iti cet—na. Viruddhobhayāropasāmagrīdvayasamājādubhayāropa eka eva bhavati sa eva saṃśayaḥ, na tvekāropasāmagryā aparāropasāmagrīpratibandhaḥ, avirodhāt. Na cobhayāropasāmagryā ekaniścayasāmagrīpratibandha iti vācyaṃ pratyekāropasāmagryatiriktāyāstasyā abhāvāt. Na ca sāmagrīdvayāt kāryadvayaṃ samūhālambanavadupapatteḥ. Tasmāt prāmāṇyaniścayasāmagrīsattvāt na tatsaṃśayassyāt.*

If it be said that at the time of non-perception of specific characters in the substantive if there is remembrance of one of the alternatives there takes place predication of that alternative and if there is remembrance of both alternatives there takes place doubt, so that the generating conditions of doubt are stronger than those of certainty and (as a consequence) if there takes place remembrance of both alternatives there should be doubt rather than certainty[1]; then (we say) no. Out of the compresence of the generating conditions of the predications of two mutually contradictory (characters) there arises predication of both, and this is doubt[2]. It cannot be that the generating conditions of the predication of one should be hindrance to the generating conditions of the predication of the other, for there is no incompatibility. It cannot also be said that the generating conditions of the predication of both are hindrance to the generating conditions of the certainty about one (of the two), for there is no generating condition of the predication of both other than the conditions of the predication of each.[3] Nor can it be said that the two sets of conditions should give rise to two (separate) effects, for it can be accounted for as in the case of a *samūhālambana*. Therefore since the generating conditions of certainty about truth are present there should be no doubt about that (truth).[4]

Notes

24.1. It was pointed out that unless the rule '*yanniścayasya yatra pratibandhakatvaṃ tanniścayasāmagryāstatra pratibandhakatvam*' were accepted there would follow doubt where in fact there should be certainty. The Mīmāṃsaka against whom the point was directed might still insist that there is no harm if this were so, for in fact—he might add in self-defence—where both the conditions of certainty and the conditions of doubt are together present the latter shall prevail. The conditions of doubt are stronger and shall make those of certainty ineffective. Consider the following case: let us suppose there is non-perception of the specific marks of any of the alternatives. Let us further suppose that under such circumstances one remembers one of the alternatives. As a rule there should take place a predication (may be, erroneous) of that remembered alternative character. But if instead there takes place remembrance of both the alternatives, then there would arise doubt. Now when both the alternatives are remembered, one of them is also remembered, so that both the conditions of certainty and the conditions of doubt are then present together. Yet only doubt takes place, not certainty. From this it follows that the conditions of doubt are stronger than those of certainty.

24.2. This Mīmāṃsaka argument is rejected by Gaṅgeśa. The hypothetical case may be otherwise accounted for. In fact there are two sets of conditions, present together, for the predication of two different and mutually contradictory characters; there is no separate condition of doubt. This being so, the result is a compound predication of both the mutually contradictory characters. Where this sort of compound predication of two mutually contradictory characters (e.g. of 'manhood' and 'absence of manhood') takes place (as in 'Is this a man or not?'), we give it the name of 'doubt'. There is therefore no point in distinguishing between the conditions of doubt and the conditions of certainty and then in arguing that where both are present the former are stronger!

[It may be noted here that in this reply Gaṅgeśa accepts an interpretation of doubt which is usually attributed to the author of *Ratnakoṣa* and to which Gaṅgeśa himself does not really subscribe. According to the author of *Ratnakoṣa*, a doubt is nothing but a joint assertion of two contradictory characters: there are no separate causal conditions of doubt quâ doubt. According to Gaṅgeśa however in case of doubt the two contradictory assertions have never equal strength, there always being a greater inclination in favour of one of them. Therefore, each of them is more (or, less?) than a simple assertion.]

24.3. In the hypothetical case, there are (i) conditions for the predication of, let us say, A; and (ii) conditions for the predication of not-A. Let us call these C_A and C_{not-A} respectively. There are (iii) also conditions for the joint predication of A and not-A. Let us call these last ones $C_{A,\ not-A}$. Now out of $C_{A,\ not-A}$ follows doubt as explained in the note above.

But why are there no separate assertions of A and not-A which would be the consequences of C_A and $C_{A\ not-A}$ respectively? Actually there is only doubt. Should we suppose that C_A and C_{not-A} have ceased to produce their separate effects owing to the presence of $C_{A,\ not-A}$ which acts as hindrance to their separate effects? Admitting this would by implication amount to admitting the Mīmāṃsaka's plea explained in 24.1, that the conditions of doubt are stronger than the conditions of certainty.

Gaṅgeśa sees no need for postulating such a relation between C_A and C_{not-A} on the one hand and $C_{A,\ not-A}$ on the other.

For $C_{A, not-A}$ is nothing other than C_A and C_{not-A}. Actually the separate effects are there, and it is their compresence—A and not-A being contradictory characters—that constitutes doubt.

24.4. Therefore Gaṅgeśa concludes, going back to the original point raised, that the possibility of doubt about truth cannot be explained by the Mīmāṃsakas. For, according to the Mīmāṃsakas the conditions that give rise to the apprehension of a knowledge are also conditions of the apprehension of the truth of that knowledge. These conditions being present, they also, like the apprehension of truth itself would ward off the possibility of doubt about that truth.

25. *Dharmijñānaṃ ca saṃśayahetuḥ. Anyathā saṃśaye dharminiyamaḥ koṭyutkaṭatvañca na syāt.*

And knowledge of the substantive is (a) cause of doubt.[1] (For) otherwise there would not have been determination regarding the substantive[2] and intensity of alternatives in doubt.[3]

Notes

25.1. It was urged against the Mīmāṃsakas that since according to them apprehension of a knowledge was also apprehension of the truth of that knowledge there could not be doubt about its truth soon after the knowledge, for doubt presupposes apprehension of the substantive which in the present case is nothing other than the knowledge whose truth is under consideration. The Mīmāṃsaka may now try to evade the difficulty by suggesting that apprehension of the substantive need not be taken as a cause of doubt. Anticipating this, Gaṅgeśa emphasises the indispensability of the apprehension of the substantive for a doubt. Two reasons are offered in support of this.

25.2. In every doubt there is a necessary reference to a substantive. Two mutually contradictory characters are simultaneously predicated of one and the same substantive. A doubt has the form, 'Is S p or not-p?' (for example, 'Is this a man or not?').

Now unless S were perceived (unless, for example, the yonder object were perceived) it could not appear as a constituent of the expression for the doubt. No doubt has the bare form 'p or not-p?'*

25.3. Gaṅgeśa holds, contrary to the opinion of some Naiyāyikas, that in a doubt the two alternatives do not present themselves with equal weight. Why should this be so unless they are ascribed to one and the same substantive? With regard to one substantive S_1, p may carry more weight than not-p. In another, S_2, not-p may be weightier than p. This fact that in a doubt one alternative may be more weighty than the other shows, according to Gaṅgeśa, that the substantive plays a determining role in it. Knowledge of the substantive must therefore be regarded as a necessary condition of a doubt. (It may be noted that Raghunātha does not agree with Gaṅgeśa in this respect: he does not look upon the so-called *koṭyutkaṭatva* or relative strength of the alternatives as a decisive matter at all and argues that it is not a true *jāti*.)**

26. *Atha pītaḥ śaṅkha ādarśe mukhamityādibhramo viśeṣadarśanepi yathā doṣāntarāt, tathā niścitepi prāmāṇye doṣāntarāt tatsaṃśaya iti cet, na tadvadevātrāpi pravṛttiprasaṅgāt. Sākṣātkāribhrame sākṣātkāriviśeṣadarśanaṃ virodhi sākṣātkāribhrame sākṣātkāryeva viparītaniścayaḥ pratibandhakaḥ na tvānumānikādiḥ. Saṃśaye tu niścayasāmānyam. Anumānādinā tanniścaye kadācidapi tasyānutpādāt. Diṅmohādau tathā darśanāt, tacca na—pittādinā pratibandhāt.*

If it be said that[1] just as in spite of certainty about specific

*Mathurānātha explains "*dharminiyamaḥ na syāt*" thus; "*Anantadharmīndriyasannikarṣe'pi yasyaiva dharmiṇo jñānaṃ tatraiva saṃśaya viparyayo vā, yasya tu na jñānam na tatra iti niyamo na syāt*" (*Māthurī*, Asiatic Soc. edn., p. 219). Mere contact with the substantive is not enough, for many substantives may be in contact with the senses. Doubt arises only with regard to that substantive which is known, not with regard to all those which are not known.

**Mathurānātha explains "*Koṭyutkaṭatvam*" thus: "*dharmijñānasya bhramahetutve saṃśayasya viparyayasya kiñcidaṃśe utkaṭatvam kiñcidaṃśe'nutkaṭatvañceti na syādityarthaḥ*" (*Māthurī*, p. 210).

characters there arises, owing to other *doṣas*, error like (perception of) yellowness in the conch-shell or (perception of) the face in the mirror, so also (there may arise) doubt about truth, due to *doṣa*, in spite of (prior) ascertainment of truth, then (we say) no. For, (if it were so) there should be here (appropriate) activity in the like manner as there.[2] What opposes perceptual error is perceptual certainty about specific characters. Only perceptual certainty of the contradictory, but not others like the inferential, acts as hindrance to perceptual error. In the case of doubt however certainty in general functions as hindrance.[3] If there is certainty through inference etc. doubt never arises. If it be said that this is seen in the case of illusion about direction etc., then (we say) no. For, there is hindrance by biles etc.[4]

Notes

26.1. The Mīmāṃsaka has been asked to explain how on his theory it could be possible for us to have doubt about the truth of a knowledge soon after the knowledge takes place. He has already offered some suggestions which have been rejected. He now suggests a new way out. May it be that the doubt is due to some *doṣa*? Elsewhere it is found that even if a person knows for certain that conch-shell is white he may still see it as yellow owing to some defect in his visual sense organ, if for example he has jaundice. Similarly, although we know for certain our faces are not inside the mirror we do nevertheless see our faces inside it. In spite of a prior certainty to the contrary error may arise if there is some frustrating circumstance, some *doṣa* somewhere. So here also even if we may have apprehended the truth of a knowledge it is still quite possible that owing to some *doṣa* there arises subsequently doubt about its truth.

26.2. Gaṅgeśa rejects this plea on two grounds. His first reply is that there is an important difference between the two cases which is likely to be overlooked. In the case of the conch-shell although we falsely see it yellow yet our activity is oriented in accordance with the earlier certainty that it is in fact white. Similarly we do not act in any way in accordance with the perception of our faces within a mirror. We rather act in accordance with the right belief that our faces are not where they appear to be. In the present case however once we come to doubt the truth of a knowledge our activity is no more in accordance with the earlier certainty about it. In view of this major difference between the two cases, the analogy fails.

26.3. Gaṅgeśa's second reply is that though in case of a perceptual error only a perceptual certainty to the contrary acts as a hindrance, in the case of a doubt it is otherwise. Any prior certainty, perceptual, inferential or of any other kind, is adequate to hinder the rise of a doubt regarding the same. Once a certainty about truth is there, the possibility of a doubt about that truth immediately after is excluded. Besides, we may add that this prior certainty about truth is a perceptual certainty, except on the Bhāṭṭa theory.

Regarding the rule that perceptual error is counteracted only by perceptual certainty to the contrary, Gadādhara adds a qualification to it. What impedes perceptual error, Gadādhara points out, is not mere perceptual certainty, but such perceptual certainty as is derived from the same sense-organ that is also involved in the error. By this he wants to exclude cases like the certainty derived from touch that the pencil dipped in water is straight which does not disallow visual perception that the same pencil at the same time is bent.

26.4. Gaṅgeśa's text in this and the next sentence of the paragraph is extremely misleading. Here he may quite reasonably be taken to be reinforcing the Mīmāṃsā argument by citing another example of a perceptual error which arises in spite of prior certainty to the contrary. But as already argued such instances do not establish the Mīmāṃsā conclusion.

The last sentence, especially the "*tacca na*" presents great difficulty. It cannot be taken as such, for in that case the entire chain of argument would be broken and would be rendered pointless. We may possibly have to supply a *pūrvapakṣa* sub-argument for the "*tat*" and then deny it. The following seems to be a likely move. Gaṅgeśa has conceded that in the case of perceiving a conch-shell to be yellow or in the case of error of direction, certainty to the contrary does not suffice to counteract the error, for that certainty is only mediate not perceptual. To this it may be asked, why is it that the certainty about the conch-shell being white is not perceptual when all the conditions of perception are present? Gaṅgeśa may then be taken to be replying that the certainty about the conch-shell being white is not perceptual since there are *doṣas* which render that impossible. There may for example be jaundiced eyes due to, as Indian medicine says, defect in the biles. But I am not quite sure if this is a correct interpretation of the text here.

27. *Na ca jātyaiva kaściddoṣo'sti. Na ca prāmāṇyasaṃśayādviṣayasaṃśayavat prāmāṇyajñāne prāmāṇyasaṃśayāt prāmāṇyasaṃśaya iti vācyam. Prāmāṇyajñāne'pi svataḥ prāmāṇyagrahe tatsaṃśayānupapatteḥ.*

And there is no class essence of *doṣa*.[1] It cannot also be said that just as doubt about the object arises out of doubt about the truth (of the knowledge of that object), so doubt about truth may arise out of doubt about the truth of the knowledge of truth.[2] For, truth being apprehended intrinsically in the knowledge of truth itself, there would be no possibility of doubt about it.[3]

Notes

27.1. The Mīmāṃsaka had contended that in spite of prior certainty error or doubt may be due to some *doṣa* or defect or frustrating circumstance. Gaṅgeśa now gives his other reply. He says that there is no generic character called *doṣatva*. In other words, there is nothing common, no class character belonging in common to all the so-called *doṣas*. There is no generic character which is present in all those cases where we have error or doubt.*

*Pakṣadhara Miśra understands the sentence "*Na ca jātyā eva kaścit doṣo'sti*" in a different way. "*Jātyā*" means according to him "by birth" (*Janmanā*). Gaṅgeśa is then taken to mean that there is no generic character called 'being born of unfamiliar circumstances' (*anabhyāsadaśājanmā na*

27.2. The Mīmāṃsaka makes another attempt to explain the possibility of the said kind of doubt. Distinction is made between doubt about the truth of a knowledge and doubt about the object of that knowledge. The former usually precedes the latter. Let us suppose, I have a knowledge of the form 'S is p'. At first I may doubt whether my knowledge was true or not. This doubt would have the form 'Is my knowledge that S is p true or not?' From this doubt there would arise another doubt having the form 'Is S really p or not?' Now the Mīmāṃsaka makes use of this distinction to explain the possibility of doubt about truth. Let, as before, the primary knowledge be k_1. In the secondary knowledge K_2 we apprehend—on the Miśra and the Bhāṭṭa theories—the truth of K_1. The object of K_2 is the truth of K_1. Now if for any reason there arises doubt regarding the truth of K_2, then this doubt would give rise to another doubt, namely, one about the truth of K_1 in accordance with the rule that doubt about the truth of a knowledge causes doubt about the object of that knowledge.

27.3. Gaṅgeśa rejects this explanation on the ground that on the Mīmāṃsa theory, the truth of K_2 also should be apprehended *svataḥ* so that doubt in its truth would be no easier to explain. Either K_2 is known or it is unknown. If it is known its truth is also known for certain on the Mīmāṃsā theory so that there cannot be any more doubt about that. If on the other hand K_2 is unknown then in the absence of knowledge of the substantive there cannot be any doubt concerning any of its properties.

28. *Nanu jñānamātraṃ na virodhibuddhinivartakaṃ, bhramottaraṃ bādhakajñānodayāt, kintu ananyathāsiddham. Ata eva tena vināpi tajjñānaṃ sambhavatīti anyathāsiddhatayā śaṅkitaṃ tanniścayaṃ paribhūya jñānaviṣayatvādviṣaye yathā saṃśayastathā prāmāṇye tanniścayasyānyathāsiddhi-*

doṣaḥ). This has reference to the fact that doubts about truth—on the possibility of which Gaṅgeśa's argument rests—take place generally in the case of those knowledges which are yet unfamiliar. Now lest the Mīmāṃsaka might count this unfamiliarity itself as a *doṣa* which is responsible for the occurrence of the doubt in spite of an initial certainty, Pakṣadhara takes Gaṅgeśa to mean that there is no generic character of that description. We however have followed the interpretations of Raghunātha and Gadādhara.

śaṅkayā taṃ paribhūya bhavati saṃśayaḥ. Na ca vyavasāyasya jñānatve ghaṭaviṣayakatve ca yathānuvyavasāyaviṣayatvānna saṃśayastathā prāmāṇye'pi na syāt, anuvyavasāyasya pramātvaniyamāditi vācyam. Ajñāne aviṣaye ca jñānatvaviṣayatvayoranuvyavasāyenāgrahaṇaniyamāt tadviṣayatvamanyathāsiddhaṃ prāmāṇyaviṣayatvañca tena vināpi sambhavatīti tatra saṃśaya iti cet.

It may be said that knowledge in general does not negate the opposite idea, for (even) after error there arises the correcting knowledge. But it is only such knowledge as is not otherwise established.[1] Therefore a knowledge which is infected with the suspicion that it can be otherwise established, that is to say by the thought that knowledge about this object is possible even without the object being present, is thereby weakened. (And as a consequence) Just as doubt in an object may arise from its being an object of knowledge[2]; so there arises doubt in truth through the weakening of the certainty about truth by the suspicion of its being possible otherwise. The following reply cannot be given: Just as there never arises doubt whether the property of being a knowledge and the property of having (the) pot as its object belong to the primary knowledge, because they are objects of *anuvyavasāya*, so also there should not be doubt about truth, since as a rule the *anuvyavasāya* is true.[3] For, in what is not knowledge and in what does not have an object, the *anuvyavasāya* never apprehends the property of being a knowledge and the property of having an object so that having these two objects is not established otherwise. Truth however can be an object even when it is not there, so that doubt about it is possible.[4]

NOTES

28.1 The Mīmāṃsaka is offering a fresh suggestion as to how the possibility of doubt about truth can be accounted for on his theory. The mere fact that we apprehend truth *ab initio* does not rule out the possibility of doubt. For knowledge in general does not act as hindrance to the opposite knowledge (in the present case, the opposite one is the doubt). If every certainty excluded the possibility of its opposite, then correction of error would have been an impossibility. Correction implies the birth of a certainty opposing the prior belief in the false. We should therefore say that only when a knowledge is accompanied by a definite awareness that it is *not* possible, or cannot arise, in the absence of its object—which is the same as saying that it is *ananyathāsiddha*—that it excludes the possibility of the opposite belief. When I know for example that unless S were really p I cannot know S to be p, then my knowledge that S is p can never suffer subsequent contradiction.

28.2. When however a knowledge is accompanied by the suspicion that its object may not be there, in other words when there is the awareness that I may well have the knowledge without the object being there, the force of the certainty is thereby weakened* and it may be followed by rise of the opposite mental state, possibly by a doubt. It is in such cases that the prior certainty about truth may leave room for subsequent doubt about it. Doubt presupposes—as is well known—perception of a generic character and non-perception of specific marks. Now, the generic character may be the simple property of being an object of awareness, the specific characters then being reality or unreality of that object. From the bare fact that something is an object of knowledge, we may come to doubt whether that something is really there or not. Likewise when the truth of a primary knowledge becomes the object of the corresponding *anuvyavasāya*—as on the Miśra theory—there may still be room left for doubt regarding that truth through the awareness of its '*anyathāsiddhatva*'.

28.3. The Naiyāyika might reply to the above argument thus: doubt about the truth of the primary knowledge is ruled out on the Mīmāṃsā theory. The primary knowledge has the property of being the object of secondary knowledge, and we never entertain any doubt as to whether the primary knowledge has the additional properties of being a knowledge and having this

*"*Paribhūya*" in the text is explained by Gadādhara as meaning '*svāvirodhinaṃ kṛtvā*' (=making compatible with itself).

object* as its object. If this be so why should we have to doubt whether it also possesses truth or not?

The Naiyāyika not only offers the analogy of 'truth' with the two properties of 'being a knowledge' and 'having an object' but also advances in his own support a universal major premise to the effect that all *anuvyavasāya* is as a rule true (*anuvyavasāyasya pramātvaniyamāt*).** If this be so, the secondary knowledge apprehending the truth of the primary knowledge cannot be in error. There can therefore be no doubt about the truth of the secondary knowledge and also no doubt about the truth of the primary knowledge.

28.4. To this rejoinder by the Naiyāyika, the Mīmāṃsaka replies thus: he points out that the general rule that *anuvyavasāya* is always true has a limited scope. The rule is unacceptable if it is given an unrestricted interpretation so as to mean that *anuvyavasāya* is true in all respects, i.e. with regard to all aspects of its object. The rule however does hold good insofar as *anuvyavasāya* can never err with regard to the two properties of *jñānatva* and *saviṣayakatva* to which reference has been made above. For where these two properties are absent, i.e. where there is no knowledge at all and so no object at all, the *anuvyavasāya* does not apprehend *jñānatva* and *saviṣayakatva*.*** With regard to these aspects then *anuvyavasāya* cannot be established otherwise; in other words, it is *ananyathāsiddha*, and therefore indubitable. But with regard to the truth of the primary knowledge the case is different. Even when the primary knowledge lacks truth, it is liable to be known as true. In this respect then the *anuvyavasāya*

*Raghunātha explains that it is wrong to say that the *ghaṭaviṣayakatva* of the knowledge. 'This is a pot' is indubitable. It is only *ghaṭatvaprakārakatva* which is not doubted. In other words, whereas it is open to doubt whether a real pot is the object, it is certainly beyond doubt that potness is a qualifier of the knowledge. Raghunātha therefore comments that what is meant by Gaṅgeśa is that it cannot be doubted that a knowledge has some object or other (*kiñcidviṣayatva*).

**Thus Vācaspati writes, in connection with the truth of *anuvyavasāya*: "...*jñānasya mānasapratyakṣasya tādṛśasyādṛṣṭavyabhicāratayā parito nirastasamastavibhramāśaṅkasya svataḥ prāmāṇyamiti*" (*Tātparyyaṭīkā*, p. 9).

***Compare Udayana in *Pariśuddhi*, "*Na hyajānannapi kaścijjānāmītyanuvyavasyati, na ca śuktikākāre jñāne rajataṃ jānāmīti syāditi*" (p. 117).

may be doubted. It is therefore possible to doubt a truth about which there was an initial certainty.

29. *Maivam. Bhramatvamanyathāsiddhatvam. Tataśca prāmāṇyaniścaye bhramatvasaṃśayena tadviṣaye prāmāṇyasaṃśaya iti phalito'rthaḥ. Bhramatvasaṃśayaśca tajjñānājñānābhyāṃ na sambhavatītyuktatvāt. Evamanyatrāpi bhramatvasaṃśayāt na viṣaye saṃśayaḥ svataḥ prāmāṇyagrahe bhramatvasaṃśayābhāvāt.*

This cannot be so. '*Anyathāsiddhatva*' is (nothing other than) erroneousness. And therefore when there is doubt regarding the falsity of the knowledge of truth there also arises doubt regarding the truth of its object: this is the meaning in short.[1] (But) doubt about falsity is not possible, whether that is known or unknown:[2] this has been already said. So also in other cases doubt about the object cannot arise from doubt about the falsity,[3] for doubt about falsity cannot take place if truth be apprehended intrinsically.

Notes

29.1. The suggestion offered and defended by the Mīmāṃsaka in the preceding paragraph is now rejected by Gaṅgeśa who prefers to prefix his criticism with a short statement of what the contention amounts to. The Mīmāṃsaka has contended that not all knowledge but only such as is not *anyathāsiddha* (in the sense explained above) excludes the possibility of contradictory knowledge. Knowledge of truth is *anyathāsiddha*, and so leaves room for subsequent doubt. What does *anyathāsiddhatva* really mean? The explanation given of this notion shows that it is nothing other than falsity. For a knowledge to take place even in the absence of its object is the same as its being false. If it be so, then the Mīmāṃsaka's contention is that once there is doubt about the falsity of our knowledge of the truth of the primary knowledge, then there would result a doubt about the truth of the primary knowledge itself. Gaṅgeśa now argues, in reply, that the former doubt is no more possible than the latter on the Mīmāṃsaka's theory.

29.2. Mathurānātha explains this argument thus. If the knowledge of truth is apprehended, there cannot any more be doubt about its truth, for that apprehension would also be an apprehension of the truth of the knowledge of truth. If on the other hand the knowledge of truth is not apprehended there also cannot be a doubt about its truth in the absence of *dharmijñāna*. The '*tat*' in "*tajjñānājñānābhyām*" in the text should therefore be taken to stand for the knowledge of the truth of the primary knowledge. This construction has the advantage that it helps us to make sense of "*ityuktatvāt*" in the text, for the original argument of Gaṅgeśa about the impossibility of doubt about truth has exactly this form: only, now he is concerned, not with the primary knowledge, but with the secondary knowledge.

29.3. Doubt about falsity is impossible not only with regard to the certainty about truth, but also in all other cases of knowledge (*evamanyatrāpi*). For, even in primary knowledges, if there is apprehension of truth there cannot further be doubt about falsity. Gaṅgeśa's main point then is: doubt about *anyathāsiddhatva* is no more possible on the *svataḥ* theory than doubt about truth was, so that the former doubt cannot be brought in order to explain the latter.

30. *Na ca vācyaṃ prāmāṇyasaṃśayāt na viṣaye saṃśayaḥ, mānābhāvāt. Jñānaviṣayatvāt samānadharmādeva tadupapatteḥ.* Na caivaṃ sarvatra viṣayasaṃśaye tanniścayocchedaḥ, prāmāṇyasaṃśaye'pi tulyatvāditi. Tasyāsārvatrikatvāt. Bhramatvasaṃśayaṃ vinā niścitaviṣaye saṃśayānupapatterānubhavikatvācca.*

The following cannot be said: doubt about object does not arise from doubt about truth, there being no proof (in favour of this contention). Doubt about (an) object can be accounted for through the generic property of 'being the object of knowledge'.[1] It cannot be objected that there would be everywhere doubt

*A variant reading at both places is '*utpatteḥ*' instead of '*upapatteḥ*'. See the Darbhanga edn. But it makes no difference to the content of the argument.

about the object and so cessation of all certainty about it, for the same is also the case with doubt about truth.[2]

For, doubt about truth does not occur everywhere.[3] Besides, doubt in an object about which there is certainty cannot be accounted for unless there is doubt about falsity. This is also borne out by experience.[4]

NOTES

30.1. The Mīmāṃsaka was so long relying on a premise that doubt about object (*viṣayasaṃśaya*) followed upon doubt about the truth of the knowledge of that object (*prāmāṇyasaṃśaya*). This did not help him, for Gaṅgeśa could show that the latter is not possible. The Mīmāṃsaka now abandons that premise and would prefer to explain the possibility of doubt in a different manner. As said before, doubt presupposes, among other factors, perception of a character common to the various alternatives. One such character common to the object of right knowledge and the object of error is the simple property of being an object of knowledge. Can we not say that since truth becomes an object of knowledge (in secondary knowledge) it too possesses the property of being an object of knowledge? Perception of this generic character may lead one to doubt if truth is over and above an object of right knowledge or is an object of false knowledge. In other words, there may arise the doubt, 'Is the truth apprehended real or not?'*

30.2. If doubt can be aroused by the character of being an object of knowledge, then should this not lead to universal scepticism and consequently to the cessation of all objective certainty? For indeed all objects possess this generic character and insofar all objects may be doubted. To this possible objection the Mīmāṃsaka replies by saying that the situation would be no better if we suppose instead that doubt about object is caused by doubt

*Thus Raghunātha comments : "*Niścayasattvāsattvayossādhāraṇadharmadarśanādeva saṃśaya iti...tathā ca yathā sthāṇutvādestathā pramātvāpramātvasādhāraṇajñānaviṣayatvādidarśanāt prāmāṇyasyāpīti*" (*Dīdhiti*, Kanchi edn., p. 62).

about the truth of the knowledge of that object. The latter doubt being always possible, the former doubt would also follow leading equally badly to universal scepticism. Both the hypotheses are so far on a par.

30.3. In reply, Gaṅgeśa points out that the two cases are not exactly similar. The first hypothesis, namely, that doubt about object is caused by doubt about truth does not in fact lead to universal scepticism, for doubt about truth does not occur always (*tasyāsārvatrikatvāt*). Therefore, there need not be universal doubt about object.

30.4. Gaṅgeśa supports his argument with the following consideration. Once there is certainty about object, doubt cannot arise unless there is prior doubt about the truth of that knowledge—unless i.e. there arises the possibility of error or of that certainty being *anyathāsiddha*. But in the present case—as argued before—since we possess an initial certainty about truth this certainty cannot leave room for any doubt about the knowledge being erroneous. This is also confirmed by experience.

31. *Atha tadvati tatprakārakatvaṃ prāmāṇyaṃ, tacca jñānagrāhakeṇa gṛhitameveti na tatsaṃśayaḥ. Na cāsminniścite api prāmāṇyasaṃśayāt na tatprāmāṇyamiti vācyam, etanniścayādeva niṣkampavyavahārāditi cet. Astu tāvadidaṃ prāmāṇyaṃ, tathāpi anuvyavasāyānantaraṃ vyavasāyasya prāmāṇye arthasya tadvattve ca saṃśayasyānubhavasiddhatvānnārthe tadvattvaṃ tasya viṣayaḥ.**

Now truth is the property of having a qualifier which is present in the qualificandum, and this is apprehended by the knowledge which (also) apprehends the knowledge; therefore, there cannot be doubt about it.[1] It cannot be said that since there does arise doubt about truth even after this is ascertained, this is not truth; for unwavering activity follows from certainty about it.[2] Let this be truth.[3] Nevertheless, it is confirmed by experience that after the *anuvyavasāya* the truth of the primary knowledge as well as

*This passage is extremely difficult to construe. We have depended on Raghunātha who, it seems, supplies the missing links.

the possession of that by the object come to be doubted.[4] Therefore, the possession of that by the object is not apprehended by it.[5]

NOTES

31.1. The Mīmāṃsaka now tries to show in quite another way that there is no contradiction in holding both that truth is apprehended *ab initio* and that after this apprehension of truth there may often be doubt about it. The apparent contradiction between these two is sought to be explained away by the suggestion that the truth which is apprehended *ab initio* is not the same truth as that which comes to be doubted later on. The truth which is apprehended *ab initio* is nothing other than the well known *tadvati tatprakārakatva*. This truth—or, truth in this sense—never comes to be doubted. Gaṅgeśa is not here explicit as to the precise sense of 'truth' in which truth according to the Mīmāṃsaka comes to be doubted. Raghunātha however comes to our aid and suggests that it is the other aspects of truth such as 'the property of being an apprehension other than memory' (*smṛtyanyajñānatva*) which may be taken as being objects of doubt.*

31.2. Lest it be pointed out that since truth is doubted (the doubt having the form, 'Is this knowledge true or not?') and since, as maintained by the Mīmāṃsaka, *tadvati tatprakārakatva* is not what is doubted, it therefore follows that *tadvati tatprakārakatva* is not *prāmāṇya* at all, the Mīmāṃsaka hastens to add that this apprehension is wrong. *Tadvati tatprakārakatva* is in fact truth. The reason adduced is that certainty about *tadvati tatprakārakatva* is in fact the cause of unwavering activity. The intention of the Mīmāṃsaka is then this: there are various senses of '*prāmāṇya*'. The sense in which *prāmāṇya* is apprehended

*Thus Raghunātha writes, "*Yadyanuvyavasāyānantaraṃ vyavasāyasya tadvati tatprakārakatve saṃśayaḥ syāt, syādapi tadanyathānupapattyā prāmāṇyasya svatastvanirāsaḥ, natvevaṃ, parantu smṛtyanyajñānatvādāveva ityāśaṅkate*" (*Dīdhiti*).

svataḥ is quite other than the sense in which it comes to be doubted subsequently: there is therefore no contradiction.*

31.3. Gaṅgeśa is hopelessly unclear about what he refers to by the 'this' in "*Astu tāvadidaṃ prāmāṇyam*". Again Raghunātha with his unerring understanding comes to our aid: the 'this' refers to those other senses of truth like the property of being a knowledge other than memory which come to be doubted.

31.4. Gaṅgeśa is obviously replying to the Mīmāṃsaka. Those aspects may of course be called 'truth' if you like, but when we doubt if our knowledge is true or not the object of our doubt is not truth in any of those senses. To be precise, we do not doubt in such cases if our knowledge is other than memory or not. What we doubt is whether the primary knowledge is true to the object and if the object is really such and such.

31.5. It follows therefore that neither *tadvati tatprakārakatva* nor *arthasya tadvattva* are apprehended in the *anuvyavasāya*, for it is they—and not the other aspects of truth—that come to be doubted subsequently.

32. *Nanu vyavasāyasya idantvarajatatvaviśiṣṭedaṃviṣayatve anuvyavasāya eva mānam. Tathā ca yāvadvyavasāyollikhitaprakāraviśiṣṭa eva dharmyanuvyavasāye bhāsate. Anyathā viṣayāṃśe tasya nirvikalpakatve idaṃ rajataṃ jānāmīti tadākāro na syāt. Ato dharmiṇīdantvarajatatvavaiśiṣṭyamanuvyavasāyena gṛhītamiti dharmiṇi svataḥ prāmāṇyagrahavadrajatatvavaiśiṣṭye api svataḥ prāmāṇyajñānamavarjanīyam. Ata eva dharmyaṃśe na kadāpi prāmāṇyasaṃśaya iti cet.*

It may be said that the *anuvyavasāya* (alone) proves that the primary knowledge has for its object the *this* as qualified by 'thisness' and 'silverness'. Therefore the substantive appears in the *anuvyavasāya* as qualified by all those qualifiers that are mentioned in the primary knowledge. Otherwise, the *anuvya-*

*Hence Gadādhara: "*Smṛtyanyajñānatvarūpaprāmāṇyasaṃśayasyānubhavikatvaṃ na yāthārthyasya svatogrāhyatve bādhakam. . .*" (*Gādādharī*).

vasāya would be indeterminate with regard to the object and (consequently) it would not have the form 'I know this silver'. Therefore the relatedness of thisness and silverness to the substantive is apprehended in the *anuvyavasāya*.[1] As a consequence, just as the truth of the substantive is apprehended intrinsically, so it is impossible not to admit that truth of the relatedness to silverness is also apprehended intrinsically.[2] Therefore, there can never be doubt about the truth (of a knowledge) with regared to the substantive.

NOTES

32.1. The Mīmāṃsaka now seeks to show—as against Gaṅgeśa's conclusion in the foregoing paragraph—that it is the *tadvati tatprakārakatva* of the primary knowledge that is apprehended in the *anuvyavasāya* so that any subsequent doubt about truth cannot possibly be about this. The primary knowledge is perceived in the *anuvyavasāya*. That the primary knowledge is of such and such object is known only in *anuvyavasāya*. Consider the knowledge 'This is silver'. The *anuvyavasāya* tells us that the primary knowledge is one having for its object something possessing thisness and silverness. In fact, the *anuvyavasāya* apprehends the original object exactly as it was determined for the primary knowledge. Since the primary knowledge apprehended its object as 'this' and as 'silver', the *anuvyavasāya* would also know it as qualified by thisness and silverness. If this were not so, then the *anuvyavasāya* would have been indeterminate so far as the object were concerned; in other words, it would have either no linguistic expression for the object, or would refer to the object as a mere something. It could not in any case have the form 'I know this silver' which in fact it has. Therefore, the *anuvyavasāya* does apprehend the substantive as determined by the qualifiers, which is the same as saying that it apprehends the *tadvati tatprakārakatva* of the primary knowledge. No doubt, therefore, is possible either about the 'this' or about the 'silver'. It would follow that the doubt about truth pertains to truth in some other sense of that term.

32.2. Even according to the Naiyāyika, there is intrinsic truth in a knowledge with regard to the substantial character (here, 'thisness'). "*Dharmyaṃśa*" in the text means '*dharmitāvacchedakāṃśa*'. The knowledge 'This is silver' is unerring with regard to the predicate 'thisness' which is the limitor of the substantive. The Mīmāṃsaka now argues that the same may be said of the other qualifiers. Raghunātha points out that the Mīmāṃsaka might rely upon Vācaspati (in the *Tātparyyaṭīkā*) for ascribing to the Naiyāyika the view that no doubt affects the knowledge insofar as the substantive is concerned. Why should not the same be true of the qualifier 'silverness'?

(Actually, however, the Nyāya does not hold that knowledge is intrinsically true with regard to the substantive. It accepts, however, that no doubt is possible with regard to it. And this impossibility of doubt may be explained otherwise than by appealing to the *svataḥprāmāṇya* theory.)

33. *Maivam, idaṃ rajatañca jānāmīti, nānuvyavasāyaḥ, bahirviśeṣyake manaso'svātantryāt. Kintvidam idantvena rajatatvena jānāmīti. Tatredantvarajatatve prakāratvena bhāsete. Tatprakārakajñānavattvaṃ cātmani bhāsate. Anyathā prakāravācitṛtīyārthāsambhavaḥ. Rajatatvavaiśiṣṭyasya tadarthatve vyavasāye'pi tṛtīyārthollekhāpattiḥ. Tathā ca dharmiṇīdantvarajatatvaprakārakajñānaviṣayatve tādṛśajñānavattve cātmano'nuvyavasāya eva mānamiti na viṣaye tasya nirvikalpakatvam. Ata idantvarajatatvavaiśiṣṭyaṃ purovartini nānuvyavasāyaviṣaya iti na svataḥ prāmāṇyagrahaḥ. Tasmādar' hyāsadaśāpannajñānaprāmāṇyaṃ parato jñāyate, sāṃśayikatvādaprāmāṇyavadityācāryāḥ.*

This cannot be so. The *anuvyavasāya* is not 'I know this (and the) silver', for the mind has no independence in the case of outer objects. Rather, (it has the form) 'I know this as (qualified by) 'thisness' and 'silverness'.' There 'thisness' and 'silverness' appear as qualifiers. The possession of the knowledge which has them as qualifiers appears in the self. Otherwise, the instrumental case ending in the sense of qualifier would not be possible. If it meant relatedness to silverness, then the instrumental should have been mentioned in the primary knowledge as well.[1] The *anuvyavasāya* is not indeterminate with regard to the object because that the substantive is the object of a knowledge which has 'silvernees' as its qualifiers and this (latter) knowledge belongs to the self are evidenced by the *anuvyavasāya* alone.[2] Therefore, the relatedness of thisness and silverness to the yonder object is not the object of *anuvyavasāya*, and so truth is not apprehended intrinsically. Therefore, the truth of a knowledge that has the (mis)fortune of being unfamiliar is apprehended extrinsically, for it becomes an object of doubt, as in the case of falsity: this is maintained by the Ācārya.[3]

Notes

33.1. Gaṅgeśa now proceeds to reject the foregoing contention of the Mīmāṃsakas. The contention that the relatedness which is apprehended by the primary knowledge is also apprehended by the *anuvyavasāya* is based on a wrong conception of the nature of the secondary knowledge. The primary knowledge 'This is silver' is a knowledge of an outer object with the help of an outer sense. The corresponding *anuvyavasāya* is a mental perception. Now, as said before, mind as an instrument of knowledge has no independent capacity for apprehending outer objects. Its independent ability is limited to inner objects. When therefore the mind in *anuvyavasāya* apprehends the primary knowledge it cannot directly apprehend the objects and the objective relatedness which were apprehended in that primary knowledge. Of course, since the primary knowledge was of those objects and objective relations they also would be apprehended along with their knowledge, but their knowledge would be indirect. What is directly apprehended in the *anuvyavasāya* is the primary knowledge itself with its epistemic determinants. The form of the *anuvyavasāya* in that case is not 'I know this silver', but 'I have a knowledge of this, whose qualifiers are 'thisness' and 'silverness';' here 'silverness' and 'thisness' are epistemic qualifiers (*prakāra*) rather than ontological properties.*

*Gaṅgeśa's remarks here about the nature of *anuvyavasāya* raise serious questions vis-a-vis the generally accepted Nyāya theory that in *anuvyavasāya* the object of the primary knowledge is perceived though through an extraordinary contact of the so-called *jñānalakṣaṇā* type. If this latter theory be

What Gaṅgeśa intends to emphasise is a rather subtle distinction between ontological and epistemic categories, between *vaiśiṣṭya* i.e. ontological relatedness and *prakāratā* i.e. epistemic qualifiers. Ontologically, thisness and silverness are related to the *this* by the relation of inherence or *samavāya*: this relational situation along with the relata is apprehended by the primary knowledge. But as soon as the knowledge comes into being it arises with its own epistemological categories (called *viṣayatā*) like *viśeṣyatā, prakāratā* and *saṃsargatā,* though it must be admitted—in accordance with the rule *'viṣayanirūpyaṃ hi jñānam'*—that these epistemic determinants of a knowledge are derived from the objects of the knowledge. These epistemic categories determine the knowledge and give it its form, but the primary knowledge does not apprehend them but only the ontological situation. The *anuvyavasāya* however brings to light these epistemic determinants of the primary knowledge. The objects of the primary knowledge are also thereby known—and to that extent the rule does hold good that the object is *jñānavittivedya.* But the objects are known only as ancillary—the Naiyāyikas prefer to say as *pucchalagna*—to these epistemic determinants, but not quâ ontological objects. The 'thisness' and the 'silverness' which appear in the *anuvyavasāya* (and are expressed with the instrumental case ending denote, according to Gaṅgeśa, epistemic qualifiers and not ontological predicates. If this be so, then the *anuvyavasāya* cannot apprehend whether the *this* is really silver or not.*

---

taken literally, then it would imply that it is the outer object itself that is perceived in *anuvyavasāya* (for after all *jñānalakṣaṇā* is a type of perception). Gaṅgeśa's remark that in *anuvyavasāya* we only perceive the knowledge as having such qualifiers (and not the outer object itself with its qualifications and relations) seems incompatible with the accepted theory, and suggests a modified theory of the nature of *anuvyavasāya.* Such a theory is suggested by Pandit Ananta Kumar Bhattacharyya in his commentary *Vimarśinī* on Harirama's *'Jñānalakṣaṇāvicārarahasyam'* (Calcutta, 1958). See especially page 11 of that book.

*Thus writes Raghunātha: "*Tena purovartini rajatatvaprakārakamiti grahe api purovartini rajate rajatatvaprakārakamiti na grahaḥ*" (*Dīdhiti*). Gadādhara, as a consequence, points out, "*prāmāṇyaghaṭakaghaṭatvaprakārakatvāder niścitatvena prāmāṇyasaṃśayasya tadvadviśeṣyakatvasandeha eva paryavasānāt*" (*Gādādharī* on above).

Gaṅgeśa adds that if the instrumental were to be interpreted as denoting ontological relatedness—as sometimes it does, as for example in '*jaṭābhistāpasaḥ*' (meaning 'recognise a hermit by his matted hair')—then even the primary knowledge should have the instrumental form which, in Sanskrit at least, it does not have.

33.2. The apprehension that unless the ontological relatedness appeared in secondary knowledge the latter would be indeterminate with regard to the substantival component is not well-founded. For the substantive is apprehended in the *anuvyavasāya* as being the object of such and such knowledge, i.e. of a knowledge having such and such epistemic determinants.

33.3. Gaṅgeśa concludes this passage with statement of Udayana's argument in the *Nyāyakusumāñjali*. Udayana's formulation is: "*Evaṃ prāmāṇyaṃ parato jñāyate anabhyāsadaśāyāṃ sāṃśayikatvāt aprāmāṇyavat*".* Gaṅgeśa's formulation differs little from this. Gaṅgeśa only limits the *pakṣa*, thereby seeking to prove that not all *prāmāṇya* but only the *prāmāṇya* belonging to certain kinds of knowledges is apprehended *parataḥ*; though he too would in the long run draw the same conclusion for all *prāmāṇya*. For the present, this limited conclusion suffices to refute the *svataḥ* theory. In this inference, the main difficulty concerns the adjective '*anabhyāsadaśāpanna*'. It is difficult to determine the precise conditions of familiarity. How many times a knowledge must be repeated in order that it or its like may become familiar? Some say that a knowledge is familiar if and only if it does not permit any doubt about its truth in the third moment after its origination. Others like the author of *Dinakarī* hold that an unfamiliar knowledge is one which is of the same kind as a knowledge whose truth has not yet been ascertained (*anavadhṛta-prāmāṇyasajātīya*): but this renders the inference trivial, for if its truth has not yet been ascertained, then of course its truth is not *svataḥ*. In any case this remains a vague notion, and one inevitably falls back on the instances of completely new types of knowledge the like of which was never met before or at least was never validated. In such cases, doubt about truth is only too natural.

* *Nyāyakusumāñjali*, Chowkhamba edn., p. 220.

Where however a knowledge belongs to a familiar type instances of which have been previously validated, truth is ascertained through the simple mark of '*tajjātīyatva*' or 'belonging to that type' without undertaking the process of confirmatory verification.*

It should be noted that the objection raised by Gaṅgeśa earlier in this paragraph and explained in note 33.1. holds good, if at all, only against the Miśra version of the theory. The Prābhākaras hold the view that the primary knowledge itself apprehends its own truth; there is nothing against the possibility of a primary knowledge apprehending an ontological relatedness. In fact, according to the Nyāya it does so when it is true. (The only argument that may be raised against the Prābhākara position is that if the primary knowledge is not regarded as being self-revealing it cannot know its own truth.) The Bhāṭṭas believe, as we have seen, that truth is apprehended by an inference, and inferences admittedly have the power of apprehending outer objects. It is only the Miśras who believe that truth is apprehended by a mental perception, and only they would have to face Gaṅgeśa's criticism that mind has not the power to perceive outer objects. Even they might reply that though normally the mind has not that capacity it may nevertheless perceive an ontological relatedness through a sort of *jñānalakṣaṇā* perception. In that case, Gaṅgeśa of course would have to fall back upon this main argument that on the *svataḥ* theory subsequent doubt about truth cannot be accounted for.

34. *Nanu svāśrayagrāhyatvepi kadācitparagrāhyatvāt svasyāpyanyāpekṣayā paratvāt bhaṭṭamate ca paragrāhyatvāt siddhasādhanam. Na ca grāhyaprāmāṇyāpekṣayā paratvaṃ, grāhakasyāpi grāhyaprāmāṇyatvena tadapekṣayā paratvābhāvāt, svagrāhyaprāmāṇyāpekṣayā paratve aprāmāṇyaprasaṅgāt.*

It may be said that even if truth is apprehended by what apprehends its locus, it is sometimes apprehended by an 'other'. What is one's own may be regarded as an 'other' in relation to some-

*For a detailed account of the notion of '*abhyāsadaśāpannatva*' see the Introduction, pp. 48-50.

thing else;[1] on the Bhāṭṭa theory, of course, truth is apprehended by an 'other'. Hence the fallacy of seeking to prove what is beyond dispute.[2] Nor can 'otherness' be (defined) with regard to the truth which is to be apprehended, for even the apprehending knowledge possesses truth which is to be apprehended and when considered in relation to that truth, lacks 'otherness'.[3] If it be said that 'otherness' is to be determined with reference to that truth which is apprehended by itself, then there would be falsity.[4]

NOTES

34.1. In para 33, Gaṅgeśa has stated the inference used by Udayana. In this formulation, what is sought to be proved is that truth of knowledge is known *parataḥ*. Gaṅgeśa now points out certain difficulties in this way of putting the matter: the difficulties, it would seem, are mainly linguistic in nature. It should anyway be clear that the words '*sva*' and '*para*' are relative; their meanings depend on context. What is 'one's own' in one context is an 'other' in another. This, Gaṅgeśa is afraid, would prove ruinous to the inference, for it can be shown that even the Mīmāṃsaka would accept the thesis that truth is apprehended by an 'other' in some sense so that the *parataḥ* theory would lose its controversial character and the Naiyāyika's efforts to prove it would be rendered pointless. The Prābhākara, though believing that truth is apprehended by the knowledge itself, would nevertheless concede that it may subsequently be apprehended by inference etc. which are certainly '*para*'. In case the Prābhākara would reject this imputation on the ground that what the Nyāya upholds is that truth is apprehended *only parataḥ* (*paramātragrāhyatvam*), Gaṅgeśa hastens to add that the distinction between what is '*sva*' and what is '*para*' is in fact relative. What is '*sva*' in one context is '*para*' in another. Udayana's argument would then be guilty of the fallacy of '*siddhasādhana*'.

34.2. The Bhāṭṭas as well as the Miśras hold the view that truth is apprehended not by the knowledge whose truth it is but by the inference which apprehends that knowledge. This secondary knowledge is certainly '*para*' and insofar Udayana's argument may again be accused of '*siddhasādhana*'.

34.3. It may be suggested that what is '*para*' and what is '*sva*' have to be determined with regard to the truth that is to be apprehended. In that case, Gaṅgeśa points out, even the Naiyāyika's inferential knowledge of truth, being itself the substratum of such a truth, ceases to be *para*.

34.4. In the above arguments Gaṅgeśa is quite clearly playing a verbal game, and taking advantage of the ambiguity of the expressions '*sva*' and '*para*' and also of 'the truth that is to be apprehended'. Why not specify that truth? Let it be nothing other than '*rajatatvavati rajatatvaprakārakatva*' or the property of having 'silverness' for its qualifier in relation to a qualificandum which possesses silverness. This truth belongs to the true knowledge 'This is silver'. In that case what is '*para*' has to be determined with regard to the substratum precisely of this truth and of no other. But in that case the following difficulty would arise in the Nyāya theory. The inference, which according to the Nyāya apprehends the truth of the knowledge 'This is silver', may possibly have the form 'This is silver, and this knowledge is true'. Now such a (*samūhālambana*) knowledge is itself a substratum of the specific truth, namely, of the property designated by '*rajatatvavati rajatatvaprakārakatva*'. It is therefore '*sva*' and not '*para*'. Since however on the Nyāya theory truth is never apprehended by '*sva*', this knowledge would cease to be a genuine inferential apprehension of the truth. This is what Gaṅgeśa *may* have meant by '*aprāmāṇyaprasaṅgāt*'.*

35. *Ucyate, anabhyāsadaśāpannajñānaprāmāṇyaṃ na svāśrayagrāhyaṃ svāśrayātiriktagrāhyaṃ vā. Svāśraye satyapi taduttaratṛtīyakṣaṇavṛttisaṃśayaviṣayatvāt, aprāmāṇyasaṃśayājanyasaṃśayaviṣayatvādvā, aprāmāṇyavat. Arthe niścitepi na tanniścayānantaratṛtīyakṣaṇe'rthasaṃśayo na vā prāmāṇyasaṃśayaṃ vineti nārthavyabhicāraḥ. Vivādapadaṃ na yāvatsvāśrayagrāhakagrāhyaṃ svāśrayaniścaye sati taduttaratṛtīyakṣaṇe'prāmāṇyasaṃśayaṃ vinā vā sandihyamānatvāt aprāmāṇyavat. Yadvā anabhyāsadaśāpannaitajjñānaprāmāṇyam*

*Gaṅgeśa's intention here is obscure. The above explanation of '*aprāmāṇyaprasaṅgāt*' is suggested by Gadādhara.

etatprāmāṇyasaṃśayapūrvakālīnaitajjñānaniścayāviṣayaḥ, etajjñānaniścayānantaraṃ sandihyamānatvāt, aprāmāṇyavat.

We say:[1] the truth of a knowledge which has not become familiar is not apprehended by its own substratum, nor is it apprehended by something other than its substratum.[2] For, its substratum being present it becomes the object of a doubt which occurs in the third moment after (the occurrence of) that (substratum); or because it is the object of a doubt which is not caused by (another) doubt about falsity; as in the case of falsity.[3] If there is certainty about the object, doubt about (that) object in the third moment after that certainty does not arise; or, it does not arise without there being (a prior) doubt about truth. Hence there is no contradiction with object.[4] The truth under controversy is not apprehended by all those (knowledges) which apprehend its substratum, for even when there is certainty about its own substratum, the truth is doubted in the third moment after that without any (other) doubt about falsity, like falsity.[5] Or, the truth of *this* knowledge which has not yet become familiar is not the object of that apprehension of this knowledge which just precedes the doubt about its truth, for this truth comes to be doubted immediately after apprehension of this knowledge, like falsity.[6]

NOTES

35.1. Gaṅgeśa now offers his own syllogistic formulation which though in substance the same as Udayana's yet differs in its form. He in fact gives a number of alternative formulations.

35.2. The *sādhya 'na svāśrayagrāhyam'* is also a source of some difficulty. God's knowledge or knowledge of a Yogin apprehends, according to the Nyāya, all knowledges and also their truths. They too could be called *'svāśraya'*. To avoid this, it is suggested that the *sādhya* should be modified into *'na yāvatsvāśrayagrāhyam'*.

The addition of *'svāśrayātiriktagrāhyatva'* to the *sādhya* shows that the argument is directed against the Prābhākaras only (for, on the Bhāṭṭa and the Miśra theories truth being apprehended by an inference and the *anuvyavasāya* respectively is already *svāśrayātiriktagrāhya*). There are some though who try to interpret this as directed against Mīmāṃsakas in general. But in that case the fallacy of *siddhasādhana* may be avoided if we could regard the Miśra *anuvyavasāya* and the Bhāṭṭa inference as also '*svāśraya*': this is possible insofar as these latter have partly the same form as the primary knowledge. In that case, the Miśras and the Bhāṭṭas also would not accept the *svāśrayātiriktagrāhyatva* of truth.*

Mathurānātha suggests a reason why this second *sādhya* is added. For the fact that truth is not apprehended by its own substratum is compatible with the possibility that it is not apprehended at all, a position not acceptable to the Naiyāyikas. The second *sādhya*, a more positive notion, is inserted with a view to excluding this unwelcome possibility. But Mathurānātha raises a fresh difficulty. The inference which according to the Nyāya apprehends truth may possibly be a compound judgment of the form 'This is silver, and this knowledge is true'; in that case, this knowledge also becomes a locus of the truth, a *svāśraya*, and since it does apprehend truth, it would provide an instance which contradicts the intended inference. In order to avoid this difficulty, Mathurānātha suggests that this expression should be modified into '*svāśrayātiriktamātragrāhya*'.

35.3. In this syllogism, the *pakṣa* is '*anabhyāsadaśāpannajñānaprāmāṇyam*', i.e. truth of all such knowledge which has not become familiar. The *sādhya* is absence of *svāśrayagrāhyatva* or simply *svāśrayātiriktagrāhyatva*. In order to prove this, Gaṅgeśa advances the following *hetu*: such truth often becomes the object of doubt exactly in the third moment after the occurrence of the knowledge whose truth it is. The *hetu* belongs to the *pakṣa*. According to the Nyāya a knowledge lasts for three moments: one for its origination, one for its bare existence and a third for its destruction. Now if the *svataḥ* theory is true then the knowledge is either accompanied by apprehension of its truth in the very first moment, or is followed by its own apprehension as well as by the apprehension of its truth in the second moment. In any

*See for example the *Tippaṇi* by Pandit Bacha Jha on Vardhamāna's *Prakāśa* on Udayana's *Nyāyakusumāñjali*, especially Chowkhamba edition, p. 222.

case, in the second moment after the origination of the knowledge there would persist the certainty about its truth. This certainty would then act as hindrance against the rise of any doubt in that truth in the very next moment. The fact that such doubt does occur in the very third moment after the occurrence of the substratum proves that the truth was not apprehended prior to it.

It should be noted that when earlier Gaṅgeśa had said that *prāmāṇyasya svato grahe'nabhyāsadaśotpannajñāne tatsaṃśayo na syāt* (see para 22), he was referring not to any and every doubt about truth, but only to the doubt which occurs in the third moment after the origination of the knowledge. This is again made clear by the alternative formulation of the *hetu*: the truth under consideration is the object of a doubt which is not due to any other doubt about falsity! This is meant to exclude all subsequent doubts so as to refer uniquely to the first doubt about the truth of that knowledge.

The alternative formulation may also have been given to circumvent the following difficulty. The adjective '*anabhyāsadaśāpanna*' may mean what does not permit any doubt about its truth in the third moment after its origination. But in that case the *hetu* is already contained in the *pakṣa*, which is not very desirable. Gaṅgeśa therefore gives another *hetu* which is in substance the same as the first one but looks different and unrecognisable in the *pakṣa*. Further, as Raghunātha points out, '*anabhyāsadaśāpannatva*' is not a limitor of the *pakṣa*, i.e. is not a *pakṣatāvacchedakadharma*, but is to be treated merely as its indicator (*paricāyaka*) whose function is to show up and point out the *pakṣa* ("*Anabhyāsadaśāpanneti hetoḥ svarūpasiddhipradarśanāya svarūpakathanamātram, na tu tadviśeṣaṇameva*"). The instance or *dṛṣṭānta* adduced is falsity. Falsity of a knowledge comes to be doubted in the third moment after the origination of the knowledge whose falsity it is, and it is also, as admitted by the Mīmāṃsakas, not apprehended *svataḥ*.

35.4. Is there *vyāpti* between the absence of *svatogrāhyatva* and the property of being an object of the above discussed kind of doubt? In order to dispel doubts about this, Gaṅgeśa argues in the following manner. It is never found that once we have certainty about any object whatsoever there still occurs doubt about the same object in the third moment after that certainty. There may be doubt only if there has been a prior doubt in the truth, but not in the absence of any such prior doubt. This shows that the required *vyāpti* does in fact hold good.

35.5. This new syllogism is substantially the same as the preceding one. It only extends the scope of the *pakṣa* to all truths of knowledges, and further it is especially directed against the Bhāṭṭa and the Miśra views.

35.6. This last formulation specifies the *pakṣa* by narrowing it down to any one knowledge and its truth: say, for example, this knowledge and its truth.

36. *Na ca svapadasya prāmāṇyamātraparatvāt tadāśrayāgrāhyatve* bādhaḥ; svapadasya sambandhiparatvena samabhivyāhṛtaparatvāt. Anyathā svasya paratvāt parasya ca svatvāt tadetattvasya tadetadanyatvasya** ca svaparasādhāraṇatvāt svataṇ parato veti saṃśayo na syāt. Prāmāṇyasya svagrāhyatve bādhāt pariśeṣeṇānyathāgrāhyatvaṃ paratogrāhyatvamiti kaścit. Prathamaṃ ca prāmāṇyajñānaṃ vyatirekiṇā. Nanu prāmāṇyaprasiddhiṃ vinā vyāptyagrahāt kathamanumānam, atha vyāghātadaṇḍabhayena pramā-tadviṣayasiddhau taddṛṣṭāntena jñeyatvādinā vahneḥ pramāviṣayatvamanumeyaṃ, tataśca sāmānyatastatsiddhau na sādhyāprasiddhiḥ.*

It cannot be said (against the above syllogism) that since the word '*sva*' refers only to truth, there would be contradiction if (the *sādhya* is) the property of not being apprehended by its locus.[1] For the word '*sva*' implies its correlative term so that its meaning depends upon what is used along with it. Otherwise since the *sva* may be *para* and the *para* may be *sva* and since the property of this being such and such as well as the property of this not being such and such are common to both the *sva* and the *para*, the very

*I have preferred '*tva*' to '*tvena*' and also to '*tve na*', and in this I have followed Mathurānātha.

**Here I have combined the two readings followed by the Kanchi and the Darbhanga editions.

doubt whether *svataḥ* or *parataḥ* should not have been there.[2] Since if truth is apprehended intrinsically there would be contradiction, therefore in the end some take it to be apprehended by an other, or as apprehended *ab extra*[3]. The first knowledge of truth is through a *vyatireki* inference[4]. It cannot be objected that without a knowledge of truth there is no apprehension of *vyāpti* and so how could there be inference. For, both true knowledge and its object are established for fear of the punishment of *vyāghāta*[5], so that it is possible to infer that fire is an object of true knowledge with the help of that instance and (*hetu* like) knowability etc. Then after truth in general has been established there cannot any more be the fallacy of the *sādhya* being unknown.

Notes

36.1. After having formulated his own syllogistic arguments, Gaṅgeśa anticipates the same objections which he had advanced against Udayana's formulation. Does not the word '*sva*' refer to truth in general? In that case, however, the *sādhya*, viz. '*svāśrayāgrāhyatvam*' becomes *aprasiddha* i.e. not known to exist. (Here again Mathurānātha comes to our aid by rightly pointing out that here '*tadāśrayāgrāhyatve*' means '*tadāśrayāgrāhyatve sādhye*', and also that here '*bādhaḥ*' should be taken to mean *aprasiddhiḥ*.) For, if *any* truth is designated by '*sva*', then every knowledge whatsoever is to be regarded as *svāśraya* so that the property of not being apprehended by its own locus becomes a non-existent property. Gaṅgeśa however circumvents this difficulty with the suggestion that the word '*sva*' is a relative term and has no sense without referring to the correlative word, so that in every case it should refer to the definite truth being talked about and not indefinitely to any truth.

36.2. If the word '*sva*' is not interpreted in the above manner as inseparable from its correlative, Gaṅgeśa argues, the words '*sva*' and '*para*' would lose their opposition, for both would apply to the same things, in which case the very doubt whether truth is *svataḥ* or *parataḥ* would be rendered pointless!

36.3. Why does Gaṅgeśa say '*kaścit*'? He is referring—so says

Mathurānātha—to a possible view according to which truth is apprehended *parataḥ* though not only *parataḥ*. This would be a position which is less stronger than Gaṅgeśa's own according to which truth is apprehended only *parataḥ*.

36.4. From here begins a new topic. How is the first truth known? The difficulty involved in this question may be brought out in the following manner. Is truth already known or is it unknown? If it is already known, how was it known? If it is not already known how can it be made the *sādhya* in the first inference of the form 'This knowledge is true, because . . .'?* Gaṅgeśa solves this difficulty by suggesting that our first apprehension of truth has the form of a *vyatirekī* inference. A *vyatirekī* inference is one which is based on a *vyatireka-vyāpti*. A *vyāpti* is positive or *anvayī* if it is the presence of the *sādhya* (e.g. fire) in all loci of the presence of the *hetu* (e.g. smoke), so that we can say wherever there is smoke there is fire. A *vyatireka-vyāpti*, on the other hand, is the fact that wherever there is the absence of the *sādhya* (namely, absence of fire) there is also the absence of the *hetu* (e.g. absence of smoke). When an inference is based on the latter kind of *vyāpti* it is called a *vyatirekī* inference. *Vyatireka-vyāpti* is more technically defined as *sādhyābhāvavyāpakābhāvapratiyogitva* i.e. the property of being the counterpositive of an absence which pervades the absence of the *sādhya*. In the example made use of here, smoke is the counterpositive of an absence (namely, of its own absence) which pervades the absence of fire, and this property of being the counterpositive in that way is the *vyatireka-vyāpti* which, as an entity, belongs to the smoke—generally speaking to the *hetu*. To put it simply, an inference is a *vyatirekī* one if it is based on the knowledge that wherever there is the absence of the *sādhya* there is also absence of the *hetu*. Now in the present case, the in-

*Thus writes Udayana—"*Prāmāṇyaṃ hi samarthapravṛttijanakatvānumeyaṃ, taccānvayavyatirekānumeyamiti. Nāpyanumānenānvayagrahaḥ prāmāṇyasya kvacidapyasiddheḥ, siddhau vā kimanumānena, anumānāntarasiddhatve ạnavasthaivetyata āha*" (*Pariśuddhi*, pp. 55-6). Vardhamāna explains as follows: "*Nanu prāmāṇyaṃ kvāpi prasiddhaṃ na vā? Ādye tatra hetorvṛttāvanvayitvamavṛttāvasādhāraṇyam. Antye vyatirekanirūpaṇe sādhyasandehasiṣādhayiṣāghaṭitapakṣatvānupapattiḥ*" (*ibid*, p. 55). The knowledge 'This knowledge is true' is impossible—Vardhamāna goes on—without a prior knowledge of the property 'truth'.

ference would have some such form as 'This knowledge is true, for, it possesses the property of causing successful activity (*samarthapravṛttijanakatvāt*)'. But this inference cannot be based on the knowledge that wherever there is this property there is also truth, for the man who is for the first time apprehending truth could not possibly point to some instance—as demanded by Indian logic—where coexistence of that property and *hetu* has been previously observed. Consequently, such a person can only appeal to a different knowledge, viz. that wherever there is absence of truth there is also absence of the said property of causing successful practice. For example, one could point to any case of an error leading to frustration.

36.5. To this of course the natural rejoinder would be that since the very notion of truth has not yet been established, how could anyone apprehend the said *vyāpti* which involves that notion. Is it not the case that the original difficulty has only been pushed one step backwards, but not really solved? Gaṅgeśa's reply then can proceed only on one line, and that line he does not fail to adopt: he has to show that the notion of truth is established through the very attempt to deny it. Take the denial 'There is no true knowledge'. Such a denial—as Raghunātha aptly points out —leads to contradiction, no matter whether the notion of truth is established or not ("*pramāyā niṣedhe kriyamāṇe tatsiddhyasiddhibhyāṃ vyāghātaḥ*"—*Dīdhiti*). For, if truth is there its denial is false; if truth is a fiction, then also its denial is absurd. The denial therefore to be significant requires that there should be true knowledge which on its part implies that there must be objects of such true knowledge. Thus the existence of true knowledge and that of the objects of such knowledge are established simultaneously. Once these two notions are established in this manner it is possible to infer in any given case that what we have is an object of true knowledge. In that case it cannot be said that the *sādhya* is unknown.

(Gaṅgeśa should not be supposed to mean that everyone of us acquires his first notion of truth in this manner. What he means is that once the philosophic doubt in the notion arises, one may dispel this doubt and rehabilitate the notion in the manner outlined, viz. by showing that a denial of this notion is self-stultifying.)

37. *Viśiṣyānirṇayānnānvayitvāsādhāraṇye. Na ca prāmāṇyaṃ nānugataṃ kintu pratijñānaṃ viṣayaprakārabhedādbhinnam, tathā ca vahnijñānasya vahnyavṛttiprakārānavacchinnatvādikaṃ sādhyaṃ taccāprasiddhamiti vācyaṃ, vahnijñānasya viśeṣyāvṛttiprakārānavacchinnatvādikaṃ sādhyamānaṃ pakṣadharmatābalena vahniviṣayakapramātve paryavasyatīti cet? Tarhi prathamaṃ kasyāpi svārthaṃ prāmāṇyānumānaṃ na syāt, prāmāṇyaniṣedharūpasya parakīyavyāghātasya tadā anupasthiteḥ svayaṃ prāmāṇyaniṣedhasya taddhīpūrvakatvāt prāmāṇyamaparijñāya prāmāṇyaniṣedhena parakīyavyāghātasyāpyajñānācca pravṛttisaṃvādavisaṃvādābhyāṃ taddhetujñānavaicitryānumānepi yathoktarūpaprāmāṇyasya viśeṣyāpratīteriti.*

Since there is no specific determination there is no *anvayitva*[1] and no (fallacy of) *asādhāraṇyam.*[2] It cannot also be said that since there is no common generic truth but truth is different in each knowledge owing to differences in (its) object and qualifier, therefore the *sādhya* in the case of (a) knowledge of fire is the property of not being limited by a qualifier which is absent in fire and this *sādhya* is unknown. For, if in the case of knowledge of fire the *sādhya* is taken to be the property of not being limited by a qualifier that is absent in the qualificandum, then that would amount —by virtue of being a property of the *pakṣa*—to the (specific) truth of that knowledge which has fire for its object.[3] But in that case no one could have at first a *svārtha* inference about truth.[4] For the contradiction by the other in the form of a denial of truth is at that time absent. One cannot oneself deny truth for that denial presupposes a prior knowledge of it. Even if there is a denial of truth without a prior knowledge of truth, one remains ignorant of the contradiction in the other's denial.[5] Even if one may infer from success and failure of the activities that the knowledges causing them are different in nature, yet truth as described before is not specifically apprehended.[6]

NOTES

37.1. Gaṅgeśa has already said that the first inference of truth must be a *vyatirekī* one. But why is an *anvayī* inference said to be impossible in this case? The reason is given now. An *anvayī* inference of truth should have the following form: 'This knowledge of fire is true, for it has the capacity of giving rise to successful activity; wherever there is such capacity, there is truth.' But the inference would not be complete unless we can adduce an instance in which the relation of positive co-presence between the capacity for producing successful activity and the property of truth has been previously apprehended. But if the inference is to be the *first* inference of truth, no positive instance of the above-mentioned kind is available at hand, for no other knowledge could have been previously known to be true: hence the impossibility of an *anvayī* inference in such a case as this. A *vyatirekī* inference however does not give rise to this difficulty, for the *vyatireka-vyāpti* of the form 'Wherever there is absence of truth there is also absence of the capacity for producing successful activity' can well be apprehended in any case of *error* known to us before. Gaṅgeśa is obviously making the rather questionable assumption that though truth has not yet been known falsity has been.

37.2. Consider now the *vyatirekī* inference, 'This knowledge of fire is true, for it has the capacity of giving rise to successful practice; whatever is not true has not this capacity; as in the case of error'. Does not this inference commit the fallacy called '*asādhāraṇyam*'? The fallacy of *asādhāraṇyam* arises when the *hetu* is absent in both *sapakṣa* and *vipakṣa*.* By '*sapakṣa*' are meant those cases where the *sādhya* is known to exist for certain (*sādhyavattayā niścitaḥ*). By '*vipakṣa*' are meant those cases where *sādhya* is known for certain to be absent (*sādhyaśūnyatayā niścitaḥ*). Now a *hetu* is *asādhāraṇa* if it is absent both in *sapakṣa* cases and in *vipakṣa* cases. In effect it is present only in the *pakṣa* (which by definition is neither *sapakṣa* nor *vipakṣa*). In the present inference, the *hetu* is 'the capacity for giving rise to successful activity'. It is not present in *vipakṣa*, namely in false cognitions. It is also not known to be present in *sapakṣa*, namely in true knowledges, for no such true knowledge has, *ex hypothesis*, been yet ascertained.

* '*Yastūbhayasmādvyāvṛttaḥ sa cāsādhāraṇo mataḥ*' (*Bhāṣāparicchedaḥ*, Kārikā 73). The stock Nyāya example of this fallacy is 'Sound is non-eternal, because of soundness'.

To this objection Gaṅgeśa replies that since truth has not yet been ascertained, in other words since no *sapakṣa* has yet been known, it is too early to say that the *hetu* is absent in *sapakṣa*. The objection that the *vyatirekī* inference involves the fallacy of *asādhāraṇyam* is therefore untenable. This objection holds good only where the *sapakṣa* has been ascertained but has been found to lack the *hetu*.*

37.3. What has been established through demonstrating the absurdity of a denial of truth is nothing more than truth in general. But truth of each definite knowledge is something specific and determinate. For example, in the case of a knowledge of fire truth is 'the property of having fireness as qualifier in relation to a qualificandum which possesses fireness'. How can I then make my first inference about truth when the specific truth of the knowledge concerned is still unknown to me? It seems we are back in the same fallacy of *sādhyāprasiddhi*. Gaṅgeśa replies to this objection in the following manner. Let the *sādhya* be the general truth defined as before. But due to what is called '*pakṣa-dharmatā*' i.e. the belonging of a property to the *pakṣa*, what comes to be inferred is not the general truth, but the truth which is resident in the specific knowledge under consideration. (In the stock example of an inference 'The hill is fiery, because it possesses smoke', the *sādhya* is no doubt fire, but what is inferred is not fire in general but hill-fire, *parvatīyavahni*.)

37.4. A fresh objection is considered. If for my notion of truth I have to depend upon a demonstration of the absurdity of a denial of it, how then can I make my first *svārthānumāna* or inference-for-myself about truth in which case I do not have an other before me, where I am not arguing with another person? In a *svārtha* inference I argue out for myself. The other who is to deny truth is not there for me. If there is no denial by another person, how do I then arrive at the notion of truth?

*Thus Vardhamāna writes in *Prakāśa* on *Pariśuddhi*: "... *sapakṣatvābhāvāt tatra hetoravṛttāvapi nāsādhāraṇyamityarthaḥ. Etena nirvikalpakepi hetoravṛttāvasādhāraṇyamapāstam. Vastutaḥ asādhāraṇyasya satpratipakṣotthāpakatayā viśeṣādarśanadaśāyāmeva doṣatvenānityadoṣatvāt na prakṛte taditi bhāvaḥ*" (p. 58).

37.5. This difficulty cannot be circumvented by saying that I myself make this denial, and then establish the notion of truth through convincing myself of the absurdity involved in that denial. Such an account is not acceptable, for I cannot make a denial without having a prior knowledge of the *pratiyogi* or counter-positive. I cannot deny truth without having a prior notion of truth, and yet it is such a notion which I am, *ex hypothesis*, after. Further, even if it is granted that there is an other who denies, the situation is no more promising, for being without a prior notion of truth I am not in a position to realise the contradiction involved in the other's denial.

37.6. Is it then possible to infer truth (and falsity) from perception of the success (and failure) of the activities to which different cognitions lead us? Differences in the effects must be due to some differences in their causes, and the latter differences are nothing other than differences in truth value. Gaṅgeśa agrees that we shall indeed be justified in inferring that there must be some major difference in the characters of cognitions, some of which lead to successful practice and others to failure. But we are not entitled to infer that those that lead to success are *true* and those that do not are *false* if we do not possess some prior notion of truth and falsity.

38. *Ucyate—prāgbhavīyasaṃskārādviśeṣyāvṛttyaprakārakatvaṃ tadvati tatprakārakajñānatvaṃ vā prāmāṇyamātraṃ smṛtaṃ vahnijñānādau sādhyamānaṃ sarvanāmamahimnā pakṣadharmatābalādvahnijñānasya viśeṣyāvṛttyaprakārakatvādau paryavasyati. Svataḥ prāmāṇyaniṣedhe prāthamikaprāmāṇyajñānasyānyathopapādayitumaśakyatvāditi sampradāyavidaḥ.*

Vayantu brūmaḥ—prathamamaprāmāṇyābhāva eva prāmāṇyaṃ vyatirekiṇā sādhyaṃ, tata eva niṣkampapravṛtterupapatteḥ, tadeva vā sidhyat pakṣadharmatābalena tadvati tatprakārakatvādikamādāya sidhyati, tadanantaram arthādvā sidhyatīti vakṣyate.

Tathāhi—Ayaṃ vahnitvenānubhavo vahnitvābhāvavati vahnitvaprakārako na, avahnivṛttiprakārako na, viśeṣyāvṛttiprakārako na, vahnitvaprakārakatve sati vahnyaviśeṣyako na, vahnitvavyadhikaraṇaprakārāvacchinno na, vahnyavṛtti-

prakārako na vā; dāhasamarthaviṣayakaprayatnajanakatve sati vahnitvaprakārakaniścayatvāt, dāhasamarthaviśeṣyaka-vahnitvaprakārakaniścayatvādvā. Yannaivaṃ tannaivaṃ yathā vahnyapramā.

It is being said—mere truth, either as the property of not having for its qualifier something absent in the qualificandum or as the property of being a knowledge whose qualifier is present in the qualificandum, is remembered owing to traces left over from past lives. This (truth) when made the *sādhya* in the case of a knowledge like that of fire amounts, with the aid of pronouns and by virtue of the property belonging to the *pakṣa,* to the property of not having a qualifier that is absent in the qualificandum of (specific knowledges like) the knowledge of fire. Because, there is no other way of accounting for the first knowledge of truth in case intrinsic truth is denied. This is the view of a school (of Naiyāyikas).[1]

We however say the following. At first truth in the sense of absence of falsity is established with the help of a *vyatirekī*, for unhesitating activity is explained by it. Or, after establishing that it is possible to prove the properties like that of having a qualifier which belongs to the qualificandum with the help of the *pakṣa* possessing the property (which it does). Afterwards it may be proved from the nature of the object. This would be said (below).[2]

Thus: this knowledge having fireness as its qualifier is not a knowledge whose qualifier is fireness but whose (corresponding qualificandum lacks fireness; (it is) not a knowledge whose qualifier is present in what is other than fire; (it is) not a knowledge whose qualifier is absent in the qualificandum; (it is) not a knowledge whose qualifier is fireness but whose qualificandum is not fire; (it is) not a knowledge which is limited by a qualifier that is never present in the same locus as fireness; (it is) not a knowledge whose qualifier is absent in fire. For, it is a certain knowledge which while giving rise to effort in respect of an object which is able to burn has at the same time fireness for its qualifier; or, because it is a certain knowledge with fireness as its qualifier and something capable of burning as its qualificandum.

Whatever has not this has not that, as in the case of a false knowledge of fire.[3]

Notes

38.1. After showing certain difficulties in the suggested explanations as to how we come to have our first knowledge of truth, Gaṅgeśa offers to more. One of these two is attributed to some Nyāya school (*sampradāya*) and the other is his own view. According to the first explanation, truth in general is remembered from traces left by past lives—remembered in the sense that traces left from past lives are awakened. One could say that the notion of truth, according to this view, is *recollected* in the Platonic sense, and one could even suggest that on this view the notion is *a priori* in the original Platonic sense of that term. The notion could not have been derived from any conceivable empirical situation, for any such situation would be found to presuppose the concept of truth. It must therefore have been 'recollected'. When the general notion of truth which is *a priori* is predicated of a specific knowledge, we have virtually the specific truth of that specific knowledge.

38.2. Gaṅgeśa's own explanation is different. He does not favour the Platonic theory, though he does not give reasons why he does not accept it. Possibly, he like most philosophers thinks the notion of 'recollection' too vague to be satisfying. Our first apprehension of truth, according to Gaṅgeśa's own theory, is not of truth as a positive notion. It could only be of truth as a negative concept, understood as the absence of falsity. It is this absence of falsity which is first proved with the help of a *vyatirekī* inference (see note 36.4). Virtually, that would amount to proving the positive truth. If necessary, the positive truth may then be separately proved once the absence of falsity has been proved. Or else, the former may simply follow from the latter by implication (*arthāt*).

38.3. Gaṅgeśa next hastens to offer a series of such *vyatirekī* inferences. In each case the *pakṣa* is a specific knowledge 'This is fire'. The *sādhya* is absence of falsity (in accordance with

Gaṅgeśa's own theory outlined just now). The six different *sādhyas* are six different formulations of what amounts to the same. Thus there are six different syllogisms. The *hetu*, to put the matter short, is the capacity for producing successful effort in respect of burning. The *vyāpti* (which is to be a *vyatirekī* one) is formulated negatively. The instance adduced in favour of the *vyāpti* is any known case of error having the same judgmental form 'This is fire'.

The 'this' in 'This fire' is explained by Raghunātha as meaning that the *pakṣa* is to be taken as any substantive as determined by the corresponding determinant character (*dharmitāvaccheda-viśiṣṭe dharmiṇi vahnitvaprakārako'nubhavaḥ*). The implication is that the *pakṣa* includes *all* the various knowledges in which 'fire' functions as predicate.

There is some difficulty about the second of the six *sādhyas* i.e. about 'the absence of *avahnivṛttiprakārakatva*'. Now consider the right knowledge 'This is fire'. Here of course the qualifier 'fireness' is not present in what is not fire. But consider the true knowledge 'The substance is fire' ('*Dravyam vahniḥ*'): here one of the qualifiers namely substancehood (*dravyatva*) is present in not-fire as well, so that this knowledge though true becomes '*avahnivṛttiprakāraka*'. An inference which has this as its *sādhya* would in that case stand contradicted. It should however be noted that though substancehood is present in not-fire, it is not present in not-fire alone. Raghunātha therefore proposes to restate the *sādhya* as '*yatra vahnitvaṃ prakārastatra avahnimātra-vṛttiprakārako na*' thereby meaning 'where fireness is the qualifier there nothing should be a qualifier which resides only in not-fire'. It is now clear that the knowledge 'The substance is fire' satisfies this description, for substancehood does not reside in not-fire alone. But why does Raghunātha add '*yatra vahnitvaṃ prakārastatra*'? Consider again the following hypothetical case: a fire and a thing that is not fire (but simulates fire) are together apprehended as fire, the knowledge having the form 'These two are fires' ('*Imau vahnī*'). This knowledge has 'fireness' as its qualifier. But taking the 'thisness' which resides in not-fire we could say that even the knowledge of the fire as fire is false inso-far as that 'thisness' which resides only in not-fire has been used as a qualifier. This however is absurd, for that part of the knowledge which predicates 'fireness' of the fire is certainly true. To avoid such cases of contradiction, Raghunātha adds the qualifying phrase '*yatra* etc.', intending thereby that in a valid knowledge of fire any property residing only in not-fire should not be a qualifier precisely with regard to that substantive which is qualified by 'fireness'.

The second *sādhya* as thus rewritten contains the phrase '*avahnimātravṛttiprakārako na*'. Now '*avahnimātravṛttitvam*' means '*vahnyavṛttitve sati avahnivṛttitvam*': the qualifier of a true knowledge of fire should (*i*) not be absent in fire and (*ii*) should not be present in not-fire. It may easily be seen that the first condition, namely that the qualifier should not be '*vahnyavṛtti*' suffices to ward off the apparently recalcitrant cases discussed above. The second part, namely the further requirement that the qualifier should not reside in not-fire would then be redundant. Raghunātha points out that this is the reason why Gaṅgeśa adds his sixth *sādhya* which is '*vahnyavṛttiprakārako na*'.

Let us now turn to the two *hetus*. The first *hetu* is: '*dāhasamarthaviṣayakaprayatnajanakatve sati vahnitvaprakārakaniścayatvam*' or the property of being a certainty which has fireness as its qualifier while at the same time causing effort directed towards something capable of burning as its object. The knowledge 'This is fire' whose truth we are seeking to establish should have the capacity of causing effort which would successfully lead to something capable of burning. But the capacity for causing effort belongs, strictly speaking, to perceptual certainty, so that if this *hetu* is to be retained then the word '*anubhava*' in the *pakṣa* is to be understood in the strict sense of perceptual knowledge. If however the *pakṣa* is to be regarded as meaning all kinds of knowledge, direct and indirect, then this *hetu* is to be abandoned in favour of the second one which reads simply as '*dāhasamarthaviśeṣyakavahnitvaprakārakaniścayatvam*' meaning the property of being a certainty whose qualifier is 'fireness' and whose qualificandum is something capable of burning. But a certainty may have both 'fireness' as its qualifier and something capable of burning as its qualificandum, and yet it may be false. As an example, consider the case discussed above, namely the case of the knowledge where we apprehend two things, one fire and another not, together as fires, expressed in the judgment 'These two are fires' ('*Imau vahnī*'). Here fireness is a qualifier, and fire is a qualificandum, and yet the knowledge is not true. Raghunātha therefore proposes to further modify it so as to mean that the property of having the said qualificandum must be limited (*avacchinna*) by the other property of having the said qualifier. The net result would be that the two conditions imposed would not remain two separate conditions to be jointly satisfied, but would constitute one complex condition, namely that in the present case fireness should be the qualifier only insofar as fire is concerned: "*Dāhasamarthamātre vahnitvaprakārakatvantu phalitārthaḥ*" (*Dīdhiti*).

Raghunātha also raises the question about the necessity of '*niścayatva*' in the *hetu*. Would it not do if the *pakṣa* be simply a cognition having the requisite properties as stated in the *hetus*? Now ordinarily a *niścaya* or certainty is one which is other than doubt. We are to see if by omitting '*niścayatva*' from the *hetu*, the *hetu* would not turn out to be fallacious. The only interesting case that has to be looked into is that of doubt which would then possess the *hetu* as thus truncated, but would it also possess the *sādhya* or any of the six *sādhyas*? For this purpose, let us divide all doubts into two kinds: (*a*) I may doubt about fireness in fire. This happens when looking at real fire (at some distance perhaps) I ask myself 'Is this fire or not?' (*b*) Or, I may have doubt about 'fireness' in not-fire. This may very well happen if seeing red colour in the horizon I ask 'Is this fire or not?' Both doubts have the same linguistic form '*Idam vahniḥ na vā*'. Taking (b) first, we find that it contains neither the *hetu* nor the first *sādhya*, for its object being not-fire has not the capacity for burning and one of its qualifiers, namely 'fireness', is absent in the qualificandum which is not-fire *ex hypothesis*. So far as (b) is concerned we are not therefore put into any trouble by dropping '*niścayatva*' from the *hetu*: the truncated *hetu* does not turn out *vyabhicārī*: where the *sādhya* is absent it too is absent. Consider now (a): we find that the *hetu* as truncated is present, for the object of effort (or, according to the second *hetu*, the qualificandum of the knowledge) is a real fire which burns, and besides 'fireness' is one of the qualifiers. The first *sādhya* is also present inasmuch as the 'fireness' which is a qualifier is in fire and not in not-fire. There is also no trouble here, for the *hetu* coexists with the *sādhya*. It would seem therefore that '*niścayatva*' in the usual sense of 'being other than doubt' is redundant. Raghunātha therefore explains '*niścayatva*' in a different way and takes it to mean '*ekatra vastuto viruddhobhayāvagāhibhinnatvam*'. A knowledge would be called a '*niścaya*', according to this explanation, only if it does not have two qualifiers that are in fact (*vastuto*) incompatibles. Raghunātha says "*vastuto*", for the incompatibilily may not be apparent. In the case of doubt it is apparent; the two alternatives are logical contradictories, A and not-A. But when the two are logical contraries, the incompatibility may not at once become apparent. Now if '*niścayatva*' means the absence of such incompatibility, then—Raghunātha points out*—mere '*vahnitvaprakārakaniścayatva*' i.e. the property of being a *niścaya* which has 'fireness' as its qualifier would suffice for proving the second *sādhya*. For, in every case of knowledge where the *sādhya* is absent i.e. where a qualifier resides only in not-fire, the *hetu* also would be absent, for in all such cases two incompatible properties, one residing only in fire and the other residing only in not-fire, would be qualifying the same knowledge so that the sort of *niścayatva* explained above would be absent in such cases.

Consider now the third *sādhya* which is '*viśeṣyāvṛttyaprakārakatva*' or the property of not having a qualifier which is absent in the qualificandum. Take the already familiar case of the knowledge where fireness is predicated of two things, one fire and another not-fire. The *hetu*, namely '*dāhasamarthaviśeṣyakavahnitvaprakārakaniścayatvam*' is present (taking '*niścayatva*' in the ordinary sense of being other than doubt), but the *sādhya* is absent inasmuch as the qualifier 'fireness' is absent in one of the qualificanda, viz. in not-fire. The *hetu* then becomes an illegitimate one. It should therefore be modified into '*dāhasamarthamātraviśeṣyakavahnitvaprakārakaniścayatvam*', so that if 'fireness' is the qualifier only fire is to be the qualificandum.

Consider however another case. Fire may be either fire in grass or fire in substances other than grass. The former is called

*Raghunātha actually writes "*dvitīye ca niścayamātraṃ hetuḥ*". But mere *niścayatva* may easily be shown to be a fallacious *hetu*. Hence we should take him to mean that the *hetu* that suffices to prove the second *sādhya* is *vahnitvaprakārakaniścayatva*.

'*tārṇa*' and the latter '*atārṇa*'. Let us call the former 'grass-fire' and the latter 'not-grassfire'. Now it is possible to mistake a grass-fire as one of the other kind. In this case the qualificandum is fire and nothing else, and a qualifier is 'fireness': the *hetu* is therefore present. But one of the qualifiers 'the property of being in not-grass' (*atārṇatva*) is absent in the qualificandum (which, by hypothesis, is a grass-fire). The *sādhya* is therefore absent. The *hetu* then becomes an illegitimate one. With a view to avoiding such ruinous consequences, Raghunātha proposes further modifications in the *hetu* by way of inserting into it the adjective '*viśeṣyāvrttivahnitvanyūnavṛttyaprakāraka*' which, in effect, would lay down a fresh stipulation that there should be no qualifier which is both non-resident in the qualificandum and is pervaded by fireness. In the present case one of the qualifiers, namely '*atārṇatva*' is a property that is both non-resident in the qualificandum which is grass-fire, and is pervaded by fireness (inasmuch as wherever there is *atārṇatva* there is fireness, though not vice versa). Therefore the *hetu*, if modified as proposed, becomes absent in the *pakṣa* and so does not become illegitimate. Lest it may be objected that this new adjective inserted into the *hetu* is, in part, identical with the *sādhya* (which is but '*viśeṣyāvṛttyaprakārakatva*'), Raghunātha adds that the total qualified absence denoted by this inserted adjectival phrase is different from the mere '*viśeṣyāvṛttyaprakārakatva*' (on the same principle which shows that the absence of hilly fire is different from the absence of fire).

Consider now the following case of a knowledge (of the so-called '*samūhālambana*' type) which together apprehends a fire as a fire and a piece of cloth as a paper. The *hetu*, namely '*dāhasamarthamātre vahnitvaprakārakatvam*' is present, for-here fireness qualifies only fire and nothing else. The *sādhya* however is absent insofar as one of the qualifiers 'paper-ness' is absent in its qualificandum which by hypothesis is really a piece of cloth. In order to avoid such a possibility of reducing the *hetu* to an illegitimate one, Raghunātha suggests that the *sādhya* should be restated thus: '*Yatra vahnitvaprakārakastatra na viśeṣyāvṛttiprakārakaḥ*', which means that precisely with regard to that qualificandum which has been qualified by 'fireness' there should be no qualifier that is non-resident in the qualificandum. In this sense, of course, the *sādhya* is present in the case under consideration, and therefore the *hetu* is not really illegitimate.

39. *Tatra bādhānantaraṃ smṛtyupanīte bhrame vahnitvābhāvavati vahnitvena mama jñānaṃ vṛttamityaprāmāṇyaṃ manasaiva paricchidyate mānāntareṇa veti sarvasiddham. Evaṃ vahnyapramāyāṃ vahnitvābhāvavati vahnitvaprakārakatvādisamarthapravṛttijanakatvābhāvayorvyāptigrahe 'prāmāṇyavyāpakahetvabhāvābhāvarūpāddhetoraprāmāṇyābhāvarūpaṃ sādhyaṃ siddhyati. Yadvyāpakatayā hetvabhāvo gṛhītastadabhāva eva hetunā sādhyate. Yatra tvabhāvasya vyāpakatā hetvabhāvasya jñāyate tatra sādhyaprasiddhiraṅgaṃ, tāṃ vinā tadajñānāt. Yatra tu bhāvavyāpakatā hetvabhāvasya tatra na tadaṅgaṃ, tena vināpi vyatirekavyāptergrahāt. Ata evetaravyāpakatā ākāśatvābhāvasya gṛhītetyākāśatvenāprasiddha evetarānyonyābhāvaḥ sidhyati.*

Now after correction the erroneous knowledge is presented through memory. In it its falsity is perceived by the mind in the form 'my knowledge was of fireness in what lacks fire'. Or it may be known by other means. So far it is acceptable to all.[1] Similarly, there is apprehension of *vyāpti*, in (an) erroneous knowledge of fire, between the property of being a knowledge which has as its qualifier 'fireness' in what lacks fireness and absence of the capacity for causing successful activity. The *hetu* consequently is of the nature of the negation of the negation of itself, and this latter negation is the pervader of falsity. This *hetu* therefore can serve to prove the *sādhya* which is the absence of falsity. The *hetu* can prove the absence of that alone as whose pervader the absence of *hetu* is apprehended.[2] Where the absence of the *hetu* is known as the pervader of a negation there the *sādhya* must necessarily have been known previously, for without it that is not known. Where however the absence of the *hetu* is known as the pervader of something positive, there that is not necessary, for the *vyatireka-vyāpti* is apprehended without that.[3] Therefore, if it is known that absence of *ākāśatva* pervades what is other than *ākāśa*, then even when it is not known as *ākāśa*, its difference from what is other than *ākāśa* may be proved.[4]

Notes

39.1. Gaṅgeśa has said that the first apprehension of truth is not of truth quâ truth, but of truth taken as the absence of falsity. At this point it may be asked, whence do we then have our notion of falsity? Gaṅgeśa seems to anticipate this objection, and suggests an answer which runs as follows: as soon as an erroneous knowledge, say of fire, is corrected, we say 'My knowledge was of fire, but the object of my knowledge lacked fireness'. This amounts to saying that my knowledge was *vahnitvābhāvavati vahnitvaprakārakam*. This is the same as apprehending the falsity of my previous knowledge of fire. That knowledge itself being now dead and gone, my apprehension of it could only be through memory, though my apprehension of its truth may be, as said above, either perceptual or inferential. In any case, we do have in this way an apprehension of the falsity of the knowledge. After saying that falsity is apprehended by 'some other means', Gaṅgeśa expects no controversy about this (*iti sarvasiddham*), for, the Mīmāṃsaka also would concede that falsity is apprehended inferentially.*

39.2. The *sādhya* (of the first inference of truth) is, roughly speaking, absence of falsity, whereas the *hetu*, again roughly speaking, is the capacity for producing appropriate and successful effort. Further, we have been told that this inference is to be a *vyatirekī* one. The *vyāpti* then on which it will be based is definable as a relation of pervasion between the absence of *sādhya* and the absence of *hetu*, such that the latter absence is the pervader of the former. In the present case it should be the relation of pervasion between falsity (=absence of absence of falsity) and absence of the said capacity for producing successful effort. This *vyāpti* may well be apprehended in the instance of erroneous knowledge discussed in note 39.1.

The *hetu* of this inference also satisfies the required test for rightly functioning in a *vyatirekī* inference. For, the *hetu* should

*The inference is thus formulated by Mathurānātha in the case of a false knowledge of fire: '*vahnitvaprakārakatvena jñānaṃ pakṣīkṛtya vahnitvābhāvavadviśeṣyakapravṛttijanakatvahetunā vahnitvābhāvavadviśeṣyakatvasādhane arthādaprāmāṇyasiddheḥ*' (*Māthurī*, p, 257).

—according to the very definition of a *vyatireka-vyāpti*—possess the counterpositiveness of a negation that is the pervader of the absence of the *sādhya* (*sādhyābhāvavyāpakābhāvapratiyogitva*). This requirement is fulfilled in the present case, for, we can apprehend in any instance of erroneous cognition that wherever there is falsity (=absence of absence of falsity) there is also absence of the capacity for producing successful effort.

39.3. Gaṅgeśa anticipates a fresh objection. Let the notion of falsity be known in this manner, but what about the present *sādhya*, viz. 'absence of falsity'? It may very well be that 'absence of falsity' is a notion with which we are not yet acquainted. How then could this inference take place? In reply, Gaṅgeśa explains that acquaintance with the *sādhya* is not always necessary. In other words, *sadhyāprasiddhi* is not always a defect. The general rule is that where the absence of the *sādhya* (which is pervaded by the absence of the *hetu*) is treated as a positive entity, prior knowledge of the *sādhya* is not to be presupposed; where however the *sādhyābhāva* as pervaded by the *hetvabhāva* is regarded as a negative entity, the *sādhya* must be known previously, for otherwise its negation could not be apprehended.

Let us consider the example 'The hill possesses absence of smoke, for there is absence of fire'. In this case, the absence of *hetu*=absence of the absence of fire. The absence of *sādhya*= absence of the absence of smoke. Now the *vyāpti* may be apprehended in either of two ways. It may be either apprehended as between the absence of the absence of smoke and the absence of the absence of fire, the latter being the pervader of the former. Or, it may be apprehended as that between just smoke and fire (since the absence of the absence of smoke may be regarded as being the same as just smoke, and so in the other case). Now if in my inference I have apprehended the *vyāpti* in the second form, no prior knowledge of the *sādhya* (in this case, of the absence of smoke) is called for, a knowledge of smoke being all that is required. If however the *vyāpti* is apprehended in the first form, then of course for apprehending the absence of the obsence of smoke a prior apprehension of its counterpositive i.e. of the absence of smoke (which is the *sādhya* in our example) is necessary.

Gaṅgeśa seems to be arguing that in the present case, the

sādhya being the absence of falsity, the absence of *sādhya* may be treated simply as falsity which is a positive notion, and therefore, in accordance with the above rule, a prior acquaintance with the *sādhya* i.e. absence of falsity is not called for.

39.4. This is an example of the principle just laid down. Where it is sought to be proved that something possesses difference from what is not *ākāśa* on the ground that it possesses *ākāśatva*, one has to depend on a *vyatireka-vyāpti* which may be stated as follows: wherever there is absence of difference from what is not *ākāśa* there is absence of *ākāśatva*. This may be restated as: whatever is not *ākāśa* (or, whatever possesses identity with not-*ākāśa*, *itaratādātmya* according to Pakṣadhara) possesses absence of *ākāśatva*. If the *vyāpti* is apprehended in this form, i.e. if the *sādhyābhāva* is apprehended as a positive something, the inference would be valid even if the *sādhya* is not known previously as being the same as *ākāśa*: there would be no fallacy of *sādhyāprasiddhi*.

40. *Viśeṣaṇajñānaṃ vinā kathaṃ prāmāṇyaviśiṣṭānumitiriti cet? Prathamaṃ na kathañcit. Jñāne prāmāṇyamityanumityanantaraṃ tenaiva hetunā tatraiva prāmāṇyaviśiṣṭānumitiḥ, abhāvaviśeṣyakapratītyanantaramabhāvavadbhūtalamiti jñānavat.*

Evañca vahnitvaprakārakajñānaṃ tadvati tadabhāvavati veti saṃśayānantaraṃ tadabhāvavati tatprakārakatvavyatirekaḥ sidhyan tadvati tatprakārakatāmādāya sidhyati, tṛtīyaprakārābhāvena tena vinā sādhyasyopasaṃhartumaśakyatvāt, jñānanityatvavat.

Yadvā idaṃ vahnitvaprakārakajñānaṃ vahnitvavadviṣayakaṃ vahnitvābhāvavadviṣayakatve sati saviṣayakatvāt, yannaivaṃ tannaivaṃ yathā vahnyaprameti vyatirekyantarāttatsiddhiḥ.

How can there be inference (of something) as qualified by truth when there is no (prior) knowledge of the adjective? This is not anyhow possible to start with. After the inference 'There is truth in the knowledge', there can be inference with the help of the same *hetu* and with regard to the same (locus) that it is qualified by truth; just as the knowledge 'The floor (is) qualified by the absence' arises soon after the knowledge having (that) absence as the qualificandum.[1]

Thus after the doubt whether this knowledge with fireness for its qualifier is of something possessing fireness or of something that possesses the absence of fireness, we prove that it is not a knowledge whose qualifier is absent in its qualificandum; after this is proved the property of having a qualifier which is present in its qualificandum is proved; for, the *sādhya* cannot be established without that, there being no third (possible) form; as in the case of the eternality of knowledge.[2]

Or, this knowledge with fireness for its qualifier has for its object something possessing fireness, for it has an object although it has not for its object something lacking fireness. Whatever is not like this is also not so; as in the case of an erroneous apprehension of fire. This can thus be established through another *vyatirekī* inference.[3]

NOTES

40.1. "*Prāmāṇyaviśiṣṭa*" in the text should here be understood to mean '*aprāmāṇyābhāvaviśiṣṭa*', for till now we have inferred truth only in the negative sense of absence of falsity. The objection suggested and then answered by Gaṅgeśa is this: how can I have a *viśiṣṭabuddhi* without a prior knowledge of the *viśeṣaṇa*? This is to appeal to the celebrated Nyāya rule that a knowledge of a qualified entity presupposes a prior apprehension of the qualifiers though not as qualifiers. The inference if it is to take the form 'This knowledge is true', requires a prior knowledge of truth, and this is what we do not *ex hypothesis* have as yet. To this objection Gaṅgeśa replies that the first inference is not of the above-mentioned form. Its form is much simpler. At first we simply infer 'There is truth in this knowledge'. Subsequently we have the knowledge 'This knowledge is true'. The former has the form 'p in S', the latter has the form 'S is p'. For the former type of knowledge an acquaintance with p is not presupposed. The same happens in the case of apprehension of absence. At first we have knowledge of the form 'There is absence of jar on the floor', in which the negation functions as the substantive.

After this however we have the other knowledge 'The floor possesses the absence of jar' in which the negation qualifies the floor.

40.2. Gaṅgeśa next proceeds to show formally how the predication of positive truth in the sense of *tadvati tatprakārakatva* follows logically from denial of falsity. *Tadabhāvavati tatprakārakatva* and *tadvati tatprakārakatva* are logical contradictories, there being no other third possibility (*tṛtīyaprakārābhāvena*). When one is denied the other must have to be asserted. The example *'jñānanityatvavat'* refers according to Mathurānātha to the following inference: 'the universe is due to a knowledge, for it is an effect (*kṣitirjñānajanyā kāryyatvāt*). The universe is obviously not due to any finite knowledge, therefore (*anityajñānabādhena*) it must be due to an eternal knowledge, finiteness a.. ˍternality being logical contradictories'.

40.3. The "*vahnitvavadviṣayakam*" in the text really means *vahnitvavadviśeṣyakam*. Gaṅgeśa adds this alternative form of *vyatirekī* inference for those who refuse to identify truth with the mere absence of falsity. Since this knowledge has some object but again since its object is not what lacks fireness—as has already been proved—therefore its object does possess fireness. It is therefore true.

41. *Atiriktaviṣayatāpakṣe ayaṃ vahnitvenānubhavo'vahnivṛttivahnitvaprakārakaviṣayatāko na, vahnitvāsamānādhikaraṇavahnitvaprakārakaviṣayatāko na, viṣayatāśrayāvṛttiprakārako na veti sādhyaṃ, vahnivṛttivahnitvaprakārakaviṣayatākatvaṃ viṣayatāśrayavṛttiprakārakatvaṃ vā arthāt sidhyati, na tu prathamaṃ, sādhyāprasiddheḥ. Vahnibhrame ca viṣayatāśrayo na vahniḥ, viṣayatāyā viśeṣyavṛttitvāditi bhramatvena na siddhasādhanam. Anye tu vahnibhrame yā viśeṣaṇavṛttiviṣayatā sā viśeṣyavṛttiviṣayatāyā abhinneti na sā vahnitvāsamānādhikaraṇadharmānavacchinneti na siddhasādhanamiti.*

On the theory that there is an additional *viṣayatā*[1]: this apprehension having fireness for its qualifier is not one whose *viṣayatā* is qualified by fireness but is present in not-fire; (it) is not one whose *viṣayatā* though qualified by fireness is not present in the same locus as fireness; (it is) not one whose qualifier is absent in the locus of *viṣayatā*; this is the *sādhya*.[2] The property of having a *viṣayatā* whose qualifier is fireness and which is present in fire, or the property of having a qualifier which is present in the locus of *viṣayatā* follows by implication, but cannot be at first proved owing to the fallacy of the *sādhya* being (then) unknown.[3] In the case of an erroneous apprehension of fire however the locus of *viṣayatā* is not fire, for the *viṣayatā* resides in the qualificandum; hence its erroneous character and hence no fallacy of *siddhasādhana*. For others again according to whom the *viṣayatā* residing in the adjective and the *viṣayatā* residing in the qualificandum are—in the case of an erroneous knowledge of fire—identical, such *viṣayatā* is not limited by a property that is not in the same locus as fireness: hence no fallacy of *siddhasādhana*.[4]

NOTES

41.1. Without introducing any new argument, Gaṅgeśa restates the already formulated syllogisms in the language of those amongst the Naiyāyikas who believe in an additional *viṣayatā*. All this, it must be borne in mind, adds nothing to the main trend of the discussion and only complicates the language further more. But in fairness to Gaṅgeśa one must say it is not his fault. He had to put the matter in the language of some others.

The Naiyāyikas generally speaking admit certain epistemological categories (*jñānīya padārtha*)* which fall into three broad groups: *viṣayatā* and *viṣayitā*, the former pertaining to the object of knowledge, the latter to the subject. A real by being an object of knowledge gives rise to both at the same time. The *viṣayatā* again is of three kinds: *viśeṣyatā*, *prakāratā* and *saṃsargatā*, i.e.

*See Introduction pp. 30-34. For an exhaustive discussion of the nature and status of these Nyāya categories see Kalidas Bhattacharyya, "The Indian Concepts of Knowledge and Self", *Our Heritage* (Bulletin of the Dept. of Postgraduate Training and Research, Sanskrit College, Calcutta) Vol. II: Part II, Vol. III: Part I & Part II.

the substantival, the adjectival and the relational components in the total object of knowledge. Now here Gaṅgeśa is referring to a theory—upheld by some Naiyāyikas—that apart from these three there is another, an additional *viṣayatā* which belongs not to the adjectival nor to the relational component but, in a pre-eminent sense, to the substantival alone. Further, it is held that the *viśeṣya* and the *prakāra* i.e. the qualificandum and the qualifier do not qualify the knowledge directly. They directly belong to the additional *viṣayatā*, and it is through this *viṣayatā* (which directly qualifies the knowledge) that the knowledge is said to have such and such *prakāra*.* One reason for postulating such an additional *viṣayatā* seems to be that, according to the Naiyāyika, there is *viṣayatā* but no *viśeṣyatā*, *prakāratā* and *saṃsargatā* in the object of *nirvikalpa* knowledge. But on the whole this theory would seem to me to be an attempt to rehabilitate the importance of the substance-attribute category in epistemological analysis, an importance which had suffered greatly: hence the attempt to locate the additional *viṣayatā* in the substantival component.

41.2. What now Gaṅgeśa does is to restate the *sādhyas* of the previously formulated syllogisms (see para 38) in the language of this new theory. For example, '*avahnivṛttiprakārako na*' is now restated as '*avahnivṛttivahnitvaprakārakaviṣayatāko na*'. The change consists in the simple fact that whereas in the earlier formulation the qualifier was directly ascribed to the knowledge now it is made to qualify a *viṣayatā* which is then made to qualify the knowledge.

41.3. Truth defined as *tadvati tatprakārakatva* which amounts in the case of a knowledge of fire to *vahnitvavati vahnitvaprakārakatva*, must be restated in the new locution as *vahnivṛttivahnitvaprakārakaviṣayatākatva*: the *viṣayatā* of a true knowledge of fire is qualified by fireness and resides in fire. In general, truth on this theory may be defined as *viṣayatāśrayavṛttiprakārakatva* i.e. the property of having a qualifier that is present in the locus of

*Mathurānātha thus expounds the theory: "*atiriktaviṣayatāpakṣa iti viṣayatā viśeṣyavṛttiratiriktaḥ padārthaḥ saiva ca saprakārikā saviśeṣyikā ca na tu jñānaṃ saviśeṣyakaṃ saprakārakaṃ veti mata ityarthaḥ*" (*Māthuri*).

viṣayatā (this locus being nothing other than the qualificandum or *viśeṣya*). Truth in either of these senses follows by implication from the negation of falsity, but cannot be at first directly proved.

41.4. I follow Mathurānātha in explaining these two sentences. Take a case of error 'This is fire'. Here fire is the *viśeṣaṇa*. The *viṣayatā* of this knowledge has 'fireness' for its qualifier. This *viṣayatā* resides also in fire, and so is in the same locus as fireness. Therefore the second *sādhya* is present in error, for the error, as we have shown, is *vahnitvāsamānādhikaraṇavahnitvaprakārakaviṣayatāka*. Now, in order to avoid this it is being pointed out that on the theory of an additional *viṣayatā*, the *viṣayatā* belongs only to the *qualificandum*, here to 'this', and not to 'fire' which is here adjectival.

42. *Na ca maṇijñānasya prāmāṇyānumāne maṇiprabhāyām maṇibhrameṇa pravṛttasya maṇiprāptau maṇigocaraprayatnajanakamaṇitvaprakārakaniścayatvamanaikāntikamiti vācyam. Maṇiprabhāviṣayakajñānena bhinnaviṣayatayā maṇigocaraprayatnānutpādāt. Maṇiprāptistu nāntarīyakatvāt Jñānaprayatnayorasamānakālatve'pi anubhavasmaraṇayoriva manasā käryyakāraṇabhāvagraha iti nāsiddhiḥ. Abhāvasādhyake ca nirvikalpakasya prathamaṃ sapakṣatvenāniścayānnāsādhāraṇyam.*

It cannot be said that in the case of inferring the truth of a knowledge of (a) jewel, (the *hetu*, viz.) the property of being a certainty which has jewel-ness as its qualifier and which causes effort leading upto arriving at the jewel, is *anaikāntika*, since a person who is led to act through mistaking the lustre of the jewel for the jewel itself does succeed in getting the jewel.[1] For, the knowledge which has the lustre of a jewel for its object cannot give rise to effort for reaching the jewel since the object is different. Reaching the jewel however is a secondary consequence.[2] The inference again is not invalid, for though the knowledge and the effort belong to different times yet the causal relation between them is apprehended by the mind, as in the case of experience and memory. When the *sādhya*[3] is a negative one, there is no *asādhāraṇya*, for, the *nirvikalpaka* is not at the beginning ascertained as possessing the *sādhya*.

NOTES

42.1. Suppose that I see a jewel from a distance. My knowledge is expressed in the judgment 'This is a jewel'. If I am to infer the truth of this knowledge I am to take as the *hetu* its capacity for causing such effort as leads me successfully to getting at the jewel. It is however possible that what I see from the distance is not the jewel but its lustre and consequently I have mistaken the light of the jewel for the jewel itself. But the knowledge thus mistaken may very well lead me to success in getting at the thing. In that case, the above *hetu* is not valid, being present in an instance where the *sādhya* is absent.

42.2. To the above objection, Gaṅgeśa replies by pointing out that the mistaken knowledge of the jewel has not the capacity of leading you upto the jewel. For, the object of the mistaken knowledge is not the jewel but its light; as a rule, a knowledge and the *pravṛtti* it causes must have the same object. The *pravṛtti* caused by the mistaken knowledge was really directed towards the light of the jewel, and not towards the stone itself. If the jewel itself was reached that is only a secondary consequence but certainly not the consequence towards which the *pravṛtti* was directed.

42.3. When the *sādhya* is negative in character being the absence of falsity, is not the *hetu* illegitimate for being *asādhāraṇa*?* The *hetu*, as we have seen, is *asādhāraṇa* if it is absent both in cases where the *sādhya* is known for certain to reside and also in cases where the *sādhya* is known for certain to be absent. Now in the present inference (i.e. in the inference of the truth of a knowledge of fire), the *hetu* is the capacity for producing effort which leads up to something able to burn, and the *sādhya* is absence of falsity. The inference being a *vyatirekī* one the instance adduced is a negative one, namely a case of false knowledge of fire where the said *hetu* is absent. The *hetu* is therefore absent in what is called

*See 37.2 above.

vipakṣa. Is it also absent in those instances where absence of falsity is known for certain to reside? If it were absent in such cases also, then the *hetu* would be rendered *asādhāraṇa*. Gaṅgeśa however adds that such apprehension is unfounded. For, this being the very first instance of an inference of truth no instance has as yet been ascertained as possessing truth. But one may ask, is not *nirvikalpa* knowledge known to lack falsity? We may reply 'no'. *Nirvikalpa* of course does lack falsity, but it has, *ex hypothesis*, not yet been known to lack it.

Why not then take all sundry objects like pots and jars as cases of *sapakṣa*, for they at least may be said even at this stage to lack falsity, falsity being a specifically epistemic character? Two replies are possible: it may be said as before that since 'absence of falsity' is being established now for the first time we do not even know pots and jars to possess it. Raghunātha however after suggesting the last mentioned objection reminds us that our apprehensions on this score are unfounded: "*tathā niścayepi na kṣatiḥ, vyatirekiṇi sādhyasāmānādhikaraṇyagrahasyākiñcitkaratvāt*".* Even if the *sapakṣa* cases are determined and are found to lack the *sādhya* there is no harm in the case of a *vyatirekī* inference. In other words, *asādhāraṇya* is no fallacy in the case of such inferences.

Gadādhara explicates Raghunātha's point in the following manner. An illegitimate *hetu* does not permit inference either by directly obstructing it or by opposing the causes of the inference.** Now a *hetu* by being *asādhāraṇa* hinders inference in one of the following three ways: it may hinder inference by making it impossible to apprehend the *sāmānādhikaraṇya*, or presence in the same locus, of the *hetu* and the *sādhya*. Since in the case of *asādhāraṇya* the *hetu* does not belong to *sapakṣa* instances, it follows that the copresence between the *hetu* and *sādhya* is not to be apprehended. Or, if the *hetu* does not belong to *sapakṣa* it might be supposed to belong to *vipakṣa*; such a *hetu* would then help the

**Dīdniti* (Kanchi edn.), p. 239.

**"*Tallakṣaṇaṃ tu yadviṣayakatvena jñānasyānumitivirodhitvaṃ tattvam*". Further, "*anumitivirodhitvaṃ ca anumititatkāraṇānyataravirodhitvam*". (*Siddhāntamuktāvalī* on *Kārikās* 71-72).

setting up of a counter-syllogism technically called *satratipakṣa*,* which arises when the *pakṣa* is shown with the help of the same *hetu* to possess the absence of the original *sādhya*. Finally, an *asādhāraṇa hetu* may also give rise to doubt as to whether the *sādhya* really belongs to the *pakṣa* or not. For, an *asādhāraṇa hetu* is one that belongs only to the *pakṣa* (*pakṣamātravṛtti*), and on knowing this one may have further doubt whether the additional property (in this case, the *sādhya*) really belongs to it or not.**

In none of these three ways, Raghunātha assures us, can the *hetu*, though *asādhāraṇa*, vitiate a *vyatirekī* inference. With regard to the first, it is clear that in a *vyatirekī* inference we need not apprehend the co-presence of the *hetu* and the *sādhya*; what is required is the apprehension of *vyāpti* between the absence of the *sādhya* and the absence of the *hetu*. The second possibility is also excluded, for the case of error which has been used as instance in the inference is known to be *vipakṣa* to which the *hetu* is known not to belong. Finally, the sort of doubt which might arise is not an obstruction to inference and therefore may very well precede the inference.*** From all these it follows that the objection that the *hetu* in the inference in para 38 is illegitimate is untenable.

43. *Tathāyaṃ pṛthivītyanubhavaḥ pṛthivītvābhāvavati pṛthivītvaprakārako na, apṛthivīvṛttiprakārako na, viśeṣyāvṛttiprakārako na, pṛthivītvaprakārakatve sati pṛthivyaviśeṣyako na, pṛthivītvavyadhikaraṇaprakārāvacchinno na, pṛthivyavṛttiprakārako na vā; gandhavadviśeṣyakapṛthivītvaprakārakaniścayatvāditi vyatirekī. Pṛthivītvabhramaḥ pṛthivītvābhāvavati pṛthivītvaprakāraka iti na bhramatvena siddhasādhanaṃ, na vā gandhavadviśeṣyaka iti na vyabhicāraḥ. Pṛthivītvavati pṛthivītvaprakārakatvādikamarthāt sidhyati.*

*"*Viruddhayoḥ parāmarśo hetvoḥ satpratipakṣatā*" (*Bhāṣāpariccheda*, *Kārikā* 77).

**"*Evamasādhāraṇadharmajñānamapi kāraṇam. Yāthā śabdatvasya nityānityavyāvṛttatvena śabde gṛhītatvācchabdo nityo na veti saṃśayaḥ*" (*Muktāvalī*, on *Kārikā* 130).

***"*Grāhyasaṃśayasya tatsāmagryāścānumityavirodhāt*" (*Gādādharī*, p. 240).

Likewise the knowledge 'This is earth' is not one whose qualifier is earthness but whose qualificandum lacks earthness; (it is) not a knowledge whose qualifier is present in what is other than earth; (it is) not a knowledge whose qualifier is absent in the qualificandum; (it is) not a knowledge whose qualifier is earthness but whose qualificandum is not earth; (it is) not a knowledge which is limited by a qualifier that is not present in the same locus as earthness; nor is it a knowledge whose qualifier is absent in earth. For, it is a certainty whose qualificandum possesses smell and whose qualifier is earthness. This is a *vyatirekī* (inference). An erroneous apprehension of earthness has earthness for its qualifier but its substantive lacks earthness; hence there is no *siddhasādhana*; nor does the qualificandum (of the error) possess smell, hence no *vyabhicāra*. The property of having earthness as its qualifier in what possesses earthness follows by implication.[1]

NOTES

43.1. Gaṅgeśa is merely giving another example of a *vyatirekī* inference whose form is exactly the same as that of the one he has already given in para 38. Just as there capacity for burning was regarded as the distinguishing feature of fire, so here smell is treated, in conformity with the physical theory of the Vaiśeṣikas, as the distinguishing property of earth. In both cases, the experience of the distinguishing property—in the one case, the experience of burning and in the other the experience of smell—is regarded as confirmatory experience.

It may however be asked, how is the *hetu* to be apprehended and what after all is the difference between the *hetu* and the *sādhya* such that the former can be whereas the latter cannot be directly apprehended? Gaṅgeśa takes up this issue partly in para 48 below. In the mean time we may derive some help from *Siddhāntamuktāvalī* and the commentary *Dinakarī* on Kārikā 136. There it is argued that the *hetu* may very well be directly perceived. This would happen when (*i*) I perceive my own knowledge (in *anuvyavasāya*) to have earthness for its qualifier, and (*ii*) if I also perceive smell in the object of knowledge. If these two conditions are fulfilled I perceive the fact that my knowledge has earthness for its qualifier and that its qualificandum possesses smell. But that the fact that the qualificandum possesses earthness determines (or limits) the fact that earthness qualifies the knowledge is too much to be directly perceived; it has to be inferred.* But this does not remove all our doubt. The distinction between *'gandhavati pṛthivītvaprakārakatvam'* and *'gandhavadviśeṣyatvāvacchinnagandhatvaprakārakatvam'* is clear and important. One understands why the former can while the latter cannot be directly perceived. But the really important question is, why is not *'pṛthivītvavati pṛthivītvaprakārakatvam'* perceived? To this however we return later on.

44. *Viṣayatāpakṣe ayaṃ pṛthivītvenānubhavaḥ apṛthivīvṛttipṛthivītvaprakārakaviṣayatāko na, pṛthivyavṛttipṛthivītvaprakārakaviṣayatāko na, pṛthivītvasamānādhikaraṇapṛthivītvaprakārakaviṣayatāko na, viṣayatāśrayavṛttiprakārako na veti sādhyam. Pṛthivītvasamānādhikaraṇapṛthivītvaprakārakaviṣayatākatvādikam arthāt sidhyati. Anye tu pṛthivītvāsamānādhikaraṇaprakārāvacchinnaviṣayatākatvābhāvaḥ sādhyaḥ, gandhāsamānādhikaraṇāprakārakagandhasamānādhikaraṇa-prakārakaviṣayatāpratiyogijñānatvāt. Tena saṃśayavyavacchedaḥ niścayatvaṃ vā vivakṣitamityāhuḥ.*

On the theory that there is (an additional) *viṣayatā*[1]: this apprehension having earthness for its qualifier is not one whose *viṣayatā* is qualified by earthness but is present in not-earth; (it is) not one whose *viṣayatā* though qualified by earthness is absent in earth; (it is) not one whose *viṣayatā* though qualified by earthness is not present in the same locus as earthness; (it is) not also one whose qualifier is absent in the locus of (its) *viṣayatā*: such is the *sādhya*. Properties like having a *viṣayatā* whose qualifier is earthness and which is present in the same locus as earthness follow by implication. Others however (regard) the absence of the property of having a *viṣayatā* which is limited by a qualifier that does not belong to the same locus as

*"*Na ca hetujñānaṃ kathaṃ jātamiti vācyam. Pṛthivītvaprakārakatvasya svatogrāhyatvāt, tatra gandhagraheṇa gandhavadviśeṣyakatvasyā'pi sugrahatvāt, tatprakārakatvāvacchinnatadviśeṣyakatvaṃ paraṃ na gṛhyate, saṃśayānurodhāt*" (*Muktāvalī* on *Kārikā* 136).

earthness as the *sādhya*; the *hetu* being the property of being a knowledge whose *viṣayatā* (*i*) has a qualifier that is in the same locus as smell and (*ii*) has no qualifier that does not belong to the same locus as smell. Doubt is thereby excluded. Or, it may be said that certainty is what is intended.[2]

NOTES

44.1. As in the case of the earlier inferences about the truth of the knowledge 'This is fire', so also here Gaṅgeśa is merely repeating. He is simply restating the syllogism in the language of those who believe in an additional *viṣayatā*. For all these, see notes on 41.

44.2. By adding (in the *hetu*) the clause that the *viṣayatā* has no qualifier that does not belong to the same locus as smell, doubt is in effect excluded from purview, for in the case of the doubt 'Is this earth or not?' one of the qualifiers is absent in the locus of smell. Doubt may by excluded also by remembering that the word '*jñāna*' in the *hetu* is intended to mean only certain apprehension.

45. ***Śītā pṛthivītyanubhavaḥ pṛthivyaṃśe pramaiva, pramābhramarūpe ca samūhālambane na vyabhicāraḥ, aṃśe tasyāpi pramātvāt; viśeṣyabhedena viṣayatābhedācca. Na ca prakārabhedena viṣayatābhedaḥ, mānābhāvāt.***

The apprehension 'Earth is cold' is true in the part 'earth'.[1] There is no *vyabhicāra* in the case of a *samūhālambana* knowledge which is both true and false, for even that is, in part, true.[2] Also because the *viṣayatā* differs with the difference in the qualificandum. There is no difference in *viṣayatā* with difference in the qualifier, for there is no proof.[3]

NOTES

45.1. The inference was to the effect that a true knowledge of earth does not possess a *viṣayatā* whose qualifier is earthness but which resides in not-earth. But this seems true of even a false knowledge 'The earth is cold' (which is false insofar as heat and cold are not, according to the Vaiśeṣika physics, properties of earth). The *sādhya* of the foregoing inference would then seem to be common to both truth and error. In reply to such an objection Gaṅgeśa points out that the knowledge 'The earth is cold' is indeed partly true and it is of this part that the above *sādhya* holds good.

45.2. What about a *samūhālambana* or collective apprehension which is both true and false, a knowledge—to take an example—in which earthness is predicated of two things, one of which is a piece of earth while the other is not? In such a knowledge the *hetu*, namely the property of being a certainty which has earthness as qualifier and whose qualificandum possesses smell, is present, but the *sādhya* is absent, for it *is* a knowledge whose *viṣayatā* resides in not-earth (inasmuch as one of the things of which earthness is predicated is a not-earth). If the *hetu* can be present where the *sādhya* is absent, the *hetu* becomes *vyabhicāri*. Gaṅgeśa answers to this objection by pointing out that the *hetu* as much as the *sādhya* is present in the knowledge only insofar as the earth is concerned, i.e. insofar as the predicate 'earthness' is predicated of a piece of earth.

45.3. Gaṅgeśa's answer explained in note 45.2 implies that if there are a number of different *viśeṣyas* in a knowledge, there would be the same number of different *viṣayatās*. In the present case if we assume that the knowledge is 'These two (a lump of earth and a glass of water) are earth', there shall be two *viśeṣyatās*, one corresponding to the lump of earth and the other corresponding to the glass of water. This accords well with the theory of additional *viṣayatā* which is supposed to reside directly only in the qualificandum. It is also implied that the *viṣayatā* does not vary with the *prakāra*, so that it cannot be maintained that since the qualifier is one, namely 'earthness', there is therefore only one *viṣayatā*.

Gaṅgeśa's solution then to the difficulty about the *samūhālambana* knowledge wherein the same qualifier is referred to more than one *viśeṣya* is that the knowledge possesses more than one *viṣayatā*. With reference to some one of these *viṣayatās* the *sādhya* must be present in the knowledge whereas with regard to the other or others the *sādhya* may be absent.

46. *Yattviyaṃ pṛthivītyanubhavaḥ pṛthivītvasamānādhikaraṇadharmāvacchinnapṛthivīviśeṣyakaviṣayatākaḥ, pṛthivītvavyadhikaraṇadharmānavacchinnapṛthivīviśeṣyakaviṣayatākaḥ, pṛthivyavṛttidharmānavacchinnapṛthivīviśeṣyakaviṣayatāko vā; gandhāsamānādhikaraṇadharmāprakārakaviṣayatāpratiyogijñānatvāt, agandhavadavṛttipṛthivītvaprakārakaviṣayatākatvāt; gandhasamānādhikaraṇaviṣayatāpratiyogijñānatvādveti. Tanna, sādhyāprasiddheḥ. Kintu arthādeva tatsidhyati.*

Regarding (the inference): the apprehension 'This is earth' is one whose *viṣayatā* has for its qualificandum earth and is limited by a property that is in the same locus as earthness; (or it is) one whose *viṣayatā* has earth for its qualificandum and is not limited by a property that is not in the same locus as earthness; or (it is) one whose *viṣayatā* has earth for its qualificandum and is not limited by a property that does not reside in earth. For, it is a knowledge having a *viṣayatā* that has not for its qualifier any property that does not belong to the same locus as smell; (or) because its *viṣayatā* has earthness for its qualifier and does not reside in what lacks smell; or because it is a knowledge having a *viṣayatā* that resides in the same locus as smell. This cannot be (so), for the *sādhya* is not known. It can be proved however by implication.[1]

NOTES

46.1. All that Gaṅgeśa does in this paragraph is to formulate syllogisms with positive *sādhyas*. But he rejects such an attempt on the already advanced ground that a positive notion of truth is as yet—*ex hypothesis*—unknown and so cannot be made the *sādhya* of an inference. We have no other way than to begin with *vyatirekī* inferences with negative *sādhyas* and then to establish the positive truth by implication in the manner explained in 40.2.

47. *Evaṃ yatprakāravyāpyatayā yadgandhasnehasamarthapravṛttijanakatvakaracaraṇādikamavagataṃ tadvati tatprakārakajñānatvameva prāmāṇye liṅgam.*

Thus: if (properties like) smell, smoothness, capacity for producing successful effort[a], (human) limbs etc. are apprehended as being pervaded by a qualifier, then the property of being a knowledge having the same qualifier in something that possesses the (said pervaded) property can serve as the mark of truth.[1]

Notes

47.1. Gaṅgeśa here lays down a general rule regarding all inferences seeking to prove the truth of knowledges. The point is, what is to serve as the proper *hetu* in such inferences. The *hetu* whatever it may be must belong to the *pakṣa* which is here some knowledge or other. As such the *hetu* must be an epistemological entity (*jñānīya padārtha*). It cannot be the simple objective property belonging to the object of that knowledge.

The general rule may now be formulated thus: let p be the qualifier of the knowledge under consideration. Suppose also that we have apprehended beforehand another property q as being pervaded by p. In other words, it is being supposed that we know already that wherever there is q there is p. In that case, the truth of the knowledge 'This is p' can be inferred from the property of having p for its qualifier in a qualificandum which possesses q.

To illustrate now, let p be 'earthness' and let q be smell. It is assumed we know already that smell is pervaded by earthness: wherever there is smell there is also earthness. In that case, if we know that the knowledge 'This is earth' has earthness for its qualifier—as we surely know in *anuvyavasāya*—and also that its qualificandum possesses smell, then we can infer that that knowledge is true.

As smell is to earthness, so smoothness is to waterness, and the possession of hands, feet etc. to the property of being a human body.

The commentary *Dinakarī* on *Siddhāntamuktāvalī* (on Kārikā 136) formulates the general rule thus: "*vyāpyavati vyāpakaprakārakatvasya vyāpakavati vyāpakaprakārakatvavyāpyatvāt*". If the *vyāpya* or pervaded property is smell, and the *vyāpaka* is earthness, then *gandhavati pṛthivītvaprakārakatva* (or, the property of having earthness for its qualifier in a qualificandum which possesses smell) is itself pervaded by—and so the *vyāpya* of—*pṛthivītvavati pṛthivītvaprakārakatva* (or, the property of having earthness for its qualifier in a qualificandum which possesses earthness). The latter then can be inferred from the former. And we see that the truth of the knowledge 'This is earth' is nothing other than this pervader (*vyāpaka*) property.

47.2. The commentators have rightly questioned the propriety of including *samarthapravṛttijanakatva* (which is a property of a knowledge, not of an object) in the list along with smell etc. (which are first-order objective properties). Gaṅgeśa may be justified thus. He is here giving a formula that should be applicable to all knowledges. Smell is a first-order objective property whose presence in the qualificandum leads us to infer the truth of the primary knowledge 'This is earth'. '*Samarthapravṛttijanakatva*' however is included to account for those cases where we infer the truth of our knowledge of the truth of the primary knowledge (*prāmāṇyajñānaprāmāṇyānumāna*). The latter inference takes the form 'This knowledge of earth is true'. The qualifier of the knowledge is 'truth'. Now if the *appropriate samarthapravṛttijanakatva* has been apprehended as the *vyāpya* of (or, as pervaded by) the truth of this knowledge, then *samarthapravṛttijanakatvavati pramātvaprakārakatva* (or, the property of having 'truth' as a qualifier in a qualificandum which possesses the capacity for producing appropriate successful activity) may be used as mark for inferring *pramātvavati pramātvaprakārakatva* (or, the property of having 'truth' as a qualifier in a qualificandum which possesses truth). This is virtually inferring the truth of the knowledge 'This knowledge is true'.

This shows that it would not be true to say that according to Gaṅgeśa we always infer truth from the mark of *samarthapravṛttijanakatva*. The pragmatic test is not the only test of truth. We also infer truth by the appropriate sense verification. That a thing is a lump of earth is verified, for example, by, experiencing smell in it. But this inference by which the knowledge is known to be true may itself be subjected to doubt? Then the pragmatic test is said to offer a sure mark. I do not think there has been a very clear distinction between these two kinds of tests.

48. *Nanu vahnijñānasya dāhasamarthaviṣayatvaṃ na dāhasamartho'yamiti vyavasāyagamyaṃ jñānaviṣayatayostadaviṣayāt. Nāpi tadanuvyavasāyagamyaṃ purovartidāhasāmarthyasya tadagocarāt. Vyavasāyopanītadāhasāmarthyasya ca bhāne tadasāmarthyāt. Anyathā vyavasāyopanītasya purovartini vahnitvasya anuvyavasāyaviṣayatve svataḥprāmāṇyagrahāpatteḥ. Evaṃ pṛthivījalajñānayorgandhasnehavadviṣayakatvagraho'pyanupapanna iti.*

Ucyate. Vahnitvaprakārakajñānānuvyavasāye sati tatra viṣaye dāhasāmarthyajñānānantaraṃ smṛtyupanīte vahnivyavasāye smṛtyupanītadāhasāmarthyaviṣayakatvaṃ, evaṃ jalapṛthivījñānayoḥ smṛtyupanītayoḥ jñānopanītasnehagandhavadviṣayakatvaṃ manasā paricchidyate; gandhādimatyeva mama pṛthivītvādyanubhava iti gandhādimattvaparicchedānantaramanubhavāt. Smṛtyupanīte dhūmādau vyāptiparicchedavat cakṣuṣā candane saurabhajñānavacca.

It may be said that the fact that knowledge of fire has for its object something capable of burning cannot be apprehended by a primary knowledge of the form 'This is capable of burning', for the knowledge as well as (its) *viṣayatā* are not its objects.[1] Nor can it be apprehended by *anuvyavasāya*, for the capacity for burning that belongs to the yonder object cannot be apprehended by it. It is also incapable of manifesting the capacity for burning as presented through the primary knowledge. For, otherwise, if the *anuvyavasāya* could apprehend the fireness in the yonder object as presented through the primary knowledge, there would be *svataḥprāmāṇya*.[2] Likewise, the apprehension of the fact that knowledges of earth and water have for their objects things possessing smell and smoothness (respectively) cannot be accounted for.

(To this) It is being replied. After there has taken place *anuvyavasāya* of a primary knowledge having fireness as its qualifier, there takes place an apprehension of the capacity for burning in the object there. After which the property of having an object capable of burning is presented through memory in the primary knowledge of fire which is (also) presented through memory. Likewise, the property of having an object that possesses smoothness or smell is presented through memory—and mentally perceived—in the (primary) knowledge of water or earth which (also) is presented through memory. For, the awareness 'My apprehension of earthness etc. is in something that possesses smell etc.' is apprehended only after the possession of smell etc. have been apprehended, just as *vyāpti* is apprehended in smoke etc. as presented through memory and just as fragrance is visually known in a sandalwood.[3]

Notes

48.1. Gaṅgeśa now takes up the question we have raised earlier in 43.1. It is only natural for one to ask, how after all does Gaṅgeśa come to ascertain that the *hetu* (in the syllogisms advanced by him) resides in the *pakṣa* (i.e. in the knowledge whose truth is being proved). How, for example, am I to ascertain that the knowledge of fire under consideration possesses an object that is capable of burning (*dāhasamarthaviṣayatva*)? In fact when afterwards I burn my finger that knowledge is dead and gone. How am I to know that *that* knowledge which I had had an object capable of burning? Consider the primary knowledge 'This is capable of burning', the 'this' referring to the fire. This knowledge however does not and cannot tell me that the knowledge of fire has an object capable of burning, for neither that knowledge ('This is fire') itself nor its *viṣayatā* are amongst the objects that are apprehended by the primary knowledge 'This is capable of burning'.

48.2. The *anuvyavasāya* 'I know that this is capable of burning' fails no less to apprehend that my knowledge of fire had an object capable of burning. For the *anuvyavasāya*, being a mental perception, is incapable of knowing that a qualifier really belongs to the qualificandum, that the capacitv for burning *really* belongs to the fire before me. In case this is said to be somehow made possible by that highly ingenious mechanism of knowledge called *upanītabhāna*, then there is nothing to say against the possibility of apprehending the very truth of the knowledge under consideration by the corresponding *anuvyavasāya* and through the same mechanism of *upanītabhāna*, which would really amount to admitting the *svataḥ* theory.

48.3. In reply to this objection, Gaṅgeśa gives an outline of the way the presence of the *hetu* in the *pakṣa*—to take an example, the fact that a knowledge of fire has an object capable of burning —comes to be apprehended. The process involves the following stages:—

i. The primary knowledge 'This is fire'.
ii. The *anuvyavasāya* of i 'I know that this is fire'.
iii. A primary apprehension 'This is capable of burning' (the *this* in iii and the *this* in i being the same).
iv. Memory of i.
v. 'My knowledge of fire has an object that is capable of burning', which is a mental perception constituted by the presentation of i and iii through memory i.e. through *jñānalakṣaṇā*.

Now, Gaṅgeśa adds that i and iii are *presented* through memory and thereby render v possible exactly in the same manner in which fragrance is visually perceived in a piece of sandalwood or *vyāpti* is apprehended in the remembered instances of smoke and fire.

49. *Tarhi pṛthivītvajñāne gandhavadviśeṣyakatvavat cakṣuṣā gandhavati pṛthivītvopanayānantaramiyaṃ pṛthivīti pṛthivītvaprakārakānubhave upanīte pṛthivītvavati pṛthivītvaprakārakatvaṃ, tathā tatraiva jñāne ghaṭatvaprakārakatāvirahavat pṛthivyavṛttiprakārābhāvavattvaṃ, viśeṣyāvṛttiprakārābhāvavattvaṃ vā prāmāṇyam manasaiva paricchidyatāmiti svata eva prāmāṇyagraha itī cet, na. Jñānāntaropasthāpitajñānavṛttiprāmāṇyagrahe paratastvānapāyāt. Yāvajjñānagrāhakasāmagrīgrāhyatvaṃ yāvatsvāśrayagrāhakagrāhyatvaṃ, tajjñānaviṣayakajanyajñānājanyajanyajñānagrāhyatvaṃ vā svatastvaṃ, tadanyathāgrā-*

hyatvantu paratastvaṃ, manasā caivaṃ prāmāṇyagrahasyābhyupagame tajjñānaviṣayakajanyajñānajanyajñānagrāhyatvānna paratastvahāniḥ.

Therefore just as the property of having a qualificandum which possesses smell (is perceived) in the knowledge of earthness, so one may have a visual perception of earthness in what possesses smell, after which the apprehension 'This is earth' having earthness for its qualifier may be (extraordinarily) presented; in this (again) (one may apprehend) the property of having earthness as a qualifier in what possesses earthness[1]. Similarly in the same knowledge one could also apprehend, through mental perception, like the absence of being qualified by potness, truth in the sense of possession of the absence of a qualifier that is non-resident in the qualificandum; which amounts to intrinsic apprehension of truth.

(To this, we reply) No. The extrinsic character of truth (with regard to its apprehension) is unavoidable if the truth of a knowledge is apprehended in that knowledge as presented (extraordinarily) through another.[2]

The intrinsic character (of truth) is (nothing other than) the property of being apprehended by a knowledge that is caused by the same conditions as also give rise to all those knowledges which apprehend the knowledge; or the property of being apprehended by all those knowledges that apprehend its own locus; (or) the property of being apprehended by a knowledge that is caused, but not caused by a knowledge—which is itself caused—of that knowledge.[3] To be apprehended in any manner other than these is to be apprehended extrinsically. If mental apprehension of truth as laid down above be admitted, truth is apprehended by a knowledge that is caused by a knowledge—itself caused—of that knowledge—so that the thesis of the extrinsic character of truth is not impaired.[4]

Notes

49.1. In the manner explained in 48, it is possible to apprehend through a very complicated process the truth of the knowledge 'This is earth'. The process would be somewhat as follows:

i. I had earlier a visual perception of earthness (which is permitted on the usual version of the Nyāya system).

ii. Now I perceive something as having smell.

iii. In this something possessing smell I have an extraordinary perception of earthness through memory or *jñānalakṣaṇā*.

iv. The primary knowledge 'This is earth' is now presented through memory.

v. In the knowledge 'This is earth' as thus presented, the property of having earthness as qualifier and having a qualificandum which possesses earthness comes to be apprehended.

vi. It is also seen that 'pot-ness' is not a qualifier of this knowledge and thus we come to apprehend that it does not have a qualifier that is not resident in earth or that is not resident in the qualificandum.

I do not think this is Gaṅgeśa's own view, for he does not hold that truth is in any case perceived. What he has allowed and accounted for is the perception of the fact that the knowledge 'This is earth' has 'earthness' for its qualifier in a qualificandum which possesses smell (*gandhavati pṛthivītvaprakārakatva*), but I do not think he would allow that we can in a like manner perceive that the knowledge 'This is earth' has 'earthness' for its qualifier in a qualificandum which possesses earthness. If he did allow that a mental, though extraordinary perception of the latter is possible then the whole theory of inference of truth developed with so much of meticulous detail would be rendered pointless. It is of course quite another issue whether he is justified in holding that the one can be perceived whereas the other can only be inferred. But in any case I do not know what Gaṅgeśa would say with regard to the primary knowledge 'This is smell': it would seem, he would allow we can perceive its truth though in an extraordinary manner. But then the distinction between 'This is smell' and 'This is earth' has to be worked out. Is it the distinction between a sense-datum statement and a physical object one?

In any case, Gaṅgeśa is here concerned with an objection. The point of the objector is understandable. If Gaṅgeśa's account in 48 were correct then even truth should be apprehended in the same manner, which would amount to the *svataḥ* theory.

49.2. Gaṅgeśa explains that even if the account of apprehension of truth explained in 49.1 were true that would not amount to the *svataḥ* theory, for even on this account truth of a knowledge is apprehended in an indirect manner through the original knowledge being extraordinarily presented in a subsequent knowledge.

49.3. For explanations of these senses of the *svataḥ* theory see relevant places earlier in this book.

49.4. On the account given by Gaṅgeśa in this passage the truth of a knowledge is apprehended subsequently on that knowledge being presented extraordinarily in another knowledge. It follows therefore that the latter knowledge presupposes a knowledge of the original knowledge, and is thus caused by *tajjñānaviṣayaka-jñāna* and therefore not uncaused by any knowledge of the original knowledge as is demanded by the *svataḥ* theroy. It may be added that the adjective '*janya*' (or, caused) in '*tajjñānaviṣaya-kajanyajñāna*' is inserted to exclude God's eternal knowledge of that knowledge, for such eternal knowledge, according to the Nyāya, is a general cause, being an invariable antecedent, of all knowledge and hence also of the first awareness of the knowledge, be it *anuvyavasāya* or inferential.

50. *Vyatirekyanantaraṃ tajjātīyatvenānvayinā prāmāṇyānumānam. Yathā—idaṃ śarīrajñānaṃ pramā, karacaraṇavati śarīrajñānatvāt, svaśarīrajñānavat. Na ca karacaraṇāntaravati karacaraṇāntaravattvajñāne vyabhicāraḥ, śarīrāṃśe tasya pramātvāt. Etena karacaraṇavati śarīrajñānatvāt ityatra karacaraṇavattvaṃ nopalakṣaṇaṃ vyāvṛttopalakṣyābhāvāt. Na ca viṣayatayā jñānaviśeṣaṇaṃ, karacaraṇavattvaprakārakaśarīrajñānatvasya vyabhicārāt, śarīramiti jñāne tadasiddheśca. Viṣayaviśeṣaṇatve karacaraṇavadviṣayakaśarīrajñānatvasya vyabhicārāt, śarīrabhramasyāpi vastutaḥ karādimadviṣayakatvāt; nāpi karacaraṇādiśūnye yaccharīratvena jñānaṃ tadanyatve satīti vivakṣitaṃ, śūnya ityatra viṣayatvaṃ saptamyartha iti karacaraṇaśūnyaviṣayakaśarīrajñānānyaśarīrajñānatvādityarthaḥ, tathā cāsiddhiḥ, śarīrajñānasya tacchūnyaśarīratvādiviṣayakatvaniyamāt. Na vā karacaraṇaśūnye yaccharīratvena jñānaṃ na bhavatīti vivakṣitam, tṛtīyārthaviṣayatve uktadoṣāt, anyasyāsambhavāditi nirastaṃ, karacaraṇa-*

vadviśeṣyakaśarīratvaprakārakajñānatvasya hetutvāt śarīra-bhrame ca karacaraṇavataḥ śarīrasya viśeṣaṇatvāt. Viṣayatā-pakṣe karacaraṇādiśūnyaniṣṭhaśarīratvaprakārakaviṣayatāpr-atiyogitvaśūnyatve sati śarīrajñānatvāditi hetuḥ.

After the *vyatirekī*, truth may be inferred by an *anvayī* inference with the property of belonging to the same class as the *hetu*.[1] As for example: the knowledge 'This is body' is true, for it is a knowledge of body in what possesses hands and feet; as in the case of one's knowledge of one's own body. It cannot be said that the *hetu* is *vyabhicārī* in the case where something possessing a different set of limbs is mistaken as possessing quite another set of limbs: for such a knowledge is true insofar as its reference to body is concerned.[2] With this are set aside the following (objections): in (the *hetu*) 'the property of being a knowledge of body in what possesses hands and feet', the property of possessing hands and feet is not an *upalakṣaṇa*, for there is nothing that could be intended for exclusion[3]; nor is it an adjective of the knowledge through *viṣayatā*, for the property of being a knowledge of body with the possession of hands and feet as its qualifier is *vyabhicārī*, and also because it is not present in the case of the knowledge 'body'.[4] If (it is taken as) an adjective of the object, then (the *hetu*) 'the property of being a knowledge of body which has for its object something possessing hands and feet' is *vyabhicārī*, for even an erroneous knowledge of body has in fact something possessing hands and feet for its object.[5] Nor can the meaning be 'being other than the knowledge of body in what lacks hands and feet'; for, if the locative in 'in what lacks' is to be understood as meaning objecthood, then the *hetu* would mean 'because of being a knowledge of body other than such knowledge of body as has for its object something lacking hands and feet'; in that case, the *hetu* is *asiddha*, for all knowledge of body has as a rule bodyness for its object and bodyness (of course) lacks it.[6] It cannot be said that what (the *hetu*) is intended to mean is 'what is not a knowledge of bodyness in what lacks hands and feet'; for the same difficulties remain even if the instrumental is taken in the sense of objecthood, and no other sense is possible.

(These objections are set aside:). For, the *hetu* is the property of being a knowledge, whose qualifier is bodyness and whose qualificandum possesses hands and feet, whereas in error about body the body as possessing hands and feet functions as the adjective.[7] On the *viṣayatā* theory, the *hetu* is the property of being a knowledge of body while at the same time lacking the counter-positiveness of the *viṣayatā* which attaches to what does not have hands and feet and which has bodyness as its qualifier.

Notes

50.1. Gaṅgeśa was so long concerned with the rather highly elusive problem as to how we get our first notion of truth. Rejecting in 38, the theory that the notion is 'recollected' from past lives (or, as we have suggested, *a priori* in the Platonic sense), he has attempted an outline of an empirical origin of the notion. It is from empirical data that we reason, with the help of a *vyatirekī* inference, to the absence of falsity. Positive truth is then shown to follow by implication. He has given in 39 an account of how we arrive at the notion of falsity. Apparently, he thinks the idea of falsity to be easier to get at than the idea of truth. Be that what it may, once we have arrived at the notion of truth in case of any particular knowledge (the notion of truth is derived from that of absence of falsity by implication, *arthādeva*), in all subsequent cases truth may directly be proved by an *anvayī* inference. The circuitous process is no longer necessary.

It should be borne in mind that Gaṅgeśa is not claiming that this is how everyone of us has arrived at the notion. I think he is more concerned with giving a *philosophical derivation* of the notion from experience without—like the Platonist—presupposing it. At the same time, he also holds that the notion is necessary in the sense that it cannot be consistently denied, which he has shown in 36. Thus there is a curious combination of the empiricist and the rationalist viewpoints.

Gaṅgeśa tells us here that we may now infer the truth of a knowledge with the help of the hetu '*tajjātīyatva*'. Correct interpretation of Gaṅgeśa's view in this connection seems extremely difficult, chiefly because on the usual Nyāya view, to which reference has been made in the Introduction, '*tajjātīyatva*' is used as the *hetu* only for the purpose of inferring the truth of those knowledges which have become '*abhyāsadaśāpanna*'. Gaṅgeśa does not explicitly say that the *anvayī* inference of which he here speaks and in which the *hetu* is '*tajjātīyatva*' is used only in connection with that restricted class of knowledges which have become 'familiar'. We leave aside for the present the difficulties connected with the notion of familiarity, for which see the introduction.

In order to make Gaṅgeśa's texts consistent with this accepted Nyāya view, we suggest that he may be understood in either of two ways:—

(*i*) It may be that when in 36 Gaṅgeśa speaks of '*prathamaṃ prāmāṇyānumānam*' he is speaking not of the general notion of truth (as we have so long supposed him to have meant) but of the truths of particular knowledges. He would then be asking, how do we first apprehend the truth of the knowledge 'This is fire', or how do we first apprehend the truth of the knowledge 'This is earth', and so on. In each case truth being something new, *in each case* we are to start with the sort of *vyatirekī* inference which he has given us. In that case, his present contention would be that in each case after once the truth (in the negative sense) has been established with the help of a *vyatirekī* inference, on subsequent occasions i.e. in cases of subsequent knowledges of the same form truth may be proved with the help of the *hetu* '*tajjātīyatva*'. For once we have proved the truth of the knowledge 'This is fire', on subsequent occasions we may say that our knowledge of fire is true by virtue of '*tajjātīyatva*'. Here obviously '*tajjātīyatva*' would mean the property of being of the same type as a knowledge whose truth has been ascertained. But having ascertained the truth of the knowledge 'This is fire' I could not possibly use the *hetu tajjātīyatva* with a view to establishing the truth of 'This is earth'.

(*ii*) Or, Gaṅgeśa may be taken to mean that we are required to acquire our first notion of truth in the circuitous method outlined by him, and it does not matter in which instance of knowledge we do that. Once however we have our first notion of truth in general, there would be no more the complaint of an unknown *sādhya* (*sādhyāprasiddhi*), and we may proceed to make use of *anvayī* inferences on all subsequent occasions of all other knowledges (and not merely of the sort of knowledge whose truth we had established at the beginning with the help of the *vyatirekī* inference). But on this interpretation, '*tajjātīyatva*' has to be understood in a different way. It could not then mean the same as before, for, the knowledge 'This is earth' (supposing we are for the first time proving *its* truth but with an *anvayī* inference) and the knowledge 'This is fire' (whose truth let us suppose was the first one to have been proved, and so by a *vyatirekī*) are not of the same kind. In any case, the entire contention at this point is difficult to construe.

Only under interpretation (*i*) is it permissible to say that according to Gaṅgeśa the *hetu* '*tajjātīyatva*' may be employed to prove the truth of those knowledges alone which have become '*abhyāsadaśāpanna*'. On the interpretation (*ii*) the truth of any knowledge may be so proved if only we have derived our first notion of truth in general with the help of a *vyatirekī* inference. The first interpretation has then the merit of conforming to the traditional Nyāya view, traceable to Vācaspati; but its drawback is that it presupposes that in every case of a new knowledge we have to institute a *vyatirekī* in order to be assured of its truth. How far the whole contention that the truth of 'familiar' knowledges is proved by the *hetu* '*tajjātīyatva*' is tenable need not be discussed here. We have recorded our criticisms in this connection in the Introduction. The merit of the second interpretation is that it makes the procedure less complicated. All that we need the *vyatirekī* for is to get our general notion of truth. But then if after we get our notion of truth in general we may infer the truth of all other knowledges by the *hetu* '*tajjātīyatva*', then in the first place the notion of '*tajjātīyatva*' becomes difficult to explain and secondly much of the Nyāya theory (for example, the theory that the test of truth is successful practice) has to be abandoned or modified beyond recognition.

Much effort has been spent over clarifying the notion of '*tajjātīyatva*' ever since Vācaspati introduced it. But I do not think that in all more than two meanings have been assigned to it. These two are: (*i*) belonging to the same class as one whose truth has been conclusively established; (*ii*) knowledge of the definiendum (*lakṣya*) accompanied by knowledge of the definiens (*lakṣaṇa*), or—better still—knowledge whose qualifier is the pervader and whose qualificandum possesses the pervaded (*vyāpyavadviśeṣyakavyāpakaprakārakajñāntava*). If p is pervaded by q, then a knowledge of q in what possesses p would be a knowledge of *tajjātīyatva.* Or, if p gives the definition of q, then knowledge of q in something that satisfies p would be a knowledge of *tajjātīyatva.** In Gaṅgeśa's own example, 'body' is definable as what possesses hands and feet. Or, possession of hands and feet is pervaded by bodyness. If then I can know that my knowledge is a knowledge of body (i.e. of the *lakṣya*) in what possesses hands and feet (*lakṣaṇasahacarita*)—or, what amounts to the same, if I can know that my knowledge has bodyness for its qualifier (*vyāpakaprakāraka*) and that it has a qualificandum which possesses hands and feet (*vyāpyavati*)—then I can infer that my knowledge 'This is a body' is true.

50.2. Gaṅgeśa apprehends an objection. It may be that I mistake one person's body as another's, or maybe I mistake one kind of body (say, an animal body) for another kind of body (say, human). In such a case the *hetu* is there, but the knowledge is not true. Is the *hetu* then *vyabbicārī*? Gaṅgeśa replies that the knowledge is true at least in this respect that it is a knowledge of body, and this is what the *hetu* is meant to establish.

50.3. The group of objections now considered pertain to the function of the phrase '*karacaraṇavattvam*' as a component of the *hetu* as formulated here. A qualifying phrase may function simply as an indicator (*upalakṣaṇa*) or as an adjective (*viśeṣaṇa*). In its former function it serves merely to indicate a thing by referring to some accidental feature which serves to distinguish it from others. One may for example point to a house as one with a crow on its top. Its sole purpose is exçlusion (*vyāvṛtti*). Now in the present case, is '*karacaraṇavattvam*' an indicator, and if so what does it serve to exclude? The objection is to the effect that there is nothing that it could serve to exclude. Mathurānātha explains it thus: "*lakṣaṇīyasya bhramavyāvṛttasya dharmāntarasya tadānīṃ jñānābhāvāt*".

50.4. If '*karacaraṇavattvam*' be regarded as an adjective (or quali-

*For a detailed account of the history of this and the allied notion see Pt. Yogendranath Tarka-Sāṅkhya-Vedāntatīrtha, "Prāmāṇyavāda", pp. 43ff, ni *Our Heritage*, Vol. VI, Part I.

fier) of the knowledge, then the *hetu* would expand into 'the property of being a knowledge of body with the possession of hands and feet as its qualifier'. Now as so expanded the *hetu* is *vyabhicārī*, i.e. it is present even when the *sādhya*, namely, truth is absent. Mathurānātha asks us to consider the case of error when we mistake a tree as being both a body and as possessing hands and feet. In this case, the knowledge is of body and has the possession of hands and feet as its qualifier, but it is false. Further, this *hetu* is absent in the simple knowledge 'body': this knowledge does not have the possession of hands and feet as one of its qualifiers.

50.5. If '*karacaraṇavattvam*' is taken as qualifying the object of the knowledge then the *hetu* would be 'the property of being a knowledge of body which has for its object something possessing hands and feet'. But this *hetu* is *vyabhicārī*. Even an erroneous awareness of a body apprehends something as possessing hands and feet so that one could say that its *object* also possesses hands and feet.

50.6. A knowledge of body has bodyness for its object. Now certainly bodyness does not possess hands and feet. Therefore it is not possible to find a knowledge of body which is not a knowledge of an object not possessing hands and feet. The *hetu* then would be rendered *asiddha*.

50 7. All these objections are answered by Gaṅgeśa by bringing out the exact nature of the *hetu* '*karacaraṇavati śarīrajñānatvāt*'. In the above inference of the truth of the knowledge 'This is body', the *hetu* is the property of being a knowledge wherein bodyness functions as a qualifier and whose qualificandum possesses hands and feet. This is not so however in the case of a false apprehension of body. In the case of error, the possession of hands and feet qualifies the body and thus qualifies the knowledge. In the latter case '*karacaraṇavattvam*' states an epistemological property, whereas in the former case it states an ontological property.

51. *Nanu nānyagṛhītaprāmāṇyaṃ jñānaṃ paraprāmāṇyaniścaya-*

rūpam, anavasthānāt. Nāpi svajñāyamānaprāmāṇyaṃ, svataḥ prāmāṇyagrahāpatteḥ. Ato'gṛhītaprāmāṇyameva jñānaṃ paraprāmāṇyaniścayarūpamāstheyam. Tathā ca vyavasāyo'pyagṛhītaprāmāṇya eva svaviṣayaṃ niścāyayatu, kiṃ viṣayaniścayārthaṃ tatprāmāṇyaniścayena. Atha vyavasāyasyāprāmāṇyadarśanānna tanmātrādarthaniścayaḥ, tarhi prāmāṇyānumiterapyaprāmāṇyadarśanānna tato'pi prāmāṇyaniścaya iti cet.

It may be objected that a knowledge whose truth is apprehended by another (knowledge) cannot be one which ascertains the truth of another, for in that case there would be infinite regress. Nor is it one whose truth is apprehended by itself. Therefore, a knowledge whose truth is not ascertained does ascertain the truth of another (knowledge). But then in the same way let the primary knowledge also ascertain its own object even if own truth remains unknown. What could then be the necessity of determining its truth in order to ascertain the object? If it be said that the object cannot be determined merely from the primary knowledge since the primary knowledge is (often) found to be false, (the reply would be that) then truth cannot any more be ascertained by the inference purporting to establish it since such inference is (often) seen to be invalid.[1]

NOTES

51.1. This is an objection against the Nyāya theory. Gaṅgeśa will reply to it in the next paragraph. The main point of the objection is that the knowledge which ascertains the truth of another knowledge must itself be known to be true. But its own truth can be ascertained either by another knowledge or by itself. In the latter case there would be *svataḥprāmāṇya*. In the former case there would be an infinite regress. If the truth of K_1 is determined by K_2, and if for this purpose K_2 itself must be known to be true and if that is possible only by another knowledge K_3, then K_3 itself must be known to be true with the help of K_4, and so on ad infinitum. A way out of this situation is to deny that a knowledge should itself be known to be true in order that it may ascertain the truth of another knowledge. In that case, K_2 may very well ascertain the truth of K_1 without itself being known to be true, so that we do not need to postulate for that purpose the infinite series of knowledges, K_3, K_4,. . . . But the objector is not satisfied. He hastens to point out that if a knowledge, itself not known to be true, may yet ascertain the truth of another knowledge, then we may say the same of the primary knowledge. The primary knowledge need not, in that case, be known to be true, in order that we may be assured of its object. Let it *ascertain* (and not merely apprehend) its object even if its own truth remains undetermined. It may be pointed out in reply that the primary knowledge often turns out to be false and so there is reason why we may suspect its veracity and why it cannot be taken as ascertaining its own object unless we are sure of its truth. But, the objection continues, the same may be true also of the inference of truth (*prāmāṇyānumiti*) of the Naiyāyika. This inference also often turns out to be false, and so we cannot accept its claim to ascertain the truth of the primary knowledge unless its own truth is ascertained, and then we shall have all the difficulties pointed out earlier in this paragraph.

52. *Na brūmaḥ jñānaprāmāṇyaniścayādevārthaniścaya iti, kintu yatrāprāmāṇyaśaṅkā nāsti karatalāmalakādijñāne tatra vyavasāya evārthaniścaya iti tata eva pravṛttirniṣkampā, yatrānabhyāsadaśāyāṃ prāmāṇyasaṃśayenārthaniścayaṃ paribhūyārthasaṃśayaḥ tatra prāmāṇyaniścayādhīnajñānādarthaṃ niścitya niṣkampaṃ pravartate nānyatheti sarvānubhavasiddham. Ata evāgṛhītaprāmāṇyameva jñānaṃ paraprāmāṇyaṃ niścāyayati, aprāmāṇyaśaṅkākalaṅkābhāvāt. Yatra tu prāmāṇyajñāne aprāmāṇyaśaṅkayā prāmāṇyasaṃśayaḥ tatra prāmāṇyajñāne prāmāṇyaniścayādeva prāmāṇyaniścayaḥ, evaṃ yāvadaprāmāṇyaśaṅkaṃ tajjñānaprāmāṇyaniścayādeva tanniścayaḥ. Na caivamanavasthā, caramajñānaprāmāṇyasya jñānābhāvena koṭismaraṇābhāvena viṣayāntarasañcāreṇa vā prāmāṇyasaṃśayānavaśyambhāvāt. Anyathā bhaṭṭamate prāmāṇyasya jñānānumitigrāhyatvenānavasthā syāt. Gurumate ca prāmāṇyasya svagrāhyatvaṃ na svagrāhyaṃ svarūpaprāmāṇyābhyāṃ bahirbhūtatvāt. Kintu paragrāhyatve anavasthānāt pariśeṣānumānena pramāṇāntareṇa vā grāhyaṃ, tathā ca tatprāmāṇyasyāpi svagrāhyatvamanyenaivetyanavasthaiva.*

We are not saying[1] that certainty about the object arises only out of certainty about the truth of the knowledge. But where there is no doubt about falsity as in the knowledge of an *āmalaka* placed on the palm, there the primary knowledge itself amounts to certainty about the object, so that unwavering activity follows from that (alone). Where, however, (as) in the case of an unfamiliar knowledge, doubt about object arises through the certainty about the object being overpowered by the doubt about the truth (of the primary knowledge), there unwavering activity ensues only after certainty about the object has been reached through ascertainment of the truth (of its knowledge), not otherwise. This is confirmed by the experience of all.[2] Therefore, the knowledge which ascertains the truth of another knowledge may itself be one whose truth has not been apprehended, since there is absence of the stain of any suspicion about (its) falsity.[3] Where, however, there arises doubt about truth (of the primary knowledge) owing to doubt about the falsity of the knowledge which apprehends that truth (of the primary knowledge), there the truth (of the primary knowledge) could be ascertained only by ascertaining the truth of the knowledge apprehending it. Thus so long as there continues to arise doubt about falsity, ascertainment of anything could only follow from certainty about the truth of the knowledge of that thing.[4] This does not lead to an infinite regress; for, doubt about truth is not inevitable, either because of the absence of the knowledge of the truth of the last knowledge, or because there is no remembrance of the alternatives, or because some other object intervenes.[5] Otherwise, there would be infinite regress (even) on the Bhāṭṭa theory that truth is apprehended by the inference of the knowledge. And on the theory of Guru, the intrinsic knowability of truth is not itself intrinsically known, for it is neither the knowledge itself nor its truth. But on the ground that extrinsic apprehension leads to infinite regress, intrinsic knowability can be apprehended either through *pariśeṣa* inference or through some other means. But the intrinsic knowability of the truth of that has to be established by another, and thus there would be infinite regress.[6]

NOTES

52.1. Gaṅgeśa now takes up the very important charge of the opponents that the Nyāya theory leads to an infinite regress. The point of the charge is that in order to act upon a knowledge I must have certainty about the truth of that knowledge. But I cannot be so certain unless I also ascertain the truth of the knowledge which apprehends the truth of the first knowledge. Gaṅgeśa argues that the charge would have been a valid one if it was his view that certainty about object required ascertainment of the truth of the knowledge of that object. Quite on the contrary, Gaṅgeśa holds that ascertainment of the truth of a knowledge is not required for the ascertainment of the object of that knowledge. Especially so far as unwavering activity is concerned, we need not have a prior ascertainment of the truth of the knowledge which causes that activity. All that is necessary is that there should be no doubt about the falsity of that knowledge. Non-apprehension of falsity is enough. Apprehension of truth is more than what is needed. Insistence on this point is one of Gaṅgeśa's great contributions to the problem.

52.2. Ordinarily, we act upon a knowledge, if that knowledge is unaccompanied by doubt about its own falsity. Unwavering activity requires *arthaniścaya* i.e. certainty about the object, but not *prāmāṇyaniścaya* i.e. certainty about truth. The former is, under normal circumstances, provided by the primary knowledge itself. The latter is not needed in that case. But cases may arise when for some reason or other there is doubt about the truth of the primary knowledge. Such a doubt upsets the certainty about the object of that primary knowledge. There is consequently doubt if the object is really so or not, and as a result there cannot be unwavering activity with respect to that object unless and until the doubt about that object is replaced by certainty. But once the initial certainty has been disturbed, it can be restored only through the roundabout way of ascertaining the truth of the knowledge of that object. The outcome then is this: ordinarily, the primary knowledge itself produces the certainty needed for activity. When, however, there is doubt, one has to reestablish the truth of the primary knowledge in order to get rid of that doubt and get back the initial certainty.

52.3 Gaṅgeśa may now formulate his answer to the objection raised in 51. The knowledge which apprehends the truth of another knowledge *may* be one whose truth has not been ascertained. K_2 may ascertain the truth of K_1, even if the truth of K_2 has not been ascertained. There is therefore no infinite regress.

52.4. This is a generalised statement. Whatever may be x, certainty about x requires—in case there has once been doubt about the truth of the knowledge of x—that we attain certainty about the truth of the knowledge of x. It does not make any difference if x stands for the object of a primary knowledge (e.g. for 'water') or if it stands for the truth of the primary knowledge (e.g. 'This is water'). Or, as Mathurānātha puts it, for activity based on a certainty it is not always necessary to ascertain the truth of that certainty ("*niścayakāryaṃ prati sarvatra niścayaniṣṭhaprāmāṇyaniścayasyānapekṣitatvāt*").

52.5. There is thus no infinite regreess. Doubt about truth does not always arise for various reasons. It may be that the last knowledge of the series is not known, and in the absence of knowledge of the substantive (*dharmi*) there cannot arise any doubt about it. Or, it may be that the alternatives 'true' and 'false' are for whatever reason not remembered. Or, it may be that some other object occupies the attention, so that the series ends abruptly. Doubt is not therefore inevitable.

52.6. Gaṅgeśa now proceeds to turn the table back on the objector. It is indeed the Mīmāṃsaka who is guilty of infinite regress. The word '*anyathā*' in the text means 'if, contrary to what Gaṅgeśa has maintained, it were always necessary to ascertain the truth of a knowledge in order to be certain about the object of that knowledge'. In that case, the Mīmāṃsā hypothesis would involve infinite regress. On the Bhāṭṭa theory, truth is known by the same inference from *jñātatā* which apprehends the knowledge. But this apprehension of truth canmot be certain unless its truth were apprehended by another inference of the same type. And this second inference would be in need of another and for the same purpose; and so on ad infinitum. The Prābhākara is no better off. How does he know that the truth of a knowledge is *svataḥ*? *This* is not self-revealing. It must be established by some kind of argument.* But that the truth of any such argument is also *svataḥ* has to be again established. Thus if we are to avoid such difficulties, we should rather admit that an initial certainty about an object does not always wait upon ascertainment of the truth of that certainty.

53. *Yattu vyavasāyasya prāmāṇyaniścayādeva pravṛtterna tasyāpi prāmāṇyānusaraṇamiti nānavasthā; na ca prāmāṇyasaṃśayādaucityavarjito viṣayasaṃśaya iti vācyaṃ, niścite saṃśayābhāvāt; anyathā svatograhe'pi saṃśaye anavastheti, tadasat. Yadi hi prāmāṇyasaṃśayānna viṣaye saṃśayo niścitatvāt, tadā viṣayaniścayārthaṃ prāmāṇyaniścayo vyarthaḥ prāthamikaviṣayaniścayādeva niṣkampapravṛttyupapatteḥ. Na hi viṣayasaṃśayamanādṛtya prāmāṇyaniścayaḥ pravṛttiheturityuktam. Anyasaṃśayādanyatra niścite kathaṃ saṃśaya iti cedanubhavaṃ pṛccha, yena svasākṣikameva prāmāṇyaśaṃśayasya viṣayasaṃśayahetutvamanumatam. Jñānaviṣayatvamapi prāmāṇyasaṃśayamāsādya viṣayasaṃśāyakam.*

It has been suggested that since activity follows from the knowledge of the truth of the primary knowledge, it is not necessary again to ascertain the truth of that knowledge (of truth), and there is therefore no infinite regress. It cannot be said that doubt about the object arises depending upon doubt about the truth (of the primary knowledge), for, there is absence of doubt regarding that of which one is certain; otherwise there can be doubt even if truth is apprehended *svataḥ* and hence the consequent infinite regress.

This is not correct. If doubt about object did not follow from doubt about truth on the ground that the object was already ascertained, then ascertainment of truth with a view to ascertaining the object would be useless—unwavering activity being

*Mathurānātha explains the *pariśeṣānumāna* thus: "*Etajjñānaprāmāṇyam etajjñānagrāhyaṃ etajjñānabhinnamātrāgrāhyatvāt*". This knowledge—to put it briefly—is intrinsically true, for its truth is not extrinsic. Or, the intrinsic truth of a knowledge may be proved by other means, *pramāṇāntareṇa*, which includes amongst others also verbal authority (*śabdādinā*).

accounted for by the primary certainty about the object. It is not correct to say that ascertainment of truth is the cause of activity independent of all reference to doubt about the object. If it be asked how could doubt about a thing of which we have certainty arise from doubt about quite another thing, we reply, "ask your own experience which would itself testify that doubt about truth is the cause of doubt about the object." The property of being an object of knowledge causes doubt about the object only through doubt about truth.[1]

Notes

53.1. By "*yattu*" Gaṅgeśa anticipates a certain mode of answering the charge of infinite regress against the Nyāya theory, and then expresses his disapproval of this answer in "*tadasat*". The charge was that if the truth of a primary knowledge is ascertained by another knowledge then the truth of that other knowledge needs to be ascertained by a third knowledge which itself needs to be validated, and so on. The answer which Gaṅgeśa now mentions and then rejects is this: since ascertainment of the truth of the primary knowlege is sufficient to cause activity, it is not any longer necessary to ascertain the truth of that second knowledge, i.e. of the knowledge of the truth of the primary knowledge. It is not necessary to ascertain the truth of the second knowledge, for, once the truth of the primary knowledge has been ascertained there cannot subsequently be any doubt in it even if there arises doubt in the truth of the second knowledge. If on the other hand the second knowledge has to be again validated in order to dispel doubt in the truth of the primary knowledge, then the same difficulty would arise even in connection with, e.g., the *svataḥ* theory. In brief, the charge of infinite regress does not hold good, for, there is no need of ascertaining the truth of the second knowledge, namely of the knowledge which ascertains the truth of the first knowledge.

Gaṅgeśa rejects this solution of the problem, for, it is based on the view that doubt about the truth of a knowledge does not cause doubt in the object of that knowledge. Gaṅgeśa rejects this proposition. He argues that if there is doubt in the truth of a knowledge there would inevitably be doubt in the object, and to remove this doubt and to make unwavering activity with regard to that object possible it is of course necessary to establish the truth of the knowledge.

In the last sentence of the paragraph, Gaṅgeśa is referring to a *pūrvapakṣa* contention that doubt about object is caused not by doubt about the truth of its knowledge but always by perception of the common character of *jñānaviṣayatva*. In para 30, Gaṅgeśa had rejected this contention on the ground that it would lead to unlimited scepticism, for everything can be doubted on that ground. Here however Gaṅgeśa argues that even if in any case doubt about object is caused by contemplation of its *jñānaviṣayatva* this can only be through the *via media* of bringing into being a doubt about the truth of the knowledge of that object. Thus, contemplation of *jñānaviṣayatva* gives rise to doubt about the truth of the knowledge of that object and the latter doubt gives rise to doubt about the object. The rule that doubt about truth causes doubt about the object therefore holds good. The primary certainty does not then act as a hindrance to doubt, for with doubt in the truth of the knowledge that primary certainty loses its capacity.

54. *Nanu liṅgapakṣavyāptyādīnāṃ jñānasya prāmāṇyāvadhāraṇe anavasthā, anavadhāraṇe hetvasiddhiḥ. Atha liṅgādijñānaṃ svaviṣayāvadhāraṇe svaprāmāṇyajñānaṃ nāpekṣate, anumānamātrocchedaprasaṅgāt, liṅgādiniścayasya ca svakāraṇādhīnasya sarvasiddhaṭvāt iti cenna—prāmāṇyasaṃśayena liṅgasyāpi sandehāt. Na hi na liṅgajñāne prāmāṇyasaṃśayaḥ, avirodhāditi. Ucyate, aprāmāṇyaśaṅkākalaṅkābhāve liṅgādijñānasyaivārthaniścāyakatvāt, tatkalaṅke tu uktaiva gatiḥ.*

Yattu vyavasāye kvacidaprāmāṇyaśaṅkā bhavati kvacinneti tvayāpi vaktavyam. Evaṃ bahuvittavyayāyāsasādhye svargasādhanaṃ yāga iti jñānaṃ na gṛhītaprāmāṇyaṃ pravartakaṃ, prāmāṇyānumiteḥ pūrvameva tasya vināśāt; kintu tajjñānasamānaviṣayakamaprāmāṇyaśaṅkāśūnyaṃ jñānāntarameva. Nanu evaṃ bahuvittavyayāyāsasādhye niṣkampapravṛttāvanupayogitvāt niṣphalaṃ prāmāṇyajñānamiti kiṃ tadupāyānusaraṇeneti cenna svargasādhanaṃ yāga iti jñānaprāmāṇye niścite tatsamānaviṣayakajñānāntare aprāmāṇyaśaṇkā na bhavatīti jñānāntaramagṛhītaprāmāṇyamapi svārthaniścaya-rūpaṃ niṣkampapravṛttiṃ janayatīti aprāmāṇyaśaṅkāprati-bandhadvārā niṣkampapravṛttāvupayujyate prāmāṇyajñāna-miti na niṣphalam.

It may be objected that if the truth of the knowledge of the *liṅga, pakṣa, vyāpti* etc. has to be apprehended, then there would be infinite regress, and if this is not apprehended there would be illegitimate *hetu*. It may be replied to the above that the knowledge of *liṅga* does not, insofar as its function of ascertaining its own object is concerned, wait upon a knowledge of its own truth, because if it did there would be an end to all inference as such and also because the ascertainment of the *liṅga* etc. is universally accepted as being dependent on its own cause. But this (reply) is not tenable, for the *liṅga* also comes to be doubted if there is doubt about the truth (of the knowledge of *liṅga*). It cannot be said that doubt about the truth of the knowledge of *liṅga* never arises, for there is no contradiction. We say that the knowledge of *liṅga* etc. does cause certainty about (its) object in case there is absence of the stain of doubt about the falsity (of that knowledge); if however there is such stain the matter could take a course as depicted (before).[1]

As regards the contention that there is sometimes doubt, and sometimes not, about the falsity of the primary knowledge, you too have to account for it.[2] Similarly, the knowledge that a sacrifice which can be performed only with immense expense and difficulty is a means to attain heaven does not become the cause of activity (even) after its truth has been ascertained; for the knowledge perishes before the inference which establishes its truth takes place. What really stimulates is rather another knowledge having the same object as that one and free from any doubt about its (own) falsity. It would not do to object that if apprehension of truth has no relevance in generating unwavering activity even in case of (such) a task attainable only through immense expenditure and trouble, then it is useless and there is no point in pursuing the means to attain it; for, the truth of the knowledge 'The sacrifice is a means to heaven' having been ascertained, no suspicion of falsity could possibly arise in the case of the other knowledge having the same object as that and hence this other knowledge, although its truth has not been ascertained, gives rise to unwavering activity which is of the nature of the ascertainment of its own object. Thus the apprehension of truth is not fruitless, for it is relevant for the purpose of unwavering activity through (i.e. acting as) the hindrance to the rise of all suspicion of falsity.[3]

NOTES

54.1. Gaṅgeśa now considers the case of inference in general. An inference depends upon knowledge of the *pakṣa*, knowledge of the *liṅga* and knowledge of the *vyāpti*. In order to be able to infer that the mountain before me possesses fire on seeing smoke there, I must have perceived the mountain which is the *pakṣa*, I must also have perceived in it the smoke which is the *liṅga* and I should also have a prior knowledge of the *vyāpti* between fire and smoke. Now, either I know the truth of each of these knowledges, or I do not. In case the truth of these knowledges has not been ascertained there cannot be inference, for the necessary causes of inference would be absent. In case I have to ascertain their truth, I have to take recourse to other inferences, and so there would be an infinite regress. One may try to resolve the difficulty by saying that if the knowledge of *liṅga* (of *pakṣa* and also *vyāpti*) had to wait for its truth to be determined before it could ascertain its own object then inference would be impossible. Gaṅgeśa rejects this on the ground that as in all other cases, here also doubt about the truth of a knowledge upsets our primary certainty about the object (of that knowledge) and gives rise to doubt about it. Therefore, if there is doubt about the truth of our knowledge of the *liṅga*, *pakṣa*, *vyāpti* etc., there would be doubt in those objects and consequently inference would not take place until truth has been determined. As before so also here the primary knowledge is enough to ascertain its object if there is no doubt about its own truth to upset that certainty. If any such doubt intervenes it has to be removed by determining the truth of the primary knowledge.

54.2. Doubt about the truth of the primary knowledge does not always take place. Sometimes it does, and sometimes it does not take place: so much should be admitted by all.

54.3. Gaṅgeśa next answers an objection which seeks to prove that ascertainment of truth is in any case a fruitless endeavour. If it is anywhere worth undertaking, it is in case of knowledges which suggest a course of action involving great effort, expense and trouble. But even here—the objection points out—ascertainment of the truth of the knowledge is useless. For by the time truth of the knowledge is inferentially established, the knowledge itself has long since perished and that knowledge, now no more, cannot cause activity in anyone. Gaṅgeśa answers this objection by arguing that although the original knowledge whose truth is now ascertained is dead and gone there may nevertheless arise another knowledge having the same object. Since the previous knowledge of the same object has been confirmed, the present knowledge—even if its truth has not been ascertained—would be free from the possibility of any doubt. This knowledge would then be able to cause activity. It follows therefore that ascertainment of truth is not useless. On the other hand, it destroys doubt in case the latter threatens one's primary certainty and thereby helps the possibility of unwavering practice.

55. *Yattvanumānasya nirastasamastavibhramāśaṅkasya svata eva prāmāṇyagraha ityuktaṃ, tat—dhūmavati vahnijñānatvamanumiteḥ prāmāṇyaniyatamanuvyavasāyenopanītam, ato viśeṣadarśanānna tatrāprāmāṇyaśaṅketi, prāmāṇyaniścayādevāprāmāṇyaśaṅkāvirahādarthaṃ niścitya niṣkampavyavahāra ityabhiprāyaḥ. Vastutastu parataḥ pakṣe na kvacidapi prāmāṇyagrahaḥ pravartaka iti. Evamanuvyavasāyasya prāmāṇyaniyatatvāt na prāmāṇyaśaṅkā. Na hyajānan jānāmīti pratyeti, na vā ghaṭajñāne paṭaṃ jānāmīti. Bhramepi anuvyavasāyena rajatatvādikaṃ vyavasāyaprakāratvenollikhyate tacca tathaiva. Yattvabhyāsadaśāyāṃ jhaṭiti pracurataraniṣkampapravṛttidarśanāt prāmāṇyaṃ svata eva gṛhyate, anyatra tu parata iti, tanna—viśeṣyaniṣṭhātyantābhāvapratiyogiprakārānavacchinnatvādikaṃ prāmāṇyaṃ svato grahītumaśakyamiti parata eva gṛhyate. Jhaṭiti pravṛttistu karacaraṇādimati śarīrajñānatvāderviśeṣasyānuvyavasāyena gra-*

hādaprāmāṇyaśaṅkāśūnyādvyavasāyādeva, na prāmāṇya-jñānaṃ pravartakamityuktam. Jhaṭiti tatsamavadhānantu svakāraṇādhīnam. Na hi pipāsūnāṃ jhaṭiti pracuratarā samarthā ca pravṛttirambhasīti, pipāsopaśamanaśaktirasya pratyakṣā iti.

Iti Mahāmahopādhyāya Gaṅgeśaviracitāyāṃ tattvacintāmaṇau pratyakṣakhaṇḍe prāmāṇyavāde jñaptivādaḥ samāptaḥ.

As regards the contention that in the case of inference truth is apprehended intrinsically[1] because it is free from doubt about all kinds of error, the (real) intention is this: the property of (an) inference's being a knowledge of fire in what possesses smoke is as a rule accompanied by truth and is presented in the *anuvyavasāya* (of the inference); since specific character is perceived, no doubt about the falsity (of the inference) could arise. Since truth is ascertained, and consequently doubt about falsity is absent, the object (also) is ascertained (by the inference) and unwavering activity follows. In fact, on the *parataḥ* theory the apprehension of truth is never the cause of activity. Similarly, there is also no doubt about the truth of *anuvyavasāya*, as this (also) is, as a rule, accompanied by truth. One who is not knowing does not introspect 'I know'. Nor does one having a knowledge of jar introspect it as 'I know a cloth'. Even in the case of error, the *anuvyavasāya* mentions 'silverness' etc. as qualifiers of the primary knowledge, and so the same holds good.[2] As regards the contention that since in the case of a familiar knowledge unwavering activity is frequently seen to follow quickly, truth in such cases is apprehended intrinsically, while in other cases it is apprehended extrinsically: (we say) it cannot hold good. For, truth in the senses of 'the property of not being limited by a qualifier that is the counter-positive of an absence residing in the qualificandum' etc. is incapable of being apprehended intrinsically and so is apprehended extrinsically.[3] Quick activity however is caused by the primary knowledge which is rendered free from all doubt about falsity by the knowledge—in the *anuvyavasāya*—of the fact that the qualificandum (i.e. the primary knowledge) possesses properties like 'being a knowledge of body in what possesses limbs'. Therefore, the apprehension of truth is not (even in these cases) the cause of activity. Quick accompaniment of it is due to its own causes.[4] It is not the case that since thirsty persons have frequently quick and successful activity directed towards water therefore they have a perception of the power of water to quench thirst.[5]

Thus ends the chapter on Knowledge (of Truth) in the *Prāmāṇyavāda* belonging to the part devoted to Perception of the work *Tattvacintāmaṇi* written by Mahāmahopādhyāya Gaṅgeśa.

Notes

55.1. Gaṅgeśa is now giving his own opinion about all those cases which have been regarded by some as indisputably possessing intrinsic truth. It is well known that Vācaspati in his *Tātparyyaṭīkā* holds the view that in the case of inference, as also in the case of *anuvyavasāya*, there is apprehension of truth right from the beginning. The same holds good also of knowledges that have become *abhyāsadaśāpanna.** Now to say that knowledge in any case is intrinsically true is inconsistent with the Nyāya standpoint, Gaṅgeśa therefore proceeds to explicate what in his view is the true intention of Vācaspati. The general point that he makes out is that in all these cases there is no scope for doubt though truth is apprehended extrinsically. In this he is following Udayana's comments on Vācaspati in his *Pariśuddhi*.

In inference there is no scope for doubt since in the *anuvyavasāya* by which the inference itself is known we also come to know its specific character of being, e.g. knowledge of fire in what possesses smoke. Smoke being pervaded by fire, perception of this character in the inference is sufficient to ward off the possibility of any doubt about its validity. However, it would be too much to claim that since there is no scope for doubt therefore truth of an inference is apprehended *ab initio*. Truth is to be inferred subsequently. The knowledge that the inference is one of fire in what possesses smoke is sufficient to ward off the possibility of doubt.

*See pp. 48-49 of the Introduction.

55.2. The same holds good of *anuvyavasāya*. This also is as a rule true, but not intrinsically true. The fact that one never introspects 'I know' when one is not actually knowing, and the fact that one never introspects 'I know a jar' when in fact one is knowing a cloth are sufficient to show that here there is no reasonable probability of doubt. Even if the primary knowledge be erroneous, its *anuvyavasāya* is not, for it accurately describes its object which is the primary knowledge. The knowledge 'This is silver' may be false, but that the knowledge has 'silverness' for its qualifier is true.

55.3. Even in the case of our most familiar instances of knowledge where we quickly react in the appropriate manner truth is apprehended *parataḥ*. How then could there be such instantaneous activity? Gaṅgeśa gives two explanations of this, which we shall discuss in 55.4. Presently, however, he gives a general argument that truth understood either as the property of not having a qualifier which is absent in the qualificandum or even as *tadvati tatprakārakatva* cannot be apprehended intrinsically (for reasons given elsewhere in the text) and so must be apprehended extrinsically (even in the case of our most familiar knowledges, *abhyāsadaśāyāmapi*, adds Mathurānātha).

55.4. In the lines "*Jhaṭitipravṛttistu . . . svakāraṇādhīnam*", Gaṅgeśa gives his own explanation of how there could be such instantaneous activity in the case of our familiar knowledges even though their truth is not intrinsically apprehended. The text however is difficult to construe, and we follow Mathurānātha's lead. Mathurānātha breaks it up into two different suggestions. According to the first, the *anuvyavasāya* apprehends the primary knowledge 'This is a body' as being a knowledge of body in what possesses limbs. This property is a mark of the truth of that knowledge, for it has been said before that *vyāpyavati vyāpakaprakārakatva* is a mark of *vyāpakavati vyāpakaprakārakatva*. Thus "*viśeṣasya*" is explained as "*prāmāṇyavyāpyasya*". Perception of what is pervaded by truth leads to an inference of the truth, and that accounts for the activity. The other explanation is simpler: the primary knowledge, not being disturbed by any doubt about its falsity, directly leads to the activity. It is not the knowledge of truth which causes the activity. Mathurānātha explains "*Jhaṭiti tatsamavadhānaṃ tu . . . svakāraṇādhīnam*" as being Gaṅgeśa's reply to a possible objection against the first of the two explanations. It may be asked, how could there be such quick inference of truth, to which Gaṅgeśa is replying that that must be due to the presence of necessary conditions. In other words, the circumstances are such that inference of truth takes place so quickly.

55.5. In this last sentence of the text, Gaṅgeśa is illustrating his point. A thirsty man has an immediate and unfailing tendency to quench his thirst on seeing water. But this does not imply that the thirsty man has a perception of the capacity of water to quench thirst. Or, it is not necessary that he should have apprehended the truth of his knowledge of water. He nevertheless acts, and the ability of the yonder object to quench thirst is determined only after the activity is successful. Prior to the activity there is only a perception of what has been elsewhere characterised as '*tajjātīyatva*' which being the mark of truth prevents doubt, and in the absence of any doubt there follows of course without any delay the appropriate activity.

All this leads to the conclusion which Gaṅgeśa has stated earlier in this paragraph and which constitutes one of his central theses, namely that "*vastutastu parataḥ pakṣe na kvacidapi prāmāṇyagrahaḥ pravartakaḥ*". One has to add the condition: "unless there has been a prior doubt in the truth of the knowledge".

APPENDIX

PRĀMĀṆYA AND WORKABILITY*

Professor Potter's very thoughtful paper[1]—the sort of constructive commentary that is needed to make oriental thought alive for us—undertakes to do three things all at once. First, he attacks the incommensurability thesis I advanced in GTT.[2] In doing so, he traces my defence of that thesis to my ascription of the so-called JTB theory of knowledge to the Indian philosophers. So much for the negative part of his paper. Happily, the rest is a bold positive construction. The second thing he does is to show a way out of the impasse created by the incommensurability thesis by suggesting a new interpretation of the concepts of '*pramā*' and '*prāmāṇya*' in Indian philosophy in general, not in any one system or other. Finally, he ascribes the faulted JTB theory to a more fundamental error, an absolute distinction between fact and value, which is then traced to a still deeper mistake, a non-cognitivist theory of value, to which much of western thought is committed but from which the main tradition of Indian thought is free. This general philosophical thesis lends philosophical support to the interpretation of *prāmāṇya* as 'workability' (rather than as 'truth'); this latter interpretation—to traverse the path regressively—destroys the JTB-theoretical assumptions on which my interpretation of the *svataḥ-parataḥ* controversy allegedly rests. My commentary shall touch on these issues in the order in which they have just been outlined.

THE INCOMMENSURABILITY THESIS

I find myself in the curious position of being expected to defend what I wrote just about twenty years ago. The incommensurability thesis was very much in the air—not in writings on Indian philosophy, but in philosophy in general amongst

*Reprinted with minor alterations from *Journal of Indian Philosophy*, 12, 1984.

linguistically oriented philosophers. The JTB theory of knowledge had not yet been cast into suspicion by the notorious Gettier paradoxes, nor had anti-foundationalism gained that wide acceptance as it has today. But to say this is not to shirk responsibility. The fact is that GTT did defend an incommensurability thesis. Whether it also accepted the JTB theory is not at all clear. I will come back to this a little later. For the present, let me stay with the incommensurability thesis.

Potter's main complaint against this thesis is that it trivialises a long and rich tradition of epistemological discussion in Indian philosophy, in which thinkers of the rank of Vācaspati and Udayana, Kumārila and Prabhākara and Dharmakīrti participated. This is indeed a very persuasive, if not logically binding, argument. I respect it. Let us see what thesis I defended in GTT, and what are its consequences.

I wrote: "... it is very much plausible that the views of the rival schools are not really mutually incompatible as they at first sight certainly appear to be. They may even be regarded in the long run as supplementing each other. The apparent incompatibility between these views then may *partly* be due to the fact that though it would seem they were giving different answers to the same question, they were *not always* unanimous in their formulation of the problems, so that *they were really* answering very different questions" (GTT, pp. 1-2).

The words 'partly' and 'not always' which I have italicised for this commentary would show that I did not want to maintain that the dispute had no real, substantive, issues at all. In fact, as I will presently argue, even when they were answering different questions while purporting to be concerned with the same problem, the differences in the *specific* questions they answered are traceable to underlying, substantive, differences in their views about common problems. If at one level, the dispute is trivialised (as in my thesis), at another level substantive issues emerge as decisive. You cannot have it both ways.

Consider the following strategies which seem to render the *svataḥ* theory analytically true: (i) Defining *prāmāṇya* as *jñānatva* so that error and other forms of *a-pramā* are not even species of *jñāna*. This answers, by implication, the Naiyāyika argument that if *prāmāṇya* were *svataḥ* (by origin) then the generating conditions of knowledge, being also the generating conditions of *a-pramā* (since *a-pramā* is a species of *jñāna*), *a-pramā* would be *pramā*. However, although in this way victory is won, the Advaitin who proposes the strategy, falls back on the thesis that error is not *jñāna*, for a *jñāna* is opposed to *ajñāna*, while error is not, also because a *jñāna* reveals its object as having had unknown existence prior to being known while error does not. Now all this puts the Advaitin under obligation, unless he has already done so, to defend the implied theory of error, which itself cannot then be definitely defended. (ii) The Prābhākara strategy is to preserve the same identification of *prāmāṇya* and *jñānatva*, not by excluding all *a-pramā* from the scope of '*jñāna*', but by including them all in a manner which does not render *a-pramā* a species of *jñāna* (which is what Nyāya does) but rather in a manner whose consequence is that there is, in reality, no *a-pramā*. We know the familiar Prābhākara theory of *a-khyāti*, which now needs to be defended.

Thus a philosopher who chooses to defend his theory on definitional grounds—unless he is a conventionalist, and no Indian philosopher was one—has to defend a substantive thesis on substantival grounds at some other point. The so-called 'incommensurability thesis' therefore does not render the Indian discussion of epistemology pointless; the thesis shows how, within a system, they hang together. The defect of the exposition in GTT was that it did *not* bring out this trade off which a philosopher makes when he so formulates his terms as to make his position analytically true. If the question, then, which he was asking was different, and the victory was won too easily, that is because at another level, a more substantive and serious encounter with the opponent either had already been or was about to be made. The issue "Is *prāmāṇya svataḥ* or *parataḥ*?" may be sought to be decided by appropriately defining '*prāmāṇya*', but then the question 'Is *prāmāṇya* this or that?' has to be dealt with substantively.

THE JTB THEORY

But the above way of making incommensurability only a surface phenomenon of deeper incompatibilities, would have the consequence of making the *svataḥ* and the *parataḥ* theories to be in the long run incompatibles. But didn't I write in the GTT, as Potter quotes me, "both the theories are in their own ways correct"? And didn't I do that by saying that the *svataḥ* theory understands by '*prāmāṇya*' a predicate of knowledge (when that word is used in standard English sense) and the *parataḥ* theory understands by it a predicate of beliefs (again in the standard English sense of 'belief')? Yes, I did in fact suggest such a 'reconciliation', and, again, the GTT did not make the following point explicit, although it was implicitly being made all along, namely, that

(a) If '*prāmāṇya*' is defined as *jñānatva* (i.e. if it is reasonable to exclude *a-pramā* from the extension of '*jñāna*'), then the *svataḥ* theory holds good; and
(b) if '*prāmāṇya*' is defined as the property of only a species of *jñāna*, then of *jñāna* so understood (i.e. understood as having two species, *pramā* and *a-pramā*), the *parataḥ* theory holds good.

One may have both (a) and (b), but one may decide—not on sweet will, but on good grounds—to regard the antecedents of anyone of them to be acceptable and so be committed to accepting the appropriate consequent. But one may still not want to deny that *if* the other antecedent were true, its consequent would follow.

Didn't the GTT uphold the JTB analysis of knowledge? It certainly did give that impression. Strangely enough, I could not have held both that *all* Indian philosophers held a JTB analysis and that the Vedānta-Mīmāṃsā concept of *prāmāṇya* concerned knowledge and not belief. Let me then first get down to what I said on pages 20-21 of GTT. I referred to the account of knowledge in terms of truth plus right to be sure *only* with a view to show how the Vedāntin's definition of *pramātva* in terms of *jñānatva* and vice versa can be explained in terms of that account. Then on page 77, where I sum up my assessment of the two parties to the *svataḥ-parataḥ* controversy, I maintain that the *svataḥ* theory takes 'knowledge' in a strong sense according to which to know is to know the truth, adding that this is not a mere linguistic stipulation. As contrasted with this, the *parataḥ* theory uses 'knowledge' in a weak sense, as a generic concept which comprehends two species: true and false cognitions. Then I add: "The belief—in spite of all the philosophical difficulties associated with it—perhaps better expresses this generic knowledge in the weak sense." On the next page, I go on to write: "As predicated of beliefs, the predicate 'true' has a significant opposite i.e., 'false' inasmuch as there are true beliefs and false beliefs. But as predicated of knowledge, the predicate 'true' has no significant opposite inasmuch as 'false' is not a predicate of knowledge in the same way as 'true' is" (p. 78).

Now if this *gave the impression* that I subscribed to a JTB theory, or that I ascribed such a theory to the Indian epistemologists, I plead guilty. Potter is quite right in his claim that such a theory cannot give an analysis of '*pramā*'. But what are the reasons he gives in support of this claim? Although at first sight he appears to be holding that the JTB theory cannot give an analysis of *pramā*, in fact his claim is much stronger than that: he insists that the JTB theory is *not acceptable at all*, even as an analysis of 'knowledge' in the western tradition (or in the English language). I will briefly remark on these two claims.

The first claim is that *pramā* cannot be explicated as justified true belief. In this I concur. It is well pointed out by Potter that the word 'belief' has no equivalent in the Sanskrit epistemological literature. Even if we leave out belief as a disposition, belief as an occurrent comes close to that variety of *jñāna* which is a *niścaya*, a certainty. What is wrong, then, in taking a *niścaya-jñāna* as an occurrent belief? Even an occurrent belief is either a feeling or an attitude which is attached to a proposition; it is a belief that, the proposition being external to the attitude. In the Indian epistemologies, a *pramā* is a *niścaya* but not tagged on to a proposition, but has itself a propositional structure (so that doubts 'about the same' would have a different structure). But this by itself may not be a very important point. A theory of belief is possible in which belief that p is one unanalysed structure. Let us not put too much weight on whether *niścayajñāna* is or is not the same as belief. Supposing it were, can we say that *pramā* is justified true *niścayajñāna*?

Pramā, of course, is true *niścayajñāna*—howsoever one may ant to explicate 'true'. It is *yathārthajñāna*. What then is the need for 'justified'? It is well known that in the western discussions on the nature of knowledge, 'justified' was inserted in order to exclude cases of someone guessing or accidentally asserting a proposition that *happens* to be true. Now within the Indian epistemologies, these and such counter-examples do not arise, for the *pramā* is not only a *niścayajñāna* but must have been *caused by* any of the acceptable *pramāṇas*. *Pramā* is *jñāna* that is a *niścaya*, that is not a memory, that is 'true' to its object, and that is brought about by any of the recognised *pramāṇas*. Since the last conjunct was assumed, one need not add "justified". The concept of 'justification', as it occurs in "justified true knowledge" has been explicated in various ways, but one explication of it, namely, the one in terms of causation, perhaps most fits in with the Indian epistemologies. The *pramāṇas* are causes of *pramā*. To be justified means to be brought about by a *pramāṇa*. Whether the resulting theory of knowledge is a JTB theory or not, makes little difference.

Why is a JTB theory, in any form, not acceptable to Potter? Not because of the Gettier sort of paradoxes. Not because it is almost impossible, within the framework of the western epistemologies, to come up with a good account of "justified", or also of "belief". He gives, as far as I can see, several general arguments: first, the JTB is committed to a correspondence theory of truth. Secondly, a JBT theory, if Potter is right, is committed to a non-cognitivist theory of value, according to which the only sorts of evidence appropriate for the truth of a belief are "empirical, perhaps mathematical" ones, but not ethically or aesthetically normative ones. The "true" in "justified true belief" is descriptive truth. Thus the JTB theory presupposes an absolute fact-value distinction. Third, JTB analysis entails that knowledge and belief are compatibles, whereas much of our *ordinary usage* of 'knowing' and 'believing' implies that they are incompatible (curiously enough, Potter introduces this argument from Vendler immediately after taking me to task for drawing conclusions about things from facts about linguistic usage.) Fourth, JTB theories presuppose a foundationalist epistemology which has recently fallen into bad repute.

Brief comments on each of these four arguments may be in order. I do not think JTB analysis is committed to any particular theory of truth. In fact, as I understand it, it is neutral as against the competing theories. It analyses 'knowledge'; but in the *analysiens*, the term 'true' occurs as unanalysed. Hence when Potter insists that "it is not at all clear that a *pramā* must be true in the sense that the justified true belief account of knowledge wants it to be", I am left wondering as to what is that sense. If that is the case, the second argument, namely, that JTB theory presupposes a non-cognitivist theory of value is also beside the point, for even 'true' in the sense of the pragmatist, as far as I can see, can be taken up into the analysiens. The third argument I concede. The fourth does not impress me a great deal. And the Nyāya itself presents a variety of correspondence theory which is not foundationalistic, as I have argued elsewhere.[3]

Prāmāṇya AS WORKABILITY

Potter's positive thesis, and the most provocative of his thoughts in the paper, is that *prāmāṇya* should be rendered not as truth but as *workability*. Potter makes several claims on behalf of this thesis: (a) that it is a correct exegesis of '*yāthārthya*' in context; (b) that it is a thesis that would be acceptable in common to all schools of Indian philosophy: (c) that it is theory-neutral; and (d) that it helps us avoid the incommensurability thesis (which on its part threatened to render much of Indian epistemology trivial): I will comment on each of these in that order.

(a) The Sanskrit word '*artha*' of course has many meanings. The *Śabda-kalpa-druma* lists the following: *viṣayaḥ*, *yācñā*, *dhanam*, *kāraṇam*, *śabda-pratipādya*, *nivṛtti* and *prayojanam*. The three philosophically relevant are: object, meaning of word, and purpose. The question whether, and to what extent these three extensionally coincide was certainly in the minds of generations of Indian thinkers. If *artha* in the sense of object was etymologised as "*arthyate anena*", i.e., as what satisfies (or frustrates) a purpose, a source of anxiety was the case of such objects as gave rise neither to a positive nor to a negative response, in other words, of objects towards which one was simply indifferent. In the epistemological literature, *artha* as *viṣaya* is also defined as that which "floats" in apprehension (*bhāsate*), or as that which is "manifested" in apprehension ("*paricchid-*

yate"). If Potter wants to bring all such meanings under one common meaning, that is not totally unwarranted, if we are simply concerned with the key word "*artha*". Thus his interpretation is, to say the least, a *plausible* one. Let him consider this key sentence from Vātsyāyana's opening statement: "*pramāṇato 'rthapratipattau pravṛttisāmarthyāt arthavat pramāṇam*". Are these two occurrences of '*artha*' in the same sense? or is the first = object, the second = purpose? or both = object? Whether it is also viable depends upon how sound are his other claims.

(b) Is "*prāmāṇya* = workability" acceptable to all the systems of Indian philosophy? or, at least, to the main participants in the *svataḥ-parataḥ* controversy? The best support, and I presume the original suggestion for Potters' idea, is to be found in the Buddhist writings. Since the Buddhist was committed to the thesis that none of the conventional *pramāṇas* yield ontological truth, he could make room for conventional truth claims only in terms of pragmatic workability. It is in this sense that Dharmottara's statement in the *Nyāyabinduṭīkā* has to be understood: "*Jñānam api pradarśitam arthaṃ prāpayat saṃvādakam ucyate.*" Here '*artha*' may be quite plausibly construed as purpose or goal. But the same notion of *saṃvāda* is understood by Pārthasārthi in *Nyāyaratnamālā* as "*tadviṣayaṃ jñānāntaram*", which amounts to saying that *saṃvāda* is cognitive coherence rather than pragmatic satisfaction. Gaṅgeśa, in his chapter on the definition of *pramā*, explains '*saṃvāda*' as *jñānāntareṇa tathā ullikhyamānatvam* (= "being mentioned similarly in another knowledge"). Gaṅgeśa in fact proceeds to assert that *pramā* cannot be defined in terms of successful practice on the ground that such a definition would not apply to cases of true knowledge where for some reason or other no practical response follows. These latter are the so-called cases of *upekṣā-pramā*. It hardly needs to be labored that many major authors did in fact regard *pramā* as 'true' (in the sense of correspondence). Consider Vidyāraṇya in *Vivaraṇaprameyasaṅgraha*: "*jñānasya arthapariccheda-sāmarthyam*", where '*artha*' cannot be "goal", if '*pariccheda*' = "*manifestation*". If *Vivaraṇa's* definition were read, favoring Potter's suggestion, as "picking out the purpose", we would want to know: does a cognition show, pick out what its goal is, or does it "pick out" the goal in the sense of "satisfying it"? Only in the latter case, would *prāmāṇya* = workability; only in the former case, could *prāmāṇya* be *svataḥ*, as *Vivaraṇa* must be able to hold.

What about Gaṅgeśa's "*tadvati tatprakārakatvam*"? Potter would want to understand by "*tadvati*", I presume: "in the object which satisfies the purpose which motivates the awareness under consideration". But the "*tat*" in "*tadvati*" and the "*tat*" in "*tatprakārakatvam*" have to be the same. If the latter means a property such as "being a silver", the former must also mean the same property. "*Tadvān*" can then mean "that which possesses that property."

The fact that Madhusūdana takes "*tadvati tatprakārakatva*" as belonging to all apprehensions, not excluding error while Gaṅgeśa takes it as picking only true ones from the false ones, is to be explained—as Madhusūdana himself does in *Advaitaratnarakṣaṇam*—by the fact that for him *tadvati tatprakārakatvam* = *tadvadviśeṣyakatve sati tatprakārakatvam*, where '*viśeṣyatā*' is a purely epistemological notion, so that even in a false cognition, its object, the qualificandum, is known as possessing *tat*. The Nyāya understanding of the same definition makes it equivalent to *tadvadviśeṣyakatvāvacchinnatatprakārakatva* which rules out that purely epistemological requirement.

(c) Now the philosophical value of Potter's thesis extends far beyond its viability as an exegesis of Sanskrit texts. He is rightly responding to a philosophical situation posed by the incommensurability thesis. In order to set aside that thesis with all its undesired consequences we have to start by assuming that all the different philosophers concerned with *prāmāṇya* were trying to explicate, or philosophically reconstruct, some one pre-philosophical notion. Let us call *that* notion *prāmāṇya*. This notion, so goes Potter's story, is that of workability. *Prāmāṇya* as workability is the pre-philosophical *explicandum;* the various definitions in the various systems are various explications of this notion, they cannot therefore replace it. By this Potter is able to preserve the univocity of "*prāmāṇya*" and free the concept of any ontological commitment i.e. render it "neutral" as between realism and idealism.

This indeed, if right, is no small achievement, especially when Potter is not introducing into Indian philosophical discourse any concept that is clearly foreign to it. On the contrary, almost every Indian philosopher—according to the standard interpretations—looks upon "successful practice" as a mark or criterion of "*prāmāṇya*", only the Buddhist is regarded as taking it as the nature of "*prāmāṇya*". It is therefore right that extensionally the class of awarenesses leading to successful response and the class of awarenesses that are, on the standard interpretation, "true" appear to coincide. Whether they coincide in intension is the issue.

First of all, I wish to place on record that I have full sympathy with Potter's project. In other words, I share his general philosophical hunch that there must be some *pre-philosophical* and *theory-neutral* concept which the different systems define, explicate, reconstruct, or what have you, depending upon what they happen to regard as the nature of theoretical enterprise in philosophy. [Consider, e.g., the concept of moral goodness of which hedonism, utilitarianism, Kantian rationalism provide some definitions. What is that pre-philosophical, theory-neutral concept which they seek to define?] If anything deserves to be called "phenomenological", then identifying such a concept must be phenomenological. In this sense, Potters' project is phenomenological.

What is disconcerting about Potter's thesis is that one of the theories of truth is assigned a special access to that pre-philosophical, theory-neutral concept. This is the pragmatic theory. The concept of workability, successful practice, however down-to-earth it may appear to be, when generalised over the entire domain of cognitive enterprise, betrays a *theoretical* commitment of *the same sort* as the other rival concepts, such as correspondence or coherence. It involves a metaphysical theory of the primacy of will, and an anthropological theory of man as a willing, projecting being. Which is all fine, but which cannot claim that theory-neutral status which is being accorded to it.

Let me propose, drawing upon certain resources of contemporary phenomenology, the conceptual structure "intention-fulfilment-frustration" to do that job, where 'intention' is detached from the concept of goal or purpose ('fulfilment' and 'frustration' likewise from their ties with the practical responsive situation) and signifies a general structure of all conscious life, cognitive or non-cognitive. Within the limits of this paper I do not propose to debate and defend this suggestion, but would like Professor Potter to take this possibility, as a general philosophical position.

(d) Does '*prāmāṇya* = workability' help us avoid the incommensurability thesis?

If the thesis is right, i.e., if there was a common univocal sense of *prāmāṇya*, then of course the issues such a '*svataḥ-parataḥ*' insofar as they were concerned with this univocal sense, would gain in substance. But this would equally be the case if we are right in ascribing *any* such common univocal sense to all the participants.

But does 'workability' in fact succeed in helping us out? I give here only one problem for Potter:

On his account, according to the *svataḥ* theory, to know an awareness is to know it as a *potential* purpose-satisfier, whereas on the *parataḥ* theory, an awareness can be called a purpose-satisfier only after actual satisfaction. So at a new point, i.e., with regard to the problem of *prāmāṇyagraha*, we have an incommensurability. They do not mean same by 'apprehension of *prāmāṇya*'. In fact, the standard Nyāya inference: *idaṃ jñānaṃ pramā saphalapravṛttijanakatvāt* renders on his thesis to: *idaṃ jñānaṃ saphalapravṛttijanakaṃ saphalapravṛttijanakatvāt*—another, example of analytical triviality.

NOTES

1. Karl H. Potter, "Does Indian epistemology concern Justified True Knowledge", *Journal of Indian Philosophy*, 12, 1984.
2. J.N. Mohanty, *Gaṅgeśa's Theory of Truth* (GTT), Santiniketan, 1966.
3. Cp. J.N. Mohanty, "Indian Theories of Truth: Thoughts on Their Common Frame-work," *Philosophy East and West*, 30, 1980, pp. 439-451.

INDEX

CORRECTIONS

Page	Line	For	Read
11	8 (from bottom)	pp. 43.	pp. 42-43
19	3 (from bottom)	right[48]a	right[48a]
123	9 (from bottom)	$C_{A\ not\text{-}A}$	$C_{not\text{-}A}$
178	10 (from top)	*'pṛthivītvavti*	*'pṛthivītvavati*
180	18 (from top)	*vyabhicāri*	*vyabhicārī*
193	last line	*vyāpakaprakār-akajñāntava*	*vyāpakaprakār-akajñānatva*